33

Masters to Managers

MASTERS TO MANAGERS

Historical and Comparative Perspectives
on American Employers

■

EDITED BY

Sanford M. Jacoby

COLUMBIA UNIVERSITY PRESS
New York

COLUMBIA UNIVERSITY PRESS
New York   Oxford
Copyright © 1991 Columbia University Press
All rights reserved

Library of Congress Cataloging-in-Publication Data

Masters to managers ; historical and comparative perspectives on
American employers / edited by Sanford M. Jacoby.
p. cm.
Includes bibliographical references and index.
ISBN 0–231–06802–6 (alk. paper)
1. Industrial relations—United States—History—Case studies.
I. Jacoby, Sanford M.
HD8066.M36   1991   331'.0973—dc20
90–2151
CIP

Casebound editions of Columbia University Press books are Smyth-sewn
and printed on permanent and durable acid-free paper

Printed in the United States of America
c 10 9 8 7 6 5 4 3 2 1

Contents

■

Contributors

Jens Christiansen, Associate Professor, Economics Department, Mt. Holyoke College, South Hadley, Massachusetts.

Daniel R. Ernst, Associate Professor, School of Law, Georgetown University, Washington, D.C.

Gerald Friedman, Assistant Professor, Economics Department, University of Massachusetts, Amherst, Massachusetts.

Howell John Harris, Lecturer in American History, Department of History, University of Durham, Durham, England.

Sanford M. Jacoby, Associate Professor, Anderson Graduate School of Management, University of California, Los Angeles, California.

Walter Licht, Associate Professor, Department of History, University of Pennsylvania, Philadelphia, Pennsylvania.

Daniel Nelson, Professor, Department of History, University of Akron, Akron, Ohio.

Peter Philips, Associate Professor, Department of Economics, University of Utah, Salt Lake City, Utah.

Daniel M. G. Raff, Assistant Professor, Graduate School of Business Administration, Harvard University, Boston, Massachusetts.

Editor's Preface

■

This volume introduces specialists and general readers to recent historical scholarship on American employers. It displays the range of work presently being done and provides a framework for locating the research in the larger scheme of American industrial history. Following an introduction, the book is divided into three parts that represent different levels of analysis. The essays in Part One, "Managing the Workplace," look at employer activities at the point of production. In Part Two, "Politics and Labor Markets," the focus shifts to the world outside the firm and to interemployer relations. Finally, Part Three, "Comparative Perspectives," compares American employers with their counterparts in other industrial countries. Each section begins with a brief overview of the material it contains.

I wish to thank all the contributors to this book. By reading and commenting on each other's work, they made this a more cogent and collective effort. For her encouragement of this project, I also thank Kate Wittenberg of Columbia University Press. Other forms of support—secretarial, financial, intellectual, and emotional—were provided by Wilma Daniels, Maury Pearl, Rose Pressey, the UCLA Institute of Industrial Relations, Alexander and Margaret Jacoby, and Susan Bartholomew. I am grateful to all of them.

Sanford M. Jacoby

Masters to Managers

Masters to Managers: An Introduction

■

SANFORD M. JACOBY

Although research on employers is hardly a new endeavor, in the past the subject failed to attract a critical mass of scholars. That is rather surprising, given the existence of venerable and sizable literatures detailing the history and current activities of labor and business organizations. Yet for various reasons—including an absence of interest in, or approval of, the employer's role in industrial relations—those literatures failed to focus on employers. During the last ten to fifteen years, however, research on employers has developed and steadily become a thriving interdisciplinary field both in the United States and abroad. Several books now are available that exhibit work being done in this field. Some discuss the industrial relations strategies of contemporary managers; others provide historical analyses of European and Japanese employers.[1] This book is the first collection specifically devoted to historical and comparative perspectives on employers in the United States.

The collection consists of eight empirical studies based on original, previously unpublished research by scholars trained in history, economics, law, and sociology. It demonstrates how scholarship is proceeding and provides a sense of the range of disciplinary approaches being taken in this expanding area. Synthetic essays and literature reviews were avoided; it was felt that these might create the impression that important issues were settled, an idea that can be deadly to future efforts and would certainly be misleading.[2] Indeed, the contributions to this book show that methodology and interpretation remain contentious issues for those conducting historical research on American employers.

The case studies presented here are attempts to illuminate the past. As such, they are concerned with questions of historical fact, develop-

1

ment, and context. Yet they are also intended to deepen our understanding of events in the contemporary workplace. Each study deals with problems of a fundamental and enduring nature; each touches on issues that are still being grappled with by today's workers, managers, unions, and policy analysts: what factors shape the employment relationship in modern society? How much scope is there for employers to exercise discretion in designing the workplace? When and why do employers discourage workers from joining labor unions? Why are workplaces so diverse within and across national boundaries? Is there a uniquely American style of industrial relations?

Those are difficult questions, and it would be misleading to suggest that this volume offers a definitive resolution of them. But the essays *do* provide conceptual and historiographical frameworks for thinking about these issues, and they contain considerable evidence to support some tentative conclusions.

HISTORIANS AND EMPLOYERS

Until recently, three fields of historical research—business history, labor history, and economic history—developed in isolation from one another, each with its own journals, ideological proclivities, and theoretical interests. Business and labor history were, to some extent, mirror images of each other. Business history was the domain of entrepreneurial biographies and company chronicles, while labor history discussed the development of trade unions and the daily concerns of various working-class groups. Studies from each field were infused with uncritical admiration for their subjects, which meant that business historians generally supported and labor historians often faulted market competition and the capitalist system. Most were case studies that proceeded by gathering an abundance of detailed and occasionally esoteric facts. Sometimes the facts were a means to the end of saying something about theoretical structures (as in the "old" institutional labor history and the "new" Chandlerian business history). But at other times, fusing facts into larger wholes was explicitly rejected, and gathering facts became an end in itself (as in the "old" business history and the "new" labor history).[3]

Economic history stood off to one side, dominated by economists and their theoretical concerns, chiefly the determinants of economic growth. Economic historians worked at a high level of aggregation, studying industries and national economies. They tended to ignore individual firms and workers, except as the latter could be counted and classified according to wage rates and demographic factors. Economic history was less homogeneous ideologically than the other two fields, split ever since its inception between proponents and critics of capitalist economic development.

Despite the seeming comprehensiveness of this three-pronged approach to industrial history, relatively little attention was given to topics that lay at the intersection of the three fields. Perhaps the most neglected area was the evolution of employers' labor policies—at the workplace, in concert with other employers, and in the political arena. Why did this gap persist? There are various explanations.

Most business historians accepted management's bias that employment and labor relations were distinctly secondary corporate functions; so at best these received cursory mention. In company histories such as the Harvard case study series, and even in more recent works such as Alfred D. Chandler's *Visible Hand*, virtually nothing was said about employment issues or the personnel function. The topics surfaced in sporadic journal articles or in the introductions to personnel textbooks but with the emphasis on ideas rather than practices. And the ideas were cast in mechanical stage theories that had one philosophy of employee relations following another in a teleology of employer enlightenment (simple paternalism, welfare work, scientific management, human relations, and so on).[4]

The branch of business history dealing with business-government relations had somewhat more to say about employer and employment issues. One example was the studies that sought either to prove or to debunk the concept of corporate liberalism by examining business attitudes toward federal regulation during the Progressive and New Deal eras. Cultural history also touched on these issues, as in studies that examined the role of businessmen in the broad cultural movements—efficiency, social reform, and modernization—that accompanied the rise of corporate capitalism. Yet neither set of studies forged strong links between businessmen's political and ideological concerns and the daily problems that confronted them in their companies. Instead, their approach was highly idealistic, probing the "business mind" or "business opinion" through the publications and pronouncements of business organizations.[5]

Labor historians, especially of the older institutional school, were more interested in the industrial relations policies of individual employers, yet rarely pursued the topic in any depth. Often the overly simple assumption was made that employers acted solely to avoid unions. The assumption could carry one far in the case of American employers. But it left unexamined historical and national variations in employer animus toward unions. As a result, the institutional labor historians ignored other, more complex motives for employers' behavior and other realms of activity, such as shopfloor and community relations.[6] The new labor history has done a better job of exploring these realms, as in studies that examine the impact of technology and managerialism on craft processes, but still tends to flatten employer motives to a monomaniacal search—in this case, for control of the shopfloor—except that now unions sometimes are portrayed as the employers' witting accomplices.[7]

It is only a slight exaggeration to say that few economic historians ever analyzed the internal workings of the black box otherwise known as the firm. Most chose instead to concentrate on commodity flows between markets and firms or on macroeconomic issues of growth and development. Neither employers nor employment mattered much to economic historians except as they related to aggregate concepts such as demand for labor and growth of the labor force. On rare occasions when the black box was opened to study labor issues, the inquiry was limited to technological innovation and inventive activity, and was pursued without regard to specific organizational contexts. None of this is surprising; neoclassical economic theorists believe that what individual employers do counts for little once relative market prices are taken into account. As two such theorists recently said, "The study of the firm as an organization . . . is not, strictly speaking, necessary; one can divine the correct 'reduced form' for the behavior of the organization without considering the micro-forces within the organization."[8]

The 1970s and 1980s marked a turning point as historians from each of these specialties began to publish influential and occasionally controversial studies of employers. In business history, pioneering works appeared on topics such as factory personnel management (Nelson), welfare capitalism (Brandes), and industrial relations policies and politics (Harris). In labor history, a group mostly of younger scholars went beyond the antinomies of "old" and "new" to produce studies that integrated top-down institutional analysis and bottom-up portraits of daily life at work. These covered a range of industries, including the railroads (Licht), electrical machinery (Schatz), department stores (Benson), and automobiles (Lichtenstein). Least affected by the new approach was economic history, although several radical economic historians (Marglin, Stone, Braverman, Edwards) wrote pathbreaking historical analyses of the labor process and of labor market segmentation. These were followed by elaborate radical syntheses (Gordon, Edwards, and Reich) and by critiques from more mainstream economic historians (Sokoloff, Landes).[9]

Underlying scholarly interest in employers are some dramatic changes in contemporary workplaces: the decline of organized labor, the emergence of innovative forms of work organization, and a new managerial concentration on employment and personnel matters. Although the changes have been felt throughout the advanced industrial world, they have affected individual nations to varying degrees. Unionization trends have shown the greatest diversity. At one extreme is the United States, which since 1970 has experienced a large drop (−13 percent) in its organized work force. At the other end are nine nations whose unionization rates rose by 5 percent or more during the same period, including Italy, France, West Germany, Australia, Canada, and the Scandinavian countries.

Innovations in work systems and management organization are occurring with greater uniformity across the advanced nations—employee participation in decision-making, job redesign, and an elevated status for the corporate personnel function. This suggests, first, that the changes in work and management structures have less to do with the decline of unions than with more universal factors such as new technology, rising education levels, and intensified competition; and second, that there is something peculiar about the union-management relationship in the United States.[10]

These events have brought a new appreciation for the pivotal role that employers play in the workplace and in the larger industrial relations system. This is not an ideological judgment. Interest in management extends across the spectrum, affecting Marxist as well as conservative scholars. Rather, it demonstrates greater realism on the part of those studying work, workers, and industrial relations. It is thought to be entirely appropriate for a social scientist's research interests to be shaped by current events. But many historians, especially those trained before the 1960s, consider any link between present and past—even if only in the choice of research topic—a form of presentism which violates the canons of historical objectivity. That attitude is changing, however. Younger historians, while careful to avoid reading the present into the past, are less inhibited in their choice of research questions. They believe that it is natural and legitimate to pursue topics inspired by present-day concerns.[11]

At the same time that historians are being drawn to questions raised by current events, social scientists are coming to have a greater respect for, and interest in, historical analysis. In the burgeoning social science literature on employers, issues are framed in historical terms and heavy use is made of historical research. With industrial relations systems in flux around the world, social scientists find themselves less able to predict the future confidently. There is a realization that, to understand where current events are leading us, it is helpful to have a historical perspective on long-term processes of change and continuity in labor-management relations and workplace organization.[12]

The impetus for research on employers also comes from more academic realms, in the form of new theoretical constructs that aid our comprehension of management policies. Economists are coming to emphasize realistic theories of the firm—those that can explain why firms exist and why they have the policies and structures that are observed at various times. This "new institutionalism" analyzes managerial motivations, firm-market (contractual) relations, and intra-firm relations, including internal labor markets. As in Nelson and Winter's evolutionary theory of the firm or in Williamson's work on corporate organization, there is explicit recognition that organizations—unlike markets—are situated in specific times and places. They have histories that, to some extent, shape their current structure and policies. Because of these insights, economists are starting to pay more attention to historical analysis, while historians—notably Chandler and his followers—are allowing economic theory to guide their historical research.[13]

Economics is not the only discipline whose ideas undergird research on employers. Although sociologists have long been interested in the study of bureaucracy, the field of organizational sociology has expanded by leaps and bounds during the past twenty years. Some of this growth comes from the increasing number of sociologists employed in business schools; some of it stems from attempts by sociologists to emulate the rigorous but antisubjectivist methods used by economists. In any event, sociology now provides a set of conceptual tools that are useful to those studying employers. Various theories examine the determinants of a firm's administrative structure and its mechanisms for employee control. Factors that have come under scrutiny include the production technology a firm uses (e.g., batch versus mass production); the "environment" in which the firm operates (a term that connotes quasibiological niches as well as cultural and political forces that affect, and are affected by, firms and their managers); and the firm's size or age. Combining an emphasis on age and on bureaucratic inertia, sociologists arrive at the conclusion that an organization's founding and history are important to understanding its present functioning.[14]

Along with their mainstream colleagues, neo-Marxist and radical social scientists have done their share of theorizing about employers, workers, and firms. Braverman's book on scientific management and the deskilling of labor, although flawed, had an enormous impact on social scientists interested in work structures and on historians studying management methods and the evolution of the labor process. Similarly, although the concept of labor market segmentation has proven to be empirically elusive, it sparked a slew of studies in fields ranging from the sociology of labor markets to the analysis of earnings structures. Segmentation theory always included a historical component, linked either to long-term economic cycles or to evolving struggles between workers and employers. Hence the theory relied heavily on historical sources and spurred additional research by labor and economic historians.[15]

As these examples suggest, research on employers and work relations involves a high degree of cross-disciplinary fertilization. Social scientific concepts and methodologies provide fresh hypotheses for, and impart statistical precision to, historical research; at the same time, exposure to historical research helps social scientists understand the importance of contingency, custom, origins, and evolution. But though research on employers provides a context for dialogue between social scientists and historians, there is also tension in their relationship.

Social scientists tend to look for recurring, universal patterns that theory can slice out of myriad case studies. Historians, however, are more inclined to emphasize unique circumstances or to interpret facts as they relate to particular historical contexts. Given these opposite orientations, it is little wonder that historians fault social scientists for putting the cart of theory before the horse of facts, a practice that is thought to produce an excessively mechanistic and deterministic view of the world. But social scientists are equally inclined to criticize historians for treating facts as ends in themselves, resulting either in a reluctance to link facts into larger patterns of meaning and causation or in an inability to create theories that transcend specific coordinates of time and place. These tensions regularly surface when historians and social scientists labor together in the same vineyards of history. As the essays in this book prove, the field of employer history is no exception.[16]

Yet it would be misleading to suggest that social scientists are themselves in agreement on important methodological issues. Among them there is considerable contention over the appropriate weight to give to material factors (economic, bureaucratic, and technological) as opposed to cultural factors (social, political, and social psychological) in the creation and operation of human institutions. The disputes range across a variety of topics. But their intensity rises when it comes to the study of work relations in business organizations, a subject situated at the confluence between material and cultural forces. Most social scientists acknowledge that employers make decisions in response to economic and bureaucratic imperatives. The debate concerns how much additional emphasis—ranging from none to a great deal—should be placed on cultural forces that arise outside the firm and that widen the array of strategies available to employers.

ANALYZING EMPLOYERS

Different ways of thinking about employers arise from debates within and across the disciplines whose boundaries overlap the field of employer studies. The view that employers' actions are driven by the exigencies of production will be called the *internal factors* approach, whereas an emphasis on external, cultural forces will be referred to as the *environmental factors* approach. A third view, the *contingent factors* approach, favors a more situational and less explicitly theoretical view of employers' activities. Each of these views is represented in the contributions to this book and has historical implications.

The *internal factors* approach portrays employers as reactive agents whose decisions are made in response to technological and economic necessity. The decisions are highly constrained: managers either choose the right technology and the right organizational form or they risk losing profits and market share to competitors who *do* make the correct choice. All else counts for little. In this view, there usually is only one right way of doing things. Employers arrive at it either by emulating successful competitors or by rationally calculating how to get the greatest amount of effort from their employees at the lowest possible cost. Often the various pressures that management must resolve are reduced to a fundamental driving force such as efficiency, transaction costs, or labor cheapening and control.

An example of the internal factors approach is business historian Alfred D. Chandler's research on the rise of the multidivisional firm in the United States. According to Chandler, large bureaucratic firms with differentiated product lines were chiefly the result of economic and technical developments: the expansion of markets, rapid increases in production throughput time, and the economies achieved by internalizing business transactions. Several of Chandler's followers have applied these ideas to the workplace, attributing the emergence of bureaucratized employment relations and internal labor markets to the same forces that brought about giant corporations.[17]

Somewhat different application of the internal factors approach is found in various radical accounts of the labor process, chief among these being Harry Braverman's *Labor and Monopoly Capital,* a blend of history and industrial sociology. For Braverman, the key to the evolution of the modern workplace lies in the continual search by employers for methods to cut labor costs and control workers' effort, chiefly by reducing employees' discretion and skill levels. Although coming from very different intellectual traditions. Braverman and Chandler both perceive the employer's world as one framed by the forces of production.[18]

Advocates of the internal factors approach, like the classical economists who first conceived of it, have the advantage of possessing a relatively simple, yet powerful and realistic, model of business decision making. After all, most employers were (and are) sober, rational businessmen not usually known for their broad interests. Even when an employer articulates an idiosyncratic philosophy of employee relations, it often stems from economic or organizational necessity. As Daniel Raff reminds us in his study of welfare work at Ford Motor Company (essay 4), businessmen "are famous for the relentless focus on reducing costs and making money."

But a weakness of the approach lies in its tendency to explain historical events in functional rather than causal terms. Institutions that persist—the multidivision firm, internal labor markets, scientific management—are assumed to be meeting a business necessity such as efficiency or control. A corollary—that observed institutions or policies were initially adopted to enhance efficiency or control—leads to functionalist statements of the sort: institution X came about because efficiency or control requirements dictated X for situations of type Y. But demonstrating that an institution met some business need is not the same as explaining the causal process by which it emerged out of earlier ones. Another weakness comes from reducing observed phenomena to manifestations of a single, articulated totality. As a result, the workplace is seen as pervaded and dominated by the logic of efficient economizing or of calculated control, each a totality that "eliminates resistance, absorbs alternatives, and assimilates critique."[19]

Several contributors to this book make use of the internal factors framework, although each is careful to qualify it in various ways. For example, Christiansen and Philips, in their analysis of the nineteenth-century Massachusetts boot and shoe industry (essay 1), make the point that efficiency itself can be given a historical interpretation: although efficiency guided the development of the shoe factory system, its path was fixed by a set of initial conditions that were unrelated to efficiency (such as wealth distribution and discrimination against women in capital markets).[20] From a different perspective, Howell Harris (essay 5) criticizes the idea that large firms and deskilled mass production were always and everywhere more profitable than alternative production and employment systems. In the early twentieth-century metalworking industry, small firms thrived because they were flexible—able to respond nimbly to sudden shifts in demand. Their viability stemmed from reliance on skilled labor and from close ties to competitors and suppliers, a combination that proved a profitable alternative to industrial integration and deskilling. In this way, Harris reorients the internal factors approach away from a mechanical determinism that sees internalization and deskilling as inevitable and toward a more historical perspective on these issues. His approach leads to such questions as: what were the conditions that permitted a given system of production and employment to thrive at certain times or places but not others? That question is especially pertinent in light of the difficulties recently experienced by America's large mass production firms.[21]

Environmental factors are usually offered as a complement to rather than a substitute for internal factors. That is, the importance of internal factors is usually acknowledged, but the idea that a particular set of those factors inevitably gives rise to a particular set of employment institutions is rejected. Instead, environmental factors—cultural norms, government regulation, social conflict, political power, and ideologies of authority—are thought to mediate the effect of internal factors, making the latter a necessary but not sufficient explanation of observed outcomes. Out of the infinitely varied forms these mediations can take comes a range of feasible employment policies and the possibility of a more strategic, less reactive posture on the part of employers. Strategy is also thought to derive from the ability of employers to act upon—not simply respond to—the forces found in the business environment. Under this approach, then, there is no one right way of doing things. Perhaps the clearest expression of this is comparative analysis, which demonstrates how a similar set of internal factors can lead to widely varying outcomes in different national settings.

Environmental factors bulk larger in personnel management than they do in such other realms of business activity as accounting, finance, or production. Employees cross the barrier between the firm and its environment, bringing with them a set of cultural and social relations that permeates the workplace. Also, employees are capable of shaping the business environment through their activities in politics, unions, and other organizations. But social relations and business objectives do not always mesh, and employees do not always agree with their employers' policies. Hence the environmental factors approach leads to a pluralist view of how employment decisions are made: that they are the result of a struggle between competing interests and need not reflect what the internal factors approach would see as "strict business necessity." Again, this approach creates a more indeterminate, less pessimistic view than is held by those who see organizations as being governed by immutable laws (whether those of Marx, Michels, Weber, or Williamson).

Here lies one explanation for economic and business historians' traditional lack of attention to employment policy: it is a subject that does not easily fit with their material approach. These historians are more likely to dwell on "hard" subjects like technology, finance, or vertical integration because internal factors bulk larger in those areas than in the workplace. But that is not to say that environmental forces can safely be ignored or given short shrift when it comes to analyzing "hard" topics. For example, comparative management studies have found that Japanese firms are enmeshed in a web of "relational" ties to customers, suppliers, and government, which function as a partial substitute for vertical integration; British and American firms also have those ties, although they are less elaborate. Efforts have been made to rationalize these national differences in terms of internal factors such as corporate growth rates. A more realistic approach, however, is one that acknowledges the role of social and political forces.[22] Economic and business historians are not the only ones at fault here. Until recently, cultural and social historians failed to extend their analytical ambit to include business and economic topics. As historian Martin J. Sklar put it, "The tendency to regard 'business' as economics or as economic history, or as consisting of 'interests' and techno-economic structures and functions, in contrast to ideas and social movements, has obstructed the study of capitalists as a social class and as involved in social movements. . . . It has largely confined the discipline of social history to noncapitalist classes and strata."[23]

Today, however, economic historians are going beyond their forebears in giving weight to environmental factors in business management, while social historians are paying more attention to business, economics, and related topics. The new directions are exemplified by several contributions to this book. In his study of French employers (essay 7), Gerald Friedman uses statistical and other methods to ana-

lyze the relationship between economic, political, and industrial relations variables. Friedman finds that French businessmen banded
together in employers' associations after 1900 as a belated response
to labor's successful use of its political influence among the leaders
and agencies of the Third Republic. In the American case, Daniel
Ernst and Howell Harris (essays 5 and 6) emphasize a similar point:
that employers turned to each other and to judicial and political
strategies because these offered potent, although not always reliable,
alternatives to the pursuit of policies centered on the individual enterprise. Joint control of the labor market obviated the need for elaborate internal labor markets; when the objective was to weaken unions,
employer associations and judicial activism were a substitute for
repression by individual employers. Finally, my own study of employers' antiunionism (essay 8) explores the possibility that American
employers were more overtly hostile to unions than their European
counterparts because they had available to them political and social
resources—not merely economic incentives—that were lacking in the
European case: noninterventionist traditions of government, a feder-
alist state, an independent judiciary, and cultural norms (such as
individualism and achievement) that were useful in mobilizing public
opinion against organized labor.

Still, there are limits to stressing the environment. Just as it is a
mistake to cut off the business firm from its social moorings, so is it
possible to overemphasize the social and cultural aspects of workplace management. This leads to what sociologists critically refer to
as the "oversocialized" view of economic institutions. As Daniel Raff
reminds us, one can go quite far with a technological and economic
explanation of a phenomenon like welfare capitalism before having to
invoke government policy, social mores, or managerial ideologies.[24]

The *contingent factors* approach is critical of determinism, whether
economic or social, mainstream or Marxist. Here the stress is on
chance, variety, hazard, and complexity. Case studies are favored
because they reveal the contextual variables that influence or override
the grand forces stressed in more sweeping accounts. Employer policy
is either seen as idiosyncratic (the great man or great woman approach) or as the result of a series of localized adjustments to historically specific, often unpredictable events. This is "management by
putting out fires" rather than a strategic method. The emphasis is on
piecemeal adjustments to unforeseen events and their unintended
consequences. Management practice is as likely to be driven by external events as it is to be divorced from them; fleeting fads coexist with
sluggish custom.

The contingent approach is an offshoot of the historicism that infuses and makes distinctive the traditional, narrative account of history. Facts and institutions are thought to be rooted in a unique historical context, the objective description of which is the historian's task. Narrative historians are skeptical of social science history, with its selective and theory-driven accounts of the past. Mechanical schema derived from abstract theory—whether stage theories of capitalism or neoclassical models of the firm—are rejected in favor of nuanced, concrete, and detailed descriptions of what "really" happened. The approach applies to employer history as well as to other realms of historical research. Whereas economic historians emphasize that internal factors (chiefly efficiency) constrain employers' policy, a contingent approach would stress that the primacy of efficiency is itself dependent on factors that vary over time. Whereas Marxist historians portray employers' policy in instrumental terms—the result of capitalists having effective control of the workplace and the state—a contingent approach would question whether the generalization holds true in all or even most historical cases.

Although critical of social science history, the contingent approach nevertheless has received empirical support from recent social scientific studies of contemporary employers. The studies find little evidence that managers act strategically through a conscious linkage of personnel policy to corporate objectives. Instead, managers are found to take things as they come, rarely acting with foresight or philosophical consistency. There is little evidence that technology, integration, or diversification is systematically related to specific personnel policies. In many instances, employers and workers are committed to an employment system that is in the long-term interests of neither; instead, the system is kept going through the inertial forces of custom and day-to-day compromises that meet short-term requirements. In these situations there is no plan, nor are there inevitable results. Finally, though many companies claim to have a definite philosophy of employee relations, few of them write it down and fewer still translate it into actual workplace practices.[25]

Deterministic or functional accounts of workplace history are sharply criticized in several of the contributions to this book. Although Marxist and mainstream accounts often portray scientific management as the dominant force in American management during the twentieth century, Daniel Nelson's careful empirical research (essay 3) suggests otherwise. Nelson finds that by the 1920s, Taylorism was neither so pervasive nor so corrosive of skill levels and worker control as has been claimed. In their studies of the French state and of the American judiciary, Gerald Friedman (essay 7) and Daniel Ernst (essay 6) find little support for an instrumentalist view of government labor policy and labor law. Just as the French state often intervened on behalf of its union supporters, so did American industrialists find the law to be far from a reliable weapon. Judges held a wide range of values that sometimes, but hardly always, overlapped the employer's interests.

Perhaps this book's most powerful brief in support of the contingent approach is Walter Licht's study of twenty Philadelphia firms (essay 2). Licht argues that no single theoretical framework comes close to capturing the variety of personnel practices that he observes. As in contemporary studies, Licht finds only a weak correlation between a firm's personnel policies and its size, technology, and ownership form. Moreover, Licht finds little evidence that personnel policies evolved in a linear fashion in response to the labor problems of successive historical periods. Instead, the Philadelphia companies were notable for the "persistence of old forms and old methods [and] the continuity of efforts."

Thus the debate—over what, if anything, systematically determines employer strategy—reflects larger, ongoing disputes within and between various scholarly disciplines. Perhaps the most that can fairly be said is that there is a danger in pushing any method—even the lack of one—too far. No single perspective on the workplace is accurate for all times and places, but some are more helpful than others in particular situations. History teaches us that employers face recurrent problems, and while each generation of employers fashions its own solutions, in doing so it relies heavily on values and institutions inherited from the past. That is, although employers make choices, their choices are constrained by custom, competition, and culture. Equivocal as these statements may sound, they echo the prudent judgments of my fellow contributors.

QUO VADIS?

Historical research on employers is a missing link that can connect the previously disparate disciplines of labor, business, and economic history to each other and to recent work being done in the social sciences. The field offers numerous unexplored opportunities to examine historical relationships between economy and society, organization and ideology, and workers and the workplace. For these reasons, the field of employer history (or industrial relations history, as others have termed it) is likely to grow in coming years. The workplace was and still is a central yet problematic feature of modern industrial society, one that continues to arouse ideas and strong feelings within us all.[26]

I hope that this book will spark the curiosity of scholars and students and interest some of them sufficiently to pursue additional studies on this subject. It has been said before but is nevertheless true in this case that more research—by historians as well as by social scientists—remains to be done. There still is much that we do not know about the employer's role in the employment relationship. But there is a problem. Corporate archives, a source for several studies in this book, are rapidly disappearing. Acquisitions, mergers, cost-cutting, and a fear of lawsuits are causing companies to dispose of their old papers and records. Even at firms that still keep archives, records are purged of controversial material or closed to the public, even to credentialed scholars.[27] Those already working in this field need to do what they can to prevent the spread of this historical amnesia. Those who wish to enter the field should have realistic expectations about the accessibility of source materials. Still, the barriers are far from insuperable, as is amply proven by the essays gathered here.

I
MANAGING THE
WORKPLACE

■

The workplace is the primary point of contact between employers and workers. Often it also has been a source of friction. During the nineteenth century, the workplace moved from the worker's home or the master's shop to larger, more mechanized sites known as factories, manufactories, and mills. Factories first appeared in the textile industry and then spread to other industries such as glass, iron and steel, shoes, and machinery. Toward the end of the century, the steel industry surpassed textiles in factory size. By 1900, a half-dozen steel mills in the United States each employed between six and ten thousand workers.

With this growth in scale, the employer's task correspondingly became more complex. Whereas the master of a small artisanal shop worked alongside his employees and knew them personally, large employers of the early twentieth century often had no idea precisely how many workers were on their payrolls. Management of the workplace was left to the firm's foremen, who were in charge of hiring, training, supervising, and motivating the workers in their departments. But the decentralized system of control by foremen proved increasingly incapable of coordinating production or resolving problems such as labor turnover, indiscipline, and strikes. Foremen were gradually displaced by more bureaucratic forms of personnel management and more sophisticated methods of employee relations.

Part One opens with Christiansen and Philips's essay on the rise of the factory system in the Massachusetts boot and shoe industry. The authors find that none of the existing explanations for the move from outwork to factory production fits the facts in this particular industry.

Although mainstream and Marxist economic historians have different interpretations of the shift to factories, both emphasize that it stemmed from problems in the workplace. Under outwork, employers allegedly were unable to sustain workers' effort or to secure suitable levels of workmanship. But Christiansen and Philips show this not to have been true in the shoe industry, in which outwork was a viable and efficient alternative to the mechanized stitching shops that appeared in the 1840s and 1850s. Yet the story becomes more complicated. With the introduction of the McKay stitcher and steam power in the 1860s, integrated factory production became more productive than outwork. The reasons for its advantage had less to do with technological factors stressed by economic historians than with the appearance of sweated labor in the form of speedups and stretchouts. Christiansen and Philips's research stands as a warning against rationalizing the past as a progression toward more efficient or more sophisticated forms of workplace organization.

Walter Licht's survey of twenty Philadelphia firms contains a similar warning against teleology. Licht observes a spectrum of personnel policies over the years 1850 to 1950, ranging from highly informal to consciously paternalistic to rationalized and bureaucratic. Although theoretical explanations for these policies abound, Licht finds that none can adequately account for the diversity he observes. Moreover, says Licht, it is a mistake to read the past as movement through stages from less to more formal policies. Some companies followed that pattern; many did not.

In their attempt to raise workers' loyalty and productivity, American employers developed two major approaches: scientific management and welfare work. Both can be traced back to the 1880s, when recurring labor unrest and the appearance of giant national firms shook the foundations of America's emerging industrial society. Halsey's "premium plan" of paying labor was developed during the mid-1880s at the same time that employers began to experiment with company towns, profit sharing, and other welfare activities. Yet it was not until the 1900s and 1910s that scientific management and welfare work became mass movements, each with its own popularizers, journals, and employer organizations. It was also in these decades that "efficiency and uplift" became cultural movements that burst the boundaries of the business firm and coursed through other institutions ranging from the schools to the military. As expressions of larger cultural movements, scientific management and welfare work have been interpreted in various ways: as part of a "search for order" by members of the middle class made anxious by industrialism; as offshoots of an "organizational revolution" whose aim was the bureaucratization and professionalization of social life; or as adjuncts of an ambitious drive by businessmen to stabilize and deradicalize American society by supporting reform legislation, social planning, and government regulation—what has come to be called "corporate liberalism."

The last two essays in this section are skeptical of recent efforts by social scientists and historians to make scientific management and welfare work into more than they were. These essays substitute fact and historical specificity for hyperbole and broad generalization. Daniel Nelson measures the precise effect of scientific management on the American workplace of the 1920s and 1930s. Rather than examine what managers and engineers said in magazines and textbooks, Nelson studies what they did. His essay brings together survey data on employer practices and case studies done at the point of production. He finds that scientific management had a modest effect on skill levels and wage methods. Wage incentives and other forms of scientific management were not nearly as widespread in practice as they were in print. And even when scientific management *was* implemented, it failed to transform the workplace in the way that Taylor and other industrial engineers had promised it would. Nelson concludes that the record of Taylorism in industry after 1920 does not support "apocalyptic views of the workers' degradation."

Perhaps the most famous example of welfare work in action was the highly publicized program introduced by the Ford Motor Company in 1913, including the five-dollar day, home visiting, and various activities aimed at "Americanizing" Ford's workers. In the final essay of this section, Daniel Raff argues that the Ford program received so much attention because it was *not* just another collection of "incidentally variegated but fundamentally homogeneous, and static [welfare] activities." Moreover, says Raff, the program had little to do with the kind of vague altruism and benevolent control that are usually seen as impelling motives for welfare work. Instead, Ford's idiosyncratic and highly expensive programs were a calculated response to the peculiar production system that the company launched at the same time as its welfare plan. This system was the mechanized assembly line, consisting of a series of dedicated machines that could be operated by semiskilled workers. Because the assembly line was so complex and tightly coupled, and because it promised to pump out a steady stream of profits, any collective action by even a small group of workers could have cost the company far more than the welfare programs. Cash, says Raff, was the sole motivator; conscience mattered not a bit.

1

The Transition from Outwork to Factory Production in the Boot and Shoe Industry, 1830–1880

■

JENS CHRISTIANSEN
PETER PHILIPS

Why the factory superceded previous methods of production remains a highly controversial issue in economic history. In this article, we analyze the transition from outwork to factory production in the Lynn, Massachusetts, boot and shoe industry of the mid-nineteenth century. We argue that existing theories about similar transitions, while containing many correct elements, ultimately fail to explain the Lynn process adequately. In particular, all these theories present one-dimensional views of the underlying forces that led to the hierarchical and centralized organization of factory production. We reject the position that this process was inevitable for reasons of technical or cost efficiency, but we also disagree with the claim that factory production was solely used to increase capitalists' control over workers. While we combine elements of previous explanations of the transition from outwork to factory production, we introduce two additional factors largely ignored in the literature: the importance of easy access to capital in stimulating factory production and the role of mechanization in inducing increased labor effort in the factories.

For neoclassical economics, the transition from outwork to factory production has long been a prime example of the "natural" progression from less efficient to more efficient methods of production. In the context of a competitive market, such increases in efficiency are always interpreted as the result of profit-maximizing behavior in which employers hire labor, purchase machines, and buy raw materials that the production process then transforms into maximum output with the best available (i.e., most efficient) technology. In this scenario, social and organizational aspects of this process—such issues as power, hierarchy, and control—do not play any role. Technology alone becomes the black box that transforms labor and other resources into final products. When better technologies become available, they are quickly adopted because ultimately they increase profits, either by cutting costs or by providing more output for the same inputs. Consequently, the fact that factories replaced outwork systems has been taken as evidence that their hierarchical and centralized organization of production was (and still is) technologically superior.

In the last two decades, this orthodox position has been challenged from different perspectives and for different reasons. In his seminal article "What Do Bosses Do?"[1] Marglin argues that employers introduced factory production so that they could supervise workers and reduce raw material usage by eliminating waste and theft. However, Marglin points out that what the employer labeled waste often occurred because workers economized on their own labor. Similarly, what the employer saw as theft was to the workers a way of appropriating materials that were by tradition due to them. In other words, changes in the production process were primarily the result of a struggle over the burdens and fruits of labor rather than an advance in society's capacity to generate output from a given amount of inputs. Hence, says Marglin, "rather than providing more output for the same inputs, these innovations in work organization were introduced so that the capitalist got himself a larger share of the pie at the expense of the worker, and it is only the *subsequent* growth in the size of the pie that has obscured the class interest which was at the root of these innovations."[2]

Marglin further argues that factory production, from the employer's perspective, increased the possibilities for sweating labor. In the outwork system, the pace and the pattern of production were only vaguely known to the employer. However, in factories, idle time and slack effort could be observed and then eliminated as a result of the employers' direct supervision of workers. But Marglin points out that this development too was a struggle over the burdens and benefits of labor—over the effort wage—rather than an advance in the productive power of society as a whole. What the employer considered slack effort was to the worker needed and earned rest. Even before the introduction of machinery, factories produced more output for given inputs than the outwork system, simply because direct supervision ensured harder work. Thus, the gain in output came from an increase in effort, not from technological superiority.

In Marglin's view, mechanization of already existing factories is also suspect. It cannot be considered merely a technical advance because it developed within an organizational context that promoted the power of employers to control workers and develop production. Thus, while mechanized factories did, in fact, raise the productive capacity of society, there is no reason to believe that mechanization was moving along a distributionally neutral or socially optimal path.

Marglin's critique of the traditional neoclassical argument has provoked a lively debate in which both Jones and Landes, for example, reaffirm the orthodox position while others, such as Williamson, challenge it, but on grounds different from Marglin's.[3]

Williamson and others criticize the orthodox position for ignoring important cost elements. They argue that the factory's superiority over the outwork system, and therefore its adoption, can be explained by taking transaction costs into consideration. Factories offered substantial savings to employers by eliminating the high information and transportation costs associated with the outwork system. Furthermore, factories offered employers greater flexibility to match a worker's skills to job requirements. Consequently, in this argument, factories replaced outwork because they represented a more efficient organization of production.

A proper evaluation of this debate must involve historical fact as much as economic logic. No single case can present all the historical issues, nor can it claim to settle all the theoretical disputes. However, this case study of the Lynn boot and shoe industry is a particularly useful one. It involves a large, vital, and long-lasting outwork system that rivaled the importance of textiles for industrial employment in mid-nineteenth-century New England. Furthermore, a wealth of statistical and descriptive material exists on the industry. In particular, the previously unused, company-level data from the Census of Manufactures manuscripts (including quantities and values of output and inputs, male and female wages, etc.) allow us to test Marglin's propositions that factory production sweated labor and economized on material usage. The more descriptive material, such as contemporary newspaper articles and government reports, enables us to assess the orthodox claim that factories emerged primarily to exploit the scale economies of new technologies. It also allows us to examine Williamson's claim that outwork systems fell of their own weight as rising transaction costs made outwork production increasingly unprofitable.

Analyzing these rich and varied historical sources, we come to the conclusion that no single theoretical approach—whether by Marglin, Williamson, or more orthodox economists—fully explains historical reality. The first shoe factories came to Lynn in the 1850s in the form of stitching shops that employed female workers to sew shoe uppers on hand- and foot-powered sewing machines—a process called binding. The reason for the emergence of stitching shops is neither, as Marglin would argue, that they saved on raw materials (in fact stitching shops used *more* material than the outwork system), nor, as orthodox proponents would claim, that they exploited economies of scale (in fact sewing machines could be used just as effectively at home— and continued to be used in the home for almost two decades). Instead, we argue that the first shoe factories were established because female workers did not have as easy access to capital as did employers —a factor that has not yet received any attention in the debate over the transition from outwork to factory production.

During the first decade of factory production (1852–1862), men's work still remained within the outwork system. Contrary to Williamson's stress on transaction costs, this is a clear indication that such costs did not matter enough to force men's work into factories. Factory production for their work came only after the mid-1860s, with the introduction and widespread adoption of the McKay stitcher and steam power. Although this sequence supports the orthodox link between power machines and the factory system, our data enable us to show that factory production was based not only on changes in technology but also on the intensification of labor.

OUTWORK PRODUCTION OF BOOTS AND SHOES,
1830–1852

Shoemaking in Lynn dates back to the middle of the eighteenth century, when the Welsh cordwainer (shoemaker) John Adam Dagyr settled in the town. He taught shoemaking skills to every man interested in learning. Over the next fifty years, this new occupation took hold, and small outbuildings—called ten-footers because of their size— sprang up in backyards all over Lynn.[4] Here, a master shoemaker would work side by side with two or three journeymen and, at times, one or two apprentices.[5] These men made the shoes by forming the upper leather into shape (lasting) and attaching the soles to it (bottoming). From the very beginning, the upper leather was sewn by their wives and daughters in nearby kitchens (binding).

Initially all shoes (and boots)[6] were produced on direct orders of the customer and for the local market only. Eventually, however, shoemakers started to produce extra stock which they sold through local shopkeepers. Before the end of the century, some shopkeepers and master shoemakers began to take boots and shoes to Salem and Boston in search of new buyers. Increasingly, footwear from Lynn found its way to many places along the Atlantic Coast and eventually even to the South, the West, and overseas.

Although some master shoemakers were involved in finding new markets for their products, the shopkeepers ultimately dominated the trade. In the early nineteenth century, these Yankee traders established themselves as manufacturers because they were able to finance large credit sales and to buy leather in large quantities at lower prices than individual shoemakers. In many cases, the shopkeepers' general merchandise stores were slowly turned into the central shops for outwork boot and shoe production. Here the raw and semifinished materials were stored and the finished products prepared for shipment. In 1837, a Lynn newspaper described a shoe manufacturer as "a wholesale dealer, who owns an establishment, purchases the various kinds of stock in large quantities; employs many individuals in the various branches of making and superintends the whole. This requires a considerable capital."[7]

One such manufacturer was Micajah Pratt, the son of a shoe dealer, who in 1812 started his own shoe business out of a two-story wooden central shop. In 1850, he expanded into a new brick building which was

> converted to a steampowered, mechanized factory around the time of his death in 1866. For a generation prior to this, he was the largest manufacturer in town, employing as many as 500 men and women in peak seasons to make about a quarter of a million pairs annually. The two generations of the Pratt family embodied the evolution of industrial roles from retail shopkeeper through central shop manufacturer to factory owner.[8]

Even though shopkeepers such as Micajah Pratt took over the shoe trade, production continued in the ten-footers and kitchens using the same tools, techniques, and gender division of labor as before: male shoemakers cut the soles out of leather from the central shop, and sewed or pegged the bottoms to uppers that had been sewn, or bound, by their wives and daughters. Both male and female workers were paid piece rates for their work.

Expansion of the Outwork System: Problems and Adjustment

From an analytical perspective, the outwork system can be seen as a device for recruiting and managing wage labor. Shopkeepers who shifted into shoe production (manufacturers or employers) did not have to seek out or train a new labor force. A production system was already in place, with a well-developed apprenticeship system for male workers and a family network that drew female binders into shoe production. But with the expansion of production in the first half of the nineteenth century, the shoe manufacturers found that the traditional outwork system no longer functioned effectively. Recruiting and managing labor now became problems.

The system imposed limits on the available labor supply, both male and female. The supply of skilled male shoemakers was limited by the craft traditions of the outwork apprenticeship system. Constraints on the supply of female labor appeared earlier and were more serious, even though female labor was unskilled, i.e., all New England girls of this era possessed the sewing skills necessary to bind the thin pieces of upper leather. The constraints resulted from the gender division of labor in the traditional outwork system. Originally, the central shop extended raw materials to male shoemakers, who passed on the task of binding to related females. This limited the pool of available female workers; there was approximately the same number of women within the outwork system as men. Between 1810 and 1830, when manufacturers attempted to increase overall production and sent larger batches to the ten-footers, the supply of female workers proved inadequate. Male shoemakers could keep pace by working longer hours; the women, however, could not do so because of household obligations.

Consequently, shoemakers sought out additional, unrelated neighborhood women to help complete the bindings of shoes on a part-time basis. At the same time, some manufacturers began to distribute the uppers directly to female workers. As early as 1830, one central shop in Lynn distributed only 20 percent of its material to shoemakers within the traditional family network, while the remaining 80 percent were sent separately to men and women unrelated to each other. By the 1840s, this practice had become widespread. As a result, the proportion of women workers rose significantly above that of men, thus compensating for women's limited working hours (see table 1.1).[9] The ability of manufacturers to tap into the pool of unskilled women outside the family network allowed the Lynn outwork system to expand production without going far afield for female labor.

Once the constraint on female labor had been removed, production increased rapidly. The apprenticeship system in Lynn could now no longer meet the increased demand for *male* shoe workers, and work had to be put out to places up to 100 miles away—in Maine, Vermont,

TABLE 1.1 Labor Productivity in the Lynn Boot and Shoe Industry, 1831–1880

Year	Total Employed	Percent Female	Output per Worker[j]	VALUE PER WORKER[k] Output	Materials	Capital
1831[a]	3,516	51%	477	$ 294	$130	
1832[b]			462			
1835[b]			469			
1837[c]	5,185	49	491	408		
1845[d]	5,928	54	406	393		
1850[e]	10,183	63	431	500	240	$123
1851[f]	10,191	63	449			
1855[g]	11,021	59	406	363		
1860[e]	9,265	40	576	486	240	118
1865[h]	11,968	40	489			
1870[e]	6,892	39	1,332	1,302	720	257
1875[i]	9,011	35				
1880[e]	8,415	32	1,490	1,490	860	346

SOURCES:

[a]*Lynn Directory*, 1832, pp. 12–15 (found in Lynn Historical Society).

[b]Alan Dawley, *Class and Community, The Industrial Revolution in Lynn* (Cambridge, Mass.: Harvard University Press, 1976), appendix A, pp. 245–47.

[c]John P. Bigelow, *Statistical Tables, Exhibiting the Condition and Products of Certain Branches of Industry in Massachusetts, for the Year Ending April 1, 1837* (Boston: Dutton and Wentworth, State Printers, 1838), pp. 11–12.

[d]John G. Palfrey, *Statistics of the Condition and Products of Certain Branches of Industry in Massachusetts for the Year Ending April 1, 1845* (Boston: Dutton and Wentworth, 1846).

[e]Calculated by authors from the manuscripts of the U.S. Census of Manufactures for Lynn, Massachusetts. Microfilms of these censuses are located at the University of Massachusetts, Amherst.

[f]*Lynn Directory*, 1851. The 1851 data appear to come from the manuscript census collection of 1850. We include the *Directory*'s published numbers for comparison with our own calculations for 1850.

[g]Francis DeWitt, *Statistical Information Relating to Certain Branches of Industry in Massachusetts, for the Year Ending June 1, 1855* (Boston: William White, State Printer, 1856).

[h]Oliver Warner, *Abstract of the Census of Massachusetts, 1865* (Boston: State Printers, 1867), pp. 150, 158–61.

[i]Carroll D. Wright, *Census of Massachusetts, 1875*, Vol. II, Boston, State Printer, 1877, pp. 391 and 611.

[j]In pairs of shoes and boots per annum.

[k]All prices in this table have been deflated by the wholesale price index (Warren and Pearson) for hides and leather products, U.S. Bureau of the Census, *Historical Statistics of the United States, Colonial Times to 1970* (Washington, D.C., 1975), p. 201.

and New Hampshire—in order to find shoemakers with sufficient skill to make at least the cheaper grade of shoes.[10] A middleman, or freighter, would bring samples of work from the outlying regions back to the central shop in Lynn. If the product was acceptable to the manufacturer, he would entrust the middleman with additional material for the rural outworkers.

However, an increase in Lynn's population kept this geographic extension of the outwork system within manageable bounds. This population growth was due both to an increase in the birthrate and to in-migration of working-age men and women attracted by the town's prosperity. From 1831 to 1850, the output of boots and shoes in Lynn rose by a factor of 2.6, and the population of Lynn rose by a factor of 2.3.[11] Shoe manufacturers could not force the apprenticeship system to recruit male newcomers, but family ties ensured that new family members found their way into the system. Moreover, the manufacturers could employ in-migrating females as binders.

Labor management problems, such as poor-quality work, slack effort,[12] waste, and theft are often regarded as the key threat to the viability of any outwork system.[13] Because the Lynn employer extended materials to the workers, these problems presented him with major risks. His risks were a function of the quantity of material sent out, the length of the production period, and his knowledge of the workers' productivity and honesty. To eliminate or at least reduce his risks, the employer adopted a number of strategies. He limited the amount of material extended to unproven workers and tried to shorten turnaround times. He also tried to increase his knowledge about his workers, often by using the services of a freighter. To ensure high and consistent quality, he carefully examined all shoes that came into the central shop and exacted penalties for inferior work, either by deducting from wages or by refusing to extend further material to incompetent workers.[14] Similarly, he attempted to deal with the issue of slack effort by imposing more definite turnaround times. If workers did not comply, no further material was extended.

However, these measures did not eliminate waste and theft. Before the 1830s, employers sent out whole leather hides to be cut into soles and uppers. Varying in size and thickness, each hide posed a unique challenge to determine the most efficient way that it could be cut into shoe parts. By tradition, all leftover scraps belonged to the cutter. Even if the worker was not cutting hides so as to increase such leftovers, the piece rate system still created waste by encouraging haste. Also, what appeared to the employer as theft might arguably be called necessary leftover by the worker. Each ten-footer had a special kitty for leftover scraps of leather, which were bought up by leather merchants. These leftovers thus provided some additional income to the workers.[15] In fact, the outwork system provided considerable opportunities for inefficient cutting and illicit sale of the material.

To eliminate waste and theft, employers in the 1830s brought skilled and trusted workers into the central shop as cutters. Their work could now be supervised, and employers paid them hourly, rather than piece-rate, wages to eliminate waste due to time pressure.[16] Marglin argues that the elimination of waste and theft was an important aspect in the move from outwork to factory production. In the case of Lynn boot and shoe production in the 1830s, however, it was sufficient for the employer to supervise only *one* crucial task directly; in all other respects, shoe production continued as an outwork system.

In the 1840s, the industry expanded further, and manufacturers went beyond Lynn in search of labor. All the risk factors mentioned above increased, as less qualified and less committed workers from outlying areas were brought into the system.[17] However, manufacturers again found ways of controlling such risks. First, only materials for cheap, low-quality shoes were sent out to the countryside; more expensive shoes continued to be put out to the better-known and more highly skilled workers closer to Lynn. Second, because of competition among freighters, the employers could force them to bear some of the risks associated with selecting distant outworkers. In effect, part of the service implicitly sold to the employer by the freighter was information about who would make a reliable outworker, information which the freighter gathered in his travels around the countryside.

Outwork: A Viable System

By 1850, boot and shoe production in New England rivaled the textile industry in output and employment. But textiles were produced in factories, while boot and shoe production remained within the outwork system. In Lynn, this system produced a large output for the national market and provided employment for a great number of people who retained a significant amount of independence and control over their own work life. The system performed so successfully because it had two significant advantages over factory production — access to labor and minimal investment of capital.

The outwork system was able to draw on a supply of cheap female labor unavailable to factories. While the textile industry had to draw women from the countryside and small towns to the factories, the outwork system could employ home workers from the larger pool of women unwilling and/or unable to leave home.[18] And because all women could sew, no elaborate apprenticeship system was needed to ensure a ready supply of binders.[19] Given this ready supply of female labor, Lynn shoe employers were able to pay low wage rates to their female workers.

Second, the outwork employer could take advantage of a well-established training system and production process, and did not have to commit any capital to buildings and equipment—apart from the central shop. Providing raw materials to the workers was his only major investment, and, as discussed above, he was able through a variety of techniques to reduce the risk involved in this investment.

However, the outwork system did present the employer with two drawbacks he could not easily overcome—exposure to the whims of the market and a constraint on craft labor. Dealing with groups of shoemakers in the ten-footers as independent and competing suppliers did indeed reduce his direct costs, but it also subjected him to the vagaries of product demand.[20] In times of strong demand, shoemakers were able to get increases in their piece-rates because of the limited supply of craft labor. As one shoemaker recalled: "We sacked the boss without scruple, when we could do better, and was [sic] sacked in turn by them when trade became slack and there were no orders on hand. . . ."[21]

The traditional outwork system also limited the supply of skilled labor. In the factories of the mid- to late nineteenth century, such craft labor constraints were typically overcome by extending the division of labor and by introducing deskilling and labor-saving technologies.[22] But shoe employers could not take these steps as long as production remained within the outwork system, where the shoemakers themselves retained control over production and had no interest in changing the traditional process. This drawback, insignificant as it was in terms of the daily functioning of the outwork system, was to present the employer with a major incentive for change to a production system that would give him much greater control.

ESTABLISHMENT OF THE FIRST FACTORIES,
1852–1862

Women's work in boot and shoe production began to change following the invention of the sewing machine in 1848. For the first time, large numbers of workers were soon to be gathered under one roof. By 1852, the first sewing machines designed for binding the thin leather of shoe uppers—work always done by women—were introduced in Lynn.[23] Initially, these machines were sold (and for a short time, a few were rented) to women who bound uppers at home.[24] Once a woman had gained some experience with the machine, she was able to sew a pair of uppers four times as fast as by hand. Because the quality of machine work was as good as, or better than, hand work, employers were willing to pay the same piece rate for both. The incomes of the relatively small number of women owning sewing machines rose considerably. In 1855, they were reported to be earning as much as $14 per week, and on average they were making $6 per week. In contrast, hand binders earned about $1.50 per week and male shoemakers earned around $5 per week.[25]

Sewing machines cost from $50 to $125, and women who could afford the initial outlay quickly recouped their investment. However, very few women were in fact able to afford the machines, and bank credit was not available to women at the time. But shoe manufacturers, with their access to capital, were able to exploit the new technology. Some of them bought machines, hired women binders, and set up so-called stitching shops. These were the first factories in the boot and shoe industry.[26]

Employers continued to pay piece rates in the new factories. Yet the fourfold productivity differential between machine work and hand work, together with the longer hours they imposed on the workers, allowed the employers to achieve two different goals simultaneously. They could pay a significantly lower piece rate in the stitching shops than in the outwork system, thus recouping their investment quickly and profiting from the productivity gains of the sewing machine. At the same time, women entering the stitching shops received total earnings comparable to those paid in textile factories but above those that could be made by hand binders at home (see table 1.2). This allowed employers to compete with textile factories in drawing women out of the home and into the stitching shops. (The few women who owned their own machines obviously made much higher earnings than any other group.)

From an analytical perspective, the decisive element that led to the establishment of the first factories in Lynn boot and shoe production was the manufacturers' recognition that in order to reap the financial benefits of the new technology they had to buy (and maintain) the machines themselves. Once the first stitching shops had been set up, high profits and strong competition among manufacturers led to a quick diffusion of the new technology and, for all intents and purposes, the exclusion of the workers from its financial benefits.[27]

Marglin would doubtless argue that stitching shops were estab-

TABLE 1.2 Average Values of Selected Variables for Stitching Shops and Outwork Firms, Lynn, Massachusetts, 1860

	MEAN (S.D.)[a]		
	Stitching Shop	*Outwork Firm*	*Z-test Stat.*[b]
Distinction criteria			
Percent female of work force	32%	49%	
Value of upper materials per female	$529	$145	
Variables with equal means			
Monthly male earnings	$22.19 ($3.09)	$22.65 ($2.14)	
Price of boots	$.94 ($.20)	$.96 ($.17)	
Value of bottom leather per male	$166 ($28)	$148 ($45)	1.65
Value of bottom leather per price of boot	.23 (.08)	.19 (.05)	1.67
Variables with different means			
Value added per laborer	$411 ($52)	$320 ($44)	5.69
Capital-labor ratio	$137 ($84)	$90 ($47)	2.14
Monthly female earnings	$10.51 ($2.03)	$7.93 ($1.77)	4.37
Value of upper materials per price of boot	.34 (.13)	.17 (.06)	100.00
N	16	34	

SOURCE: Calculations based on data from the manuscripts of the *U.S. Census of Manufactures, 1860* (microfilms at the University of Massachusetts, Amherst).

[a] Firms with stitching shops are identified as those with a female percentage of the work force smaller than 40 percent and a flow-through per female (value of upper material per female) greater than or equal to $400. Firms are identified as outwork firms if their female percentage is greater than or equal to 40 percent and their material flow-through per female is smaller than $200.

[b] The critical value for a z-test at the .05 level of significance is 1.96.

lished to economize on raw materials by eliminating waste and theft. But the data provided in the Census of Manufactures manuscripts for 1860 refute this hypothesis. The manuscripts do not tell us directly which employers had stitching shops and which continued to make use of the outwork system for binding. However, we are able to distinguish between the two groups on the basis of the following criteria: the relative number of female to male workers and the amount of raw material used per binder. Given the strict gender division of labor, whereby women only bound uppers and men carried out all other tasks, the high productivity of machine binding and the longer hours in the factories meant that employers with stitching shops needed fewer women relative to men than outwork employers. For the same reasons—high productivity and long hours—women in stitching shops used up more raw materials per year than women in the outwork system. Thus, we can identify employers with stitching shops by their relatively low percentage of female workers and relatively high volume of material usage. In 1860, there were 16 employers with stitching shops and 34 outwork employers in Lynn (table 1.2). The former employed slightly less than one female worker for every two male workers, while the latter employed equal numbers of male and female workers.[28] The average value of upper material used per female worker was almost four times higher in the stitching shops than in the outwork system.[29] Both groups produced a homogeneous product (as indicated by the almost identical average price per pair of boots) and paid the same average monthly earnings to their male workers. As expected, the average capital-labor ratio, monthly female earnings, and value added per laborer were all higher in stitching shops than in outwork.

For our purposes, the most crucial distinction between stitching shop and outwork employers lies in the value of upper materials per boot: in 1860, it was twice as high for the former as for the latter. This is a clear indication that the early factories in Lynn did not economize on raw materials. (The reason why stitching shops used twice as much raw material per boot as outwork binding awaits further research. At this point, we assume that it was easier for a binder to make mistakes using a sewing machine than sewing by hand, and that stitching shops used many binders with less experience than binders in the outwork system.)

Throughout the 1850s and into the early 1860s, men's work continued as outwork in the ten-footers. This suggests that the transaction costs that Williamson sees as decisive for the shift to factory production did not play a crucial role in Lynn. If it had been the savings on those costs that forced women's work into the factories, the very same thing should have happened with men's work. However, it was only with the advent of the McKay stitcher and steam power that men's work moved into the factories.[30]

DEVELOPMENT OF THE INTEGRATED FACTORIES, 1862–1880

When male shoemakers were brought into the factories, the outwork system finally began to disappear. In Lynn, this process began in 1862 with the introduction of the McKay stitcher.[31] This heavy-duty machine, invented in 1857, stitched the thick leather of the soles to the thinner uppers at a speed that some contemporary observers claimed to be eighty times that of hand work.[32] Thus, an immense productivity increase occurred in one key area of men's work, while all other steps —such as cutting, shaving, channeling, and lasting—were unaffected. Obviously such a machine could not be utilized to its full potential within the small confines of the ten-footers. Furthermore, lasting and bottoming had to be done in close proximity to each other, and therefore the stitching task could not be brought into the central shop by itself (as happened with cutting in the 1830s).[33] Also, any efficient use of the McKay stitcher required a commensurate increase in the scale of all other aspects of men's work. Therefore, male shoe workers had to be brought under one roof, which created the fully integrated factory.

Along with the McKay stitcher, manufacturers introduced steam-power and a very detailed division of labor in men's work.[34] One of the first shoe manufacturers to use power and to subdivide tasks was Bancroft and Purington, a small company selling a standardized product.[35] By 1865, it had a four-story factory 100 feet long and 22 feet wide. The basement contained a small steam engine, while the first floor had a leather cutting room and a finishing room. It was estimated that this factory turned out one shoe every ninety seconds.

Bancroft and Purington contracted out binding (whether to separate stitching shops or to women in the outwork system is unclear), and bound uppers were returned to the factory. Together with the cut bottoms, they were sized, sorted, and delivered to the second story. There, the lasters completed their task and returned each semifinished shoe to its appropriate size drawer. Batches of shoes were then hoisted to the top floor, where a McKay operator stitched the bottoms to every shoe. An additional 25 to 30 men and boys finished bottoming the shoes; their work was subdivided into fourteen steps, such as tacking on the heel and shaving the extra leather. The product was inspected twice to identify inferior work. It is important to note that the worker's *product* was inspected rather than the work effort of the man or boy himself. This meant that the factory used the same ex post facto inspection method that had been developed in the outwork system rather than direct supervision.[36]

The detailed division of labor in finishing did not raise labor productivity as dramatically as the McKay stitcher had done for bottoming. But it did ease the problem of finding new male labor for the expanding factories and eroded the supply constraints imposed by the apprenticeship system.[37] The detailed division of labor in the context of factory production also encouraged the invention of many mechanical devices that increased labor productivity.[38]

Productivity in the Integrated Factories

For Lynn manufacturers, the McKay stitcher and steam power opened up dramatically new ways of doing business. The speed with which these manufacturers could now produce great quantities of shoes gave them a chance to gain a growing share of the expanding but very competitive national market.[39] Initially, the owners of the large, steam-powered factories tried to estimate national demand as accurately as they could on the basis of various economic data. As the *Shoe and Leather Reporter* observed in 1869: "the greater rapidity of the machine enables him [the owner] to wait until the news as to the crops in the West and South and other incidents of the year can give a basis for estimates as to the probable amounts of orders, and then hurry through his production accordingly."[40] However, this strategy was not completely successful, and over- and under-production remained a major risk. Hence, some factories started to gear production even closer to actual demand by producing only for advance orders.

The factory system enabled the manufacturer to pursue such just-in-time production. Twice a year—in the fall and in the spring—large quantities of shoes had to be produced between the advance orders and delivery date. Thus, a prerequisite for just-in-time production was the workers' willingness to put in long, intense hours during these two busy seasons. However, given the scarcity of jobs, the workers did not have much of a choice; as a result of mechanization, employment in the Lynn shoe industry had declined steadily between 1865 and 1870—by over 40 percent—while productivity had risen sharply—by over 170 percent (see table 1.1).

Data from the 1870 Census manuscripts allow us to investigate the Lynn manufacturers' new production strategy in some detail and to compare factory and outwork production during that year. Thus we can see whether the growing productivity of the factory system was due solely to the use of new machines and steam power or whether other factors—especially increased effort and longer hours on the part of the workers—also played a role. In 1870, Lynn had 102 firms producing boots and shoes. Of these 71 reported that they used machinery, steam power, or both (51 used both, and we shall call these steam-powered factories); 31 firms produced shoes using the old-fashioned methods of the outwork system. Average annual labor productivity in the latter was 1,200 pairs of shoes per worker, while in the factories each worker produced on average 1,778 pairs (workers in steam-powered factories produced an even higher average of 1,826 pairs). Thus, labor productivity in the factory system was approximately 50 percent higher than in the outwork system.

The reason for this difference was related to the new production strategy of the Lynn shoe factories. Three factors were likely to influence whether a company practiced just-in-time production. First, such a strategy could be adopted only by those companies that were highly mechanized. They alone were able to operate at the speed necessary to fill all orders on time. Therefore, we expect that the higher the firm's capital-labor ratio, the greater would be the likelihood of just-in-time production. Second, while the new strategy reduced market risk, it was costly because it idled plant and equipment during the two dull seasons. Therefore, we expect any employer with a large capital investment to be less inclined to use such a production method. In other words, we predict a negative correlation between total capital invested and just-in-time production. A third factor was the degree to which the firm was producing ladies' shoes rather than boots. In 1870, shoe production was large scale and standardized, while boot production was a more elaborate, time-consuming process. Many of the larger factories at the time specialized in ladies' shoes. The town's biggest manufacturer, Samuel Bubier, produced only shoes.[41] In general, the higher the percentage of shoes in total production, the more likely it was that an establishment would be engaged in just-in-time production.

The results of our statistical analysis support all our expectations about the determinants of a factory owner's willingness and ability to produce in two short but intensive seasons rather than at a steady pace throughout the year (see table 1.3).[42] We find that such a strategy (just-in-time production) is negatively correlated with the total amount of capital invested and positively correlated with the capital-labor ratio and the percentage of shoes (of total production) for each company. This supports the notion that factory owners indeed practiced just-in-time production and that they were more inclined to do so when their capital-labor ratio and percentage of shoes were higher and their total capital invested was lower. In contrast, for the outwork system there is no correlation between the three factors and our measure of just-in-time production, suggesting that this strategy was not used by outwork employers.

How did this production strategy affect output? We start with the

TABLE 1.3 Determinants of Just-in-Time Production (Intensity), 1870: Ordinary Least Square Estimation (Dependent Variable: 1/months in operation per annum)

	ESTIMATED COEFFICIENTS (STANDARD ERRORS)	
	Outwork	*Factories*
Capital	−.000001	−.00000020*
	(.000001)	(.00000006)
Capital-labor ratio	.000036	.000031*
	(.000029)	(.000009)
Percent shoes	−.0068	.017*
	(.0173)	(.003)
Constant	.11*	.08*
	(.02)	(.004)
Adj. R²	.01	.35
N	31	71

* Statistically significant at the .01 level.

SOURCE: Estimations based on data from the manuscripts of the *U.S. Census of Manufactures, 1870* for Lynn, Mass. (microfilm at the University of Massachusetts, Amherst).

self-evident notions that annual output of each company is a function of capital and labor, and that this output should be greater the more months a firm operates during the calendar year. This relationship may not hold, however, if fewer months in operation are associated with longer daily workhours or more work days per week (stretch-outs) and greater work intensity (speed-ups). In other words, if stretch-outs and speed-ups more than compensate for the shorter production time, one would expect *fewer* months in operation to lead to *higher* annual output for those factories that practice just-in-time production. We find that this was, indeed, the case in the more mechanized, steam-powered factories.

For the outwork system, our statistical results show a significant positive correlation between months in operation and annual output (see table 1.4). For all factories, this correlation becomes negative, but it is not statistically significant. For steam-powered factories, however, we find that *shorter* production periods definitely led to *greater* annual output: speed-ups and stretch-outs more than offset the reduction in operating months.

To assess how important the impact of speed-ups and stretch-outs (i.e. work intensity) was on the volume of output produced, monthly

TABLE 1.4 Boot and Shoe Production Functions, 1870: Ordinary
Least Square Estimation of Log-linear Cobb-Douglas Functions

Dependent Variable	ESTIMATED COEFFICIENTS (STANDARD ERRORS)		
	Outwork	*Factories*	*Steam Factories*
Annual output			
Months in operation	.73 (.36)**	−.43 (.32)	−.75 (.33)**
Labor	.34 (.14)**	.45 (.11)*	.35 (.11)*
Capital	.82 (.11)*	.49 (.08)*	.45 (.09)*
Constant	.29 (.99)	5.85 (.93)*	7.49 (.99)*
Adj. R^2	.92	.85	.75
N	31	71	52
Monthly output 1			
Labor	.31 (.14)**	.28 (.12)**	.16 (.13)
Capital	.83 (.11)*	.59 (.09)*	.53 (.11)[b]
Constant	−.28 (.65)	2.23 (.53)*	3.40 (.78)*
Adj. R^2	.92	.80	.63
N	31	71	52
Monthly output 2			
Effective labor	.33 (.14)**	.49 (.12)*	.35 (.13)*
Capital	.83 (.11)*	.48 (.09)*	.40 (.11)*
Constant	.38 (.82)	3.62 (.69)*	4.65 (.90)*
Adj. R^2	.92	.82	.67
N	31	71	52

*Statistically significant at the .01 level.
**Statistically significant at the .05 level.
SOURCE: Estimations based on data from the manuscripts of the *U.S. Census of Manufactures, 1870* (microfilm at the University of Massachusetts, Amherst).

output rather than annual output needs to be analyzed (to eliminate the effect of months in operation). We estimate monthly output as a function of capital and labor (see table 1.4). In "monthly output 1" labor is measured as the number of workers per company, while in "monthly output 2" this number is adjusted for work intensity, thus measuring *effective* labor.[43] A comparison of the two shows that, while labor and effective labor have almost exactly the same impact on monthly output under outwork production, their effects vary significantly under factory production. In particular, although differences in the monthly output among steam factories cannot be explained by differences in the number of workers employed, effective labor—which incorporates work intensity—has a significant impact on output.

TABLE 1.5 Determinants of Wages, 1870

Dependent Variable	ESTIMATED COEFFICIENTS (STANDARD ERRORS)		
	Outwork	Factories	Steam Factories
Shoe piece-rates			
Intensity	1.03 (1.36)	.34 (2.07)	.94 (2.37)
Capital-Labor Ratio	−.00021 (.00012)	−.00030 (.00016)***	−.00036 (.00019)***
Constant	.32 (.15)**	.45 (.21)**	.41 (.24)***
Adj. R²	.05	.02	.04
N	28	50	37
Annual earnings			
Intensity	−1554 (1046)	1798 (1454)	3003 (1649)***
Capital	.0095 (.0026)*	.0022 (.0008)*	.0020 (.0008)**
Constant	425 (122)*	283 (146)*	170 (167)
Adj. R²	.36	.09	.11
N	31	69	51

*Statistically signficiant at the .01 level.
**Statistically significant at the .05 level.
***Statistically significant at the .10 level.
SOURCE: Estimations based on data from the manuscripts of the *U.S. Census of Manufactures, 1870* for Lynn, Mass. (microfilm at the University of Massachusetts, Amherst).

We conclude that the most technologically advanced shoe factories practiced just-in-time production most effectively and that their strategy was based on increased worker effort and/or increased daily working hours. Consequently, Marglin's notion that factory production was associated with sweated labor holds up in this case. However, speed-ups and stretch-outs do not automatically lead to the redistribution of income that Marglin claims to be at the heart of the transition to factory production. As long as workers are paid piece rates, they may well be compensated for increased effort as well as for longer hours.

To find out how workers' earnings changed in the transition to factory production in Lynn, we first examine how the amount of effort and daily hours (intensity) and the amount of machinery used by each worker (capital-labor ratio) affected piece rates.[44] As expected, our statistical results in table 1.5 show that the use of machinery per worker had some negative influence on piece rates in the factories,[45] but none in the outwork system. This means that the more mechanized factories were able to reduce their piece rates and still attract workers by offering the possibility of higher output per worker through mechanized production. Work intensity, on the other hand, had no impact on piece rates either in the outwork system or in the factories. Factories using the new just-in-time production method apparently did not have to pay any premium piece rates to induce workers to work harder or for longer hours. Workers received more money for making more shoes under speed-ups and stretch-outs, but no more than another worker would have made producing the same number of shoes over a longer and more leisurely work period.

But what about earnings? Did speed-ups and stretch-outs lead to higher annual earnings, or did the simultaneous reduction in months of operation cause annual earnings to fall? Table 1.5 addresses these questions. First, we find that workers' annual earnings increased with the amount of capital invested by the company (whether in outwork or in factory production). This, together with similar results on piece rates, means that workers and employers shared in the productivity benefit which resulted from the more extensive use of machinery. That is, workers received lower piece rates but higher annual earnings when they worked with more capital. Second, we find that in outwork, fewer months in operation led to lower annual earnings,[46] whereas in steam factories the reverse was true: just-in-time production, i.e. greater work intensity, created higher annual earnings. In other words, speed-ups and stretch-outs compensated for fewer months in operation.

Our statistical analysis of the Census data has led us to the conclusion that the Lynn shoe factories were based on sweated labor but with compensating earnings. This corroborates and clarifies the contemporary descriptive evidence that associates the factory system with very intense labor effort. For instance, the 1871 Bureau of the Statistics of Labor Report states: "a [shoe] manufacturer . . . remarks that the factory system really calls for more intense muscle exertion, and hence is more exhaustive than the shop system."[47] Elsewhere, this report says that a shoe factory worker often works "thirteen hours a day, with corresponding high wages, even if by so doing, he is reduced in a few weeks to a mere skeleton. Time even to eat is not taken. . . ."[48]

It is important to realize that the use of machinery in the factories did not require sweated labor for any technical reasons. Instead, sweated labor was the result of the employers' decision to use their new machinery for just-in-time production. Blewett comes to similar conclusions from a very different perspective when she argues, "Mechanization and centralization did not cause extreme seasonality in the industry, but capitalists used machines and factories to attempt to dominate the national market and increase profits."[49]

What does all this mean for Marglin's claim that "the capitalist got himself a larger share of the pie at the expense of the worker"? Our results show that manufacturers did benefit from the new production strategy because it reduced their market risks significantly and thus raised their profits. As for workers, factory production meant sweated labor. But contrary to Marglin's claim, it was not direct supervision that enabled employers to extract greater effort from the workers. After all, all the new factories continued to use outwork methods of inspecting the final *product* rather than direct supervision of the work *process*. But neither did the workers voluntarily increase their efforts in order to receive higher annual earnings. These earnings may have been the carrot that drew workers into the shoe factories. However, this was a rather small carrot. Instead, it was primarily a big stick— the decline of alternative employment opportunities—that clobbered workers into the intensified work environment of the factory.[50]

CONCLUSION

Our analysis of the Lynn boot and shoe industry confirms that no existing theory can adequately explain the transition from outwork to factory production. At first glance, a casual observer might argue along orthodox lines that "adoption of the factory system tended to lag just behind the major technological developments"—in our case the invention of the sewing machine and the McKay stitcher—and that "such a close correlation between the timing of innovation and organizational change strongly suggests some causal relationship between the two."[51] But close correlation does not necessarily imply causation and thus cannot adequately *explain* developments in the Lynn boot and shoe industry—or anywhere else, for that matter. We have shown that in the case of the sewing machine there was no compelling technical reason to set up factories. Manufacturers began to set up centralized production in the stitching shops because that was the only way in which they could reap financial benefits from the new technology; it was their easy access to capital that allowed them to change the work environment in this way within a fairly short time period. In the case of the McKay stitcher, however, centralized production was indeed required for technical reasons. But employers simultaneously forced a significant increase in workers' effort so that the resulting productivity increase was due both to new technology *and* to sweated labor.

Another observer might similarly be persuaded by the Williamsonian argument that geographic expansion of the outwork system caused it to collapse under the weight of increasing transaction costs. But in the Lynn shoe case, outwork (despite some drawbacks) was a viable and expanding system which did not decline because of its own contradictions. After the advent of factory production for women's work, men's work continued in the outwork system for at least another decade. Had transaction costs been so important, factories for men's work would have been established much earlier.

While we agree with much of Marglin's argument, we believe that his focus on the effort/supervision link and on raw material savings is too narrow. In the case of Lynn, the outwork system was indeed able to deal with problems of poor quality work, slack effort, waste, and theft. Furthermore, the first factories for women's work did not economize on raw materials, nor did the later factories use direct supervision to sweat labor.

The major organizational changes in the Lynn boot and shoe industry occurred for a number of different reasons, not all of which are dealt with by existing theories. In particular, it was access to capital that allowed Lynn manufacturers to set up factories and to reduce the workers' share of benefits from the new technology. But the underlying force behind changes in the production system in Lynn's boot and shoe industry was the employers' drive for profits. Thus, the transition from outwork to factory production was neither determined by technological necessity nor brought about by the capitalists' drive to control workers. Our analysis of the final and most significant development in the Lynn boot and shoe industry—the establishment of integrated factories after the introduction of the McKay stitcher and steam power—clearly shows that both technical and social forces determined economic change.

2

Studying Work:
Personnel Policies in Philadelphia Firms,
1850–1950

■

WALTER LICHT

This article is concerned with the formalization of personnel practices in American business enterprises. By "formalization" is meant consideration and implementation of deliberate policies on the recruitment, training, disciplining, rewarding, promoting, firing, and retiring of labor. When and why firms in the past began to forge regularized employment procedures and in what kinds of companies and which trades such practices came to emerge and prevail are key questions of concern here. Twenty case studies of firms operating in the city of Philadelphia during the last half of the nineteenth and first half of the twentieth centuries provide the grist for this exercise. The subject raises a number of methodological and theoretical issues to be dealt with at the outset.

A general plea is made here for historical point of production or labor process case studies, that is, for analyses of the actual workings of enterprises, the actual activities of those directing the productive process and those whose labors are being directed, and, of course, their interactions, be those enterprises households, tribal units, manors, plantations, or capitalist or socialist firms. In an age when a significant proportion of scholarly endeavor is devoted to the reading of texts and signs, the ascertaining of the role of discourse and ideology, a call for a materialist history, new or otherwise, is not guaranteed to garner great acclaim, but a simple point is to be made. With the exception of the most purist of practitioners of intellectual history, most efforts at dealing with values and consciousness attempt to ground perception in some reality—avoiding at all costs, of course, the taint of base/superstructure argumentation. It would be in the best interests of such efforts to get that reality as accurate as possible. Artisan ideology, bourgeois mentality, or a bureaucratic corporatist ethos, for example, cannot be thought to emerge from some material base if the actualities of home, shop, mill, or office life are not determined. Superficial reference or assumption will not hold; the problems faced by and the behaviors of patriarchs, masters, lords, bosses, entrepreneurs, and bureaucrats as well as women and children in the family, slaves, serfs, laborers, and comrades have to be known and catalogued. In fact, disjunctures between public claim and daily practice may prove of interest. Suggested then is simply the following: that the work site, in addition to the family, the community, the voluntary association, and the state, provides a valuable unit of analysis for scholars.

An interrelated methodological issue concerns sources. A good deal of social and economic life is studied through prescriptive literature. Business historians in this light certainly study firms—though usually major companies of managerial note and rarely personnel matters—but their analyses normally proceed through official plans. As open testimony of business leaders—editorials appearing in trade journals, speeches delivered at special gatherings—must be treated as normative and not as a mirror of reality, so do the announced procedures, regulations, and flow charts of managers at the point of production. Actual implementation is at issue. The same could be said for studies in the history of technology and labor history. Monographs derived from the journals of professional engineers' organizations or the papers of technical planners tell mostly of possibilities and expectation, and not necessarily of ongoing encounters and consequences. The language of labor figures is public and political as well and cannot be accepted as representative of existing circumstances without further research. Prescriptive statements, in other words, are no substitute for production-floor documentation.

Statistical surveys are equally problematic sources of information. Agricultural and manufacturing censuses, for example, provide data on inputs and outputs of enterprises but reveal little if anything about the internal organization of production (certain inferences can be drawn, but they are exactly that, inferences). Population censuses offer the means to construct occupational typologies, but the problems of labeling occupations are legion (as has often been noted, there are many kinds of "weavers" and they toil in any number of different kinds of circumstances). The real problem with relying on occupational listings, however, is that work is invariably treated in these analyses as an activity rather than as an experience. The source dictates the approach: tasks, products rendered, skill levels, and sectors of the economy provide the terms to define jobs—a person is a ditch-digger, candlestick maker, white-collar employee, or transport worker —and it is assumed that the nature and quality of the experience is thus known. Avoiding the titles and understanding the substance of jobs on a daily basis may produce more valuable ways of describing employment, as rewarding, steady, responsible, protected—"desirable"—for example, or lonely, hazardous, irregular, monotonous, exploitative—"lousy," if you will (this way of classifying occupations is deliberately fashioned on the primary and secondary labor markets distinctions drawn by labor market segmentation theorists, distinctions properly made only by studying work directly).

Finally, there is another kind of survey bearing on the subject matter of this article which also reveals the importance of point of production investigations. Surveys conducted by government agencies or such organizations as the National Association of Manufacturers and the National Industrial Conference Board provide valuable profiles on the adoption of various managerial strategies, including personnel procedures, but the dynamics of innovation cannot be fathomed from such static documents.[1] Why change occurred, what developments or incidents forced new practices, remains a mystery. Enterprise-level studies offer not only a base for study but a source of information that avoids the pitfalls of prescriptive literature and survey listings of data.[2]

If the subject of the formalization of personnel practices encourages rumination on method, theoretical issues of note also come to the fore. How is the implementation of formal procedures concerning labor recruitment, compensation, and internal allocation to be explained? The scholar is presented with a host of theories to guide research and for testing.

Standard microeconomics, for example, would first draw attention to the problems of costs and competition. Firms generally integrate vertically (and the taking on of the personnel function may be considered a form of vertical integration) when competition and falling profits demand new managerial initiatives.[3] Why companies would choose to invest time, energy, and money in new programs for labor when threatened by lowered profits rather than simply cutting the wage bill is not quite self-evident, especially since potential schemes —from grievance procedures to seniority and pension rights—risk transforming labor into a fixed cost; if, however, institutional change in personnel practices within firms comes in response to the high costs of unionization, labor shortage, or turnover (and subsequent losses in productivity), then standard economic thinking would be confirmed.

The human capital variant of neoclassical economic thinking also encourages speculation but of a less ambiguous nature. Here technology would make the difference. The adoption of new technologies would require, it may be surmised, different kinds of technically and socially trained work forces, a situation achieved only through the inception of various internal labor market mechanisms. Advocates of technological determinism and human capital theorists would share common ground here. Macro-level economic theorizing, whether Keynesian or monetarist, it should be noted, provides little help in understanding the course of structural change within the black box of the productive enterprise. Inputs affect outputs, and internal arrangements and social relations have no necessary form.

Sociological explanations are also available. A culturalist perspective might point to the role of custom and tradition or ideas and values in spurring enterprise directors to certain actions. In the city of Philadelphia with a large population of Quakers and a sizable number of leading Quaker businessmen and where family owned and operated firms persisted, this kind of argument is not easily dismissed. In fact, a group of Quaker manufacturers formed the Business Problems Group in the early 1920s for the express purpose of discussing personnel reform and the responsibilities of Christian businessmen toward labor.[4]

Organizational theorists would provide other kinds of sociological answers. Those operating in a strict Weberian vein might stress the imperatives toward greater degrees of hierarchy, specificity, and rationality within organizations and the role that increased size and complexity might play in fostering departmentalization in general and specifically the creation of specialized offices for handling employment matters. Another kind of organizational perspective would place less emphasis on the inevitability of bureaucratic development and point to the creative work of middle-level managers—their efforts to shape market conditions as much as respond to them and their personal interest in seeing to the maintenance and expansion of their prerogatives and realms of control. The personnel function can be envisioned here as the protected and growing offspring of professionally trained personnel executives. Had Alfred Chandler in his various seminal writings on managerial history chosen to deal with labor affairs, this kind of organizational understanding would probably have been in the offing.[5]

There is no single "Marxist" answer to the question of the formalization of employment practices. Marxists of different stripes would share the assumption of inherent tensions between managers and managed over the extraction of surplus labor, thus making the management of labor a continual issue. Management systems do evolve, and in terms of modern personnel practices, a Marxist explanation would point to the significance of the rise of the corporation and the subsequent need to restructure incentives and make for careers within firms as possibilities for independent producership were eliminated. This top-down form of argument has been best articulated by Harry Braverman; it rests on an assumption of management's imperative and ability to control.[6] Within the Marxist framework there are also more dialectical ways of envisioning the process. A first would be to stress fully the role of conflict in spurring executives to develop new strategies aimed at engendering greater labor discipline and loyalty; a second would be to see the push for greater procedures and programs actually and singularly coming from below, that is, labor; and in a third, formalization would be pictured as part of converging and negotiated attempts by both directors of work and the directed to secure more regularized employment conditions.[7]

In the recent work of labor market segmentation theorists, in fact, this kind of mixed Marxist view on the subject can be found. Their argument goes as follows: labor conflict, pressure, or intractibility forces those firms operating in regularized markets where costs for administrative mechanisms can be passed on to consumers to develop technological and ultimately bureaucratic methods of control— sometimes this occurs not through actual threat but through the foresight of corporate figures recognizing the need for stabilized relations. Less wealthy firms conducting business in competitive situations and unable to focus on long-range possibilities continue to hire and fire at will and manage on personalistic bases. Two different labor markets emerge as a result, consisting of jobs with different characteristics.[8]

There is a final way of looking at the question of the development of formal personnel practices which does not immediately come to mind. That is a political answer, an attention to the role of the state in affecting private-enterprise-level decision making either through legislation, regulation, example, or the demand for information. The state's role in noncapitalist settings would be obvious, but cannot be ignored in situations seemingly free of political impact.[9] Of related note is the fact that none of the previously mentioned economic or sociological frameworks contain a political element.

The subject of formalization of employment matters thus provides a great deal to mull over, both methodologically and conceptually. A number of explanations are available and although listed separately, they are by no means mutually exclusive. Standard economic arguments on the need to limit costs—caused by labor turnover, unionization, or lost productivity in general—and the Marxist emphasis on the imperatives to control labor are hardly contradictory (although certain evidence would make one view more salient than the other). Equally similar are speculations by organizational theorists and Braverman-like Marxists that place emphasis on the seeming omniscience and omnipotence of managers. Economic, technological, cultural, organizational, Marxist, and even political answers exist and are to be treated as resources; the point now is to set our sights on the workplace and attend to the details.

Painfully brief thumbnail sketches of the employment histories of twenty firms follow, firms operating at various times in the city of Philadelphia from the early nineteenth century to the present. These companies were not randomly chosen; they constitute enterprises for which records survive.[10] They do form, nonetheless, a representative sample of the diverse kinds of businesses that remain based in Philadelphia to this day. Among small-scale firms with less than 50 workers, the companies include a tannery, an iron foundry, a stone carving concern, a cutlery factory, a publishing house, an insurance office, and one paint and one varnish-producing manufactory. Five other of the twenty companies studied can be characterized as middle-level in scale, with 50 to 300 workers; included in this group are a metal works, a leatherware factory, an industrial pottery, and one carpet and one textile mill. Finally, seven Philadelphia businesses with employment forces of upwards of 15,000 were surveyed, including a department store, an insurance office, a brewery, a utility company, a locomotive plant, and one precision instrument and one hatmaking concern. The objective in considering these firms is not to formulate a statistical profile. These cases will not be used to argue that certain percentages of firms in the city acted in one way or another. Rather, these companies, representing well the scale, trade, sector, and product diversity of the production of goods and services in the city of Philadelphia in the period under study, provide a means of discovering the various paths actually taken in the development of personnel practices (and possibly ways not even conceived theoretically).[11]

The twenty firms reveal a spectrum of results—from firms operating on an absolutely informal basis to businesses with highly regularized labor practices (see table 2.1). In general, twelve enterprises conducted business with limited or moderate deliberation on personnel matters while the other eight can be characterized by industrial relations of a definite developed nature. Important distinctions are in order, however, within this broad grouping, and the case studies are best fathomed in scale or spectrum-like fashion.

INFORMALITY

An almost complete absence of formal practices is noteworthy in five firm histories. The Wetherill Paint Company provides a first example. The company, which failed to survive the depression of the 1930s, dated its origins to the opening of a dry goods store in Philadelphia by Samuel Wetherill in 1784. Among other items, Wetherill sold dye colors and ground paint lead. Increased demand for paint stuffs at the turn of the nineteenth century proved an incentive to manufacture white lead directly; Wetherill subsequently established a small plant, and eventually his sons abandoned retailing and built a larger paint factory in the 1840s to concentrate solely in production.[12]

The manufacturing of white lead at Wetherill remained unchanged from the mid-nineteenth century through the company's demise in 1933. Single plant superintendents hired, fired, and supervised teams of common day laborers, and a few skilled workmen in pouring molten lead into sheets, stacking the sheets into pots of chemicals to force corrosion, and grinding the pulverized lead. Turnover at the company was extreme because of the rigors and perils of the work and the low compensation—40 percent of the 3,600 men employed there between 1848 and 1896 worked less than one week for the firm—and the Wetherills, with labor costs never amounting to more than 10 to 20 percent of operating expenses, were never moved to alleviate circumstances.[13] Outside agencies did contribute to change; inspectors from both the company's insurance carrier and the Pennsylvania Department of Labor and Industry demanded improvements in working, especially safety conditions, during the 1910s.[14] Still, Wetherill is noteworthy for the general absence of attention to personnel matters on the part of its owners and managers.

Two other firms no longer in operation fit the same pattern. John Gay & Sons Carpet Company was established in 1876 and stayed in business until 1915. The firm produced worsted, velvet, and "Tapestry Brussel" carpets. A diverse work force was employed, from highly skilled loom fixers and handloom weavers to power loom machine

TABLE 2.1 Twenty Philadelphia Firms: Firm Characteristics (Listed by Personnel Arrangements)[a]

Company	Dates of Operation[b]	Product/ Service	Number of Employees (range at peak)[c]	Predominate Skill Level	Form of Ownership	Organization of Production	Personnel Arrangements
Wetherill Paint Co.	1784–1933	Paint	60–80	Unskilled	Proprietorship	Single product line/few processes	Informal
John Gay & Sons Carpet Company	1876–1915	Carpets	50–100	Semiskilled	Proprietorship	Single product line/multiple processes	Informal
William Horst-mann Co.	1815–1880s	Silk products	400–500	Semiskilled/ skilled	Proprietorship	Multiple product line/multiple processes	Informal
H. Swoboda & Sons	1852–	Leather hides	30–50	Semiskilled	Proprietorship	Single product line/few processes	Informal
Kelley & Hueber	1849–	Leather cases	100–300	Semiskilled	Proprietorship	Single product line/few processes	Informal
Herder Cutlery Co.	1840s–	Cutlery	25–50	Skilled	Proprietorship	Single product line/few processes	Informal: unsystematic paternalism
Lea & Febriger	1785–	Publishing	10–30	Semiskilled	Proprietorship	Single product line/few processes	Informal: unsystematic paternalism

Company	Dates	Product	Employees	Skill	Ownership	Product line/processes	Labor relations
Philadelphia Contributionship	1752–	Insurance	15–25	Semiskilled	Private corporation	Single product line/few processes	Informal: unsystematic paternalism
Richard C. Remmey Co.	1810–	Industrial ceramics	50–100	Semiskilled/skilled	Proprietorship	Single product line/few processes	Partial formalization
McCloskey Varnish Co.	1854–	Varnish	50–125	Semiskilled	Proprietorship	Single product line/few processes	Partial formalization
Ellisco Inc.	1843–	Sheet metal containers	150–250	Semiskilled	Proprietorship/private corporation	Single product line/few processes	Partial formalization
Insurance Corporation of North America (INA)	1792–	Insurance	1,000–2,000	Semiskilled	Corporation	Single product line/multiple processes	Informal/late formalization
Perseverance Iron	1850s–1981	Cast iron parts	20–30	Skilled	Proprietorship	Single product line/multiple processes	Formal/unionization
H. C. Wood Inc.	1849–	Gravestones	25–50	Skilled	Private corporation	Single product line/few processes	Formal/unionization
Christian Schmidt Brewery Co.	1860–	Beer	1,000–2,000	Semiskilled/skilled	Proprietorship	Single product line/few processes	Formal/unionization
John B. Stetson Hat Co.	1865–1960s	Hats	3,000–5,000	Skilled	Proprietorship/corporation after 1892	Single product line/multiple processes	Formal: systematic paternalism/unionization

TABLE 2.1 (Continued)

Company	Dates of Operation[b]	Product/ Service	Number of Employees (range at peak)[c]	Predominate Skill Level	Form of Ownership	Organization of Production	Personnel Arrangements
Brown Instrument Co.	1859–	Measuring instruments	1,500–3,000	Semiskilled/ skilled	Proprietorship/ corporation	Multiple product line/multiple processes	Formal: systematic paternalism/ unionization
Baldwin Locomotive Works	1832– 1940s	Locomotives	15,000–20,000	Skilled	Partnership/ corporation after 1907	Single product line/multiple processes	Formal: systematic paternalism/ unionization
John Wanamaker	1861–	Department store	5,000–7,000	Semiskilled	Proprietorship/ corporation	Multiple product line/multiple processes	Formal: systematic paternalism/ antiunionization
Philadelphia Gas Works (PGW)	1834–	Natural gas service	2,500–3,000	Mixed	Semipublic agency	Single product line/multiple processes	Formal

[a]The firms listed here have long and evolving histories as indicated in the text. Predominate characteristics are noted.

[b]Actual dates of establishment are difficult to ascertain in some instances and a general date is listed. Firms also liquidated over periods of time; termination dates are also given in a general way in certain cases.

[c]Peak employment figures are for before the 1960s.

operatives and bobbin boys.[15] Operating in a highly competitive market, Gay & Sons sought to increase productivity through increased purchases of power looms and frequent staff and wage cuts when slack periods occurred.[16]

Turnover at John Gay & Sons was extremely high largely because of seasonal factors and fluctuating business conditions.[17] A strong plant manager retained complete control over production, and the owners of the concern did not develop special personnel policies to engender diligence or loyalty (a small sales and supervisory force did receive special favors and benefits, however).[18] Most notable in the firm's history is the extent of organized unrest. Work stoppages of one kind or another occurred in every year, with serious strikes in 1878, 1879, 1882, 1894, 1900, 1902, 1903, 1906, and 1912.[19] Wage cuts or reductions in piece rates were the most frequent causes of job actions, and all grades of workers participated. The owners of the firm did join with other carpet manufacturers in the 1880s to build a united front against striking Knights of Labor–led carpet employees and agreed to the creation of citywide arbitration procedures for the industry, but the protocols were in effect for only a short period of time. John Gay & Sons offers an example of a firm in a highly competitive industry in which labor cost cutting was a daily imperative and reality; the work experience was affected accordingly.

William H. Horstmann, a German immigrant and skilled silk weaver, established a small silk weaving workshop in 1815 which would grow to become the highly successful William Horstmann Company. Horstmann built a fully integrated facility where under one roof raw silk was washed, twisted, dyed, and then woven into specialty items, such as tassels, fringe, and lace. Horstmann initially employed fellow German workers and operated under craft traditions with formal apprenticeship and journeymen training.[20]

In 1824 Horstmann introduced Jacquard looms to his shop, an event that immediately transformed the nature of his business. Some handloom weaving continued, but soon upwards of 85 percent of a growing work force would be women hired to oversee the power machinery.[21] Craft practices were dispensed with, and in 1854, the firm, under the control of Horstmann's sons, opened a five-story factory where between 300 and 500 workers manufactured silk ware. A departmentalized structure of management emerged with overseers appointed to supervise particular activities or product lines.

With expansion, high turnover became a feature of employment at the firm. Between 1850 and 1875, 50 percent of those hired remained with the firm for less than one month; 25 percent, however, did find

steady employment.[22] With the exception of a few recreational out-
ings and the creation of a company baseball team in the 1880s, there
is no evidence of special initiatives taken on personnel matters.[23] In
the 1890s the firm was incorporated, and the Horstmann family with-
drew from management; records for the firm are unavailable after
that date. Adequate labor supply and a reputation as a place where
German immigrants could find employment allowed the firm to operate with an inelaborate labor system throughout the period for
which documentation survives.[24]

Two firms still in existence today retain features of the three formerly existing companies described above. H. Swoboda & Sons, absorbed as a division of Trans-Continental Leathers, Incorporated, in
the 1960s, was established in 1852 and has survived as a producer of
specialty horsehides.[25] A general absence of concern for personnel
matters has marked its history. Labor has been hired, trained informally, and supervised first by the company's founder and then by a
succession of strong plant superintendents. Operations were gradually mechanized but without significant incident. In the early 1940s a
personnel office was created after a successful unionization campaign
by CIO organizers, but almost entirely to handle contract matters and
not to usurp powers or activities of the plant manager (benefit packages, for example, are only of very recent origin, and to this day the
company does not require high school diplomas or any form of training on the part of its blue collar work force). High labor turnover has
also been a constant and notable feature of the firm's history—despite
mechanization, the work is arduous, and noxious gases and the danger of chemical burns make the job fairly undesirable—but the firm
has never moved or been forced to develop policies to encourage
greater stability.

A much less grim but in many ways similar portrait can be drawn
for Kelley & Hueber, a manufacturer of specialty leather products,
including eyeglass cases, it major sales item.[26] The present owners
purchased the company in 1922 from a family that had established a
leather case and strap concern in 1849. Production at Kelley & Hueber has remained unchanged: fully bleached and dyed hides are cut
to pattern with mechanical cutting tools and subsequently sewn on
industrial machines and finished. The firm is known as a producer of
high-quality, small-batch, made-to-order goods.

From the 1920s through the early 1960s, one plant superintendent
directed all aspects of production. He hired and trained people from
the surrounding neighborhood: males generally in cutting and females for sewing and finishing. A family and personalistic spirit was

maintained. The owners knew workers on a first-name basis and offered occasional discretionary gratuities. The plant superintendent's personal relations and knowledge of the neighborhood and the people who came to work for the firm kept loyalty high and turnover low. Apparently little has changed since his retirement. Ready access to labor, in fact, represents a common aspect of production in the five least formalized cases of personnel relations considered to this point. Wetherill, Gay & Sons, Horstmann, Swoboda, and Kelley & Hueber differed somewhat in size, complexity, and spirit of operations, but the ability of their strong plant superintendents to hire help through personal, family, neighborhood, and ethnic connections appears a basic factor in their undeveloped employment practices.

UNSYSTEMATIC PATERNALISM

Actual concern for labor matters but lack of formal initiatives characterizes the next three case histories; as at Kelley & Hueber, and to a greater extent, warm personal relations are noteworthy and crucial. Leopold Herder, a German immigrant, established a cutlery factory in the late 1840s to manufacture custom knives and scissors.[27] Herder and later his descendants managed all aspects of production and sales. Members of the family were sent back to Germany in their early adult years to learn the cutlery trade in formal apprenticeship programs, and there they recruited skilled workers trained in metal work. Turnover was low in the firm, and a family and protective atmosphere prevailed. In the 1920s the Herder family, faced with competition from producers of stamped, standardized stainless steel cutlery, closed their manufactory to concentrate solely in retailing and repairs (and in which they are still involved). The firm represents a fairly typical family proprietorship, where a nonprogrammatic paternalism ordered relations and affairs.

A similar history is revealed in the case of Lea & Febriger, founded in 1785 by Matthew Carey and the oldest existing publishing house in the United States.[28] The firm, which came to specialize in the publication of medical texts, has remained in the same family's hands for two centuries. Family members have served as editors and managers of a small office of salespeople and clerks. The office of the nineteenth century was run quite traditionally with frock-coated male clerks who were expected to maintain prescribed high levels of decorum. College-educated women began to be hired in the first decade of the twentieth century as the office was mechanized with typewriters and billing machines.[29] The owners of the firm have been quite solicitous of the employees' needs; gifts on holidays and paid vacations were fixed practices by 1900.[30] Decorum is still an important matter at Lea & Febriger, a quaint spirit persists, and the company boasts of a loyal staff with long tenure—in short, a small office where tradition and custom have been prime motivators.

The Philadelphia Contributionship, the nation's oldest fire insurance company, founded in 1752 needless to say by Benjamin Franklin and a group of his associates, fits the same portrait, but with some differences.[31] Until 1960, the firm offered perpetual, one-payment fire insurance to customers, and the business involved minimal clerical and bookkeeping tasks. Throughout the nineteenth century, an appointed chief clerk directed the work of a small staff of male clerks, mostly relatives of board members. Expansion in services after 1900 brought mechanization of the office and the hiring of women secretarial and clerical personnel (with a few exceptions, the women hired were high school graduates with commercial course degrees).[32] Few stayed with the company for long periods of time, and until very recently the firm did little to encourage longer tenure. A career ladder developed, however, more through custom than through deliberation, for male employees, whose clerkships have been treated as training grounds for managerial positions (the social backgrounds of these recruits, it should be noted, have changed but not the purposes of their apprenticeship).[33] The Contributionship remains a small office offering two kinds of gender-specific work experiences, but to this day tradition rather than deliberate initiative determines employment practices. A visit to the Philadelphia Contributionship as well as Herder Cutlery and Lea & Febriger is an object lesson in the efficacy of custom and proprietary values.

PARTIAL FORMALIZATION

Four other firms can be characterized as having unformalized labor relations, but their histories are more complicated, with deliberate initiatives either affecting portions of the work force or occurring sporadically and not in a developmental way. The Richard C. Remmey Company, the first firm to be considered in this group, dates its founding to 1735 when John Remmey, a native of Germany, settled in New York City and established a pottery. Seventy-five years later a grandson of Remmey's moved to Philadelphia and created a ceramics works that would prosper in the production of stoneware pitchers, plates, bowls, pipes, and fire brick for use in kilns and ovens.[34]

In the late 1860s the firm, under the direction of Richard C. Remmey, moved to specialize in the manufacture of refractory materials: clay and silica fire bricks and tiles for ovens, kilns and furnaces; large-scale crucibles for mixing and melting processes; specialized ceramic pipes, and eventually insulators for electrical use. Old craft production techniques were then abandoned, mechanical shovels, conveyors, mixers, and kiln stackers adopted, a detailed division of labor effected, and a large twenty-five acre facility constructed at the turn of the twentieth century. Skills, however, were not eliminated. The Remmeys built a laboratory where college-trained engineers were hired to develop new ceramics; model, pattern, and mold makers were still required, and here firm managers maintained formal apprenticeship programs (in fact, between 1910 and 1950, the company recruited master potters from England to train apprentices and serve as model makers).[35] The majority of other production workers, however, remained in the supervision of plant superintendents who handled personnel matters on a day-to-day basis. Until the 1960s when the firm was absorbed into the U.S. Gypsum Company, employment practices at Remmey, which remained in spirit a family firm, were generally without procedure.

The McCloskey Varnish Company founded in 1854 provides another example.[36] Until the 1960s practically all labor at McCloskey's was hand labor. Resin, gums, and coloring were cooked in large open vats and the resultant varnish cooled, thinned, poured, canned, and labeled without the use of machinery. In an effort to increase output and market coverage, automatic reactors and filling and labeling devices were then adopted which have almost eliminated labor in basic production (sales and clerical forces have increased proportionately). That the firm survived with primitive technologies until very recently is testimony to the openness of the market and the reputation McCloskey garnered as a producer of high-quality varnishes, especially for industrial use.

Before World War II small groups of men worked at McCloskey in teams with little division of labor. Expansion in production during and after the war effected an initial specialization in tasks which was formalized in 1953 when new owners hired a efficiency-minded managerial staff. To boost productivity, the company also began to offer various benefits for the first time, including paid vacations, medical insurance, and pensions. The firms still operates, however, without a personnel department and without great deliberation on personnel matters. McCloskey has offered its employees steady work—the result of a stable market for its product—and smallness has allowed a boasted family spirit to prevail (despite the fact that the original family has not been involved with the company for generations). Turnover remains low, and the business has successfully resisted periodic efforts at unionization.

The case of Ellisco Incorporated takes the McCloskey Varnish story one step further on the path toward formalization. Ellisco dates its founding to 1843 when George Ellis established a metal works to manufacture tanners' and curriers' tools.[37] Little is known about the firm's history until World War I when the company entered into the production of metal cans under government contract and ownership was transferred to a family that retains control to this day. Ellisco since the First World War has become a major producer of sheet metal milk cans, industrial waste disposals, and specialized containers for chemical and pharmaceutical processing and the handling of radioactive materials. Until World War II skilled metalworkers cut and pressed objects with hand-controlled machinery; the firm in the late 1940s adopted automated technologies, and with the exception of extremely specialized items which require hand control, the machines are tended by a work force of semiskilled operatives.

Until 1938 recruitment and training of labor at Ellisco was completely in the hands of a strong plant superintendent. In that year an office was established to facilitate employee enrollment in the social security system and the gathering of data for local, state, and federal labor-related government agencies. That office evolved into a personnel department which by the late 1940s kept records, set labor policy, including new fringe benefits schedules, and controlled hiring and firing. The single plant manager, however, retained substantial power and authority. In recent years the office and sales components of the work force have dramatically increased, and here the firm has established training programs, formal requirements for employment, and promotion ladders. Attention to labor matters has affected white collar workers in this way to a far greater extent than plant employees. Control of the production work force then has been maintained through both personal and technical means; bureaucratic and organizational solutions have been forged for the office. The Ellisco example is interesting also for the way in which government orders and regulations have affected personnel arrangements. In a common but unsystematic fashion, managers at Remmey, McCloskey Varnish, and Ellisco have had to consider and implement programs for labor, but only for portions of their work forces.

The final example of a firm without a highly developed system of industrial relations is perhaps the most curious, because it involves a notably large-scale enterprise, the Insurance Company of North America (INA).[38] Formalization emerged at INA, but at a rather late date. The company was founded in 1792 by a group of Philadelphia merchants with an eye to providing maritime insurance to the city's mercantile community. It was established as a joint stock venture and became the first capital stock insurance company in the United States.[39]

Until the 1920s, when INA's daily operations were moved into a large downtown office building, the concern was managed directly by an elected board of stockholders. One board member was selected as an operating officer of the company and assigned to direct the work of a growing office of clerks, many of whom were younger relatives of company officials (as at the Philadelphia Contributionship, clerking was intended as an apprenticeship for eventual participation on the board).[40]

Growth in the first decades of the twentieth century forced the board to relinquish control over operations to a staff of hired, professional managers. When the firm occupied its new large headquarters in 1924, a committee of executive officers was established to oversee personnel matters. A set of rules and regulations was issued and formal application procedures for employment initiated. Control of operations, however, remained extremely loose and in the hands of lower-level supervisors.[41]

INA did not adopt comprehensive formalized personnel practices until after World War II. The first initiative was the creation of a training school for agents; out of this effort came the creation of a full-fledged personnel department in 1956.[42] The office was delegated responsibility for hiring and testing employees, training, and establishing work assignments, benefit schedules, promotions, and extracurricular activities. The department, the idea of one innovative executive, represented a vast departure from the more laissez-faire practices of earlier eras.

For a firm of its size, influence, and importance, INA was late in formalizing and elaborating its personnel procedures. To this day the company acknowledges that it does not compensate its large clerical force as well as other Philadelphia white collar employers and that it tends to rely on recruiting young women from Catholic high schools with commercial course degrees and skills and expects them to remain with INA for short periods of time.[43] The less dynamic role assumed in personnel matters by the firm is a reflection of this strategy and of the conservatism of its management.

Among the twelve Philadelphia businesses that have been considered as unformalized with regard to personnel matters, there appear to be two patterns. Unskilled work and/or an available labor pool allowed firms as disparate as the Wetherill Paint Company and the Insurance Company of North America to conduct operations over many generations with minimal attention to labor relations. Continued family ownership and management in the absence of overt pressure by employees seem to have been responsible for the persistence of customary and personalistic methods of administration in other instances. The importance of values—the desire to maintain a certain spirit of enterprise—cannot be discounted in these cases.[44]

The question of formalization becomes better highlighted when moving from basically null cases to positive examples. Definitive crises, points of transformation, and initiative make for less blurred and seamless histories. Eight firms provide evidence of deliberate efforts on personnel management, and within the group four different patterns are discernible.

FORMALIZATION FROM BELOW

In the case of three firms, order came almost unilaterally from below. Here, well-organized craft workers imposed official union work procedures that led to highly regularized practices. Perseverance Iron, for example, was founded as an iron foundry for the manufacture of iron stoves in the early 1850s, and the company remained in operation and in family hands until its closing in July 1981.[45] The firm operated under strict craft traditions and conditions with little mechanization throughout its history. Highly skilled pattern makers, molders, kiln men, and lathe and drill press operators participated in the making and finishing of custom cast iron parts for final assembly or replacement. Until 1916, recruitment and training were conducted by shop foremen, but the pace of production was greatly controlled by the foundry's skilled workers. In that year the firm was organized by an AFL craft union, and conditions of employment from hiring on the basis of union lists to apprenticeship arrangements, compensation, benefits, layoffs, and ultimately retirement came under strict contract regulation. The owners of the firm for their part never initiated personnel programs on or of their own accord, and the shop remained very much the province of several generations of highly permanent, kin-connected, autonomous craftsmen and staunch trade unionists.

H. C. Wood Incorporated, founded by Aaron Wood, a stonecutter of British descent, in the late 1840s, offers a similar history.[46] The firm produced marble front steps for Philadelphia town and row houses until after the Civil War when a decision was made to enter the growing lucrative market for ornamental gravestones. A tradition of hiring skilled carvers of northern Italian ancestry then began and continues to this day. These workers were also organized by an AFL craft group in the 1890s, and all aspects of labor relations have been handled through contracts and union rules ever since. The production of gravestones after the turn of the century did become highly mechanized, sandblasting with stencils replacing hand carving. Skills have been diluted accordingly, but mechanical innovation transpired with union approval and regulation and the continuation of craft standards and procedures. The firm has been marked by low turnover, family connection in employment, and few deliberate personnel initiatives on the part of Aaron Wood and his heirs.

The case of the Christian Schmidt Brewery Company is different because the firm is decidedly large scale in nature, with thousands of employees, but the basic pattern of labor relations is identical to the small shop examples of Perseverance Iron and H. C. Wood Incorporated. Christian Schmidt, a German immigrant, founded Schmidt's Brewery in 1860, and the company remained in family hands until 1976.[47] The production of beer has not changed greatly at Schmidt's in 130 years. Ingredients are cooked and allowed to ferment in large vats. Cleaning of equipment and packaging have been the only areas that have undergone thorough automation.

Since the turn of the twentieth century Schmidt's has also operated as a closed union shop, and unionization has had a singular influence on personnel matters at the company. All hiring of nonoffice and supervisory staff takes place through a union hiring hall and on the basis of union lists (a personnel office was established after World War II to handle recruitment and benefits of white collar employees). Although standardized, customary agreements and arrangements with the union—including stipulations that sons of brewmasters have first access to job openings—have resulted in the employment of successive generations of families of workers, mostly of German and Irish background; the union has also implemented and strictly controlled apprenticeship procedures, wages, hours, work assignments, vacations, promotions, seniority rights, pensions, safety measures, and medical and life insurance. Schmidt's, although a family-run firm until recently, has been notably free of personnel initiatives or paternalistic programs on the part of management as regards production workers. To this day, recreational programs are union- and not management-created and administered. The firm does boast the allegiance of its unionized employees and can point to low rates of turnover. The company was and to some extent still is considered a good firm to work for, which is greatly due to the Schmidt family's willingness to deal with the strong, cohesive unions that have been a fixture in the plant and a fixture in the community of brewery workers.

SYSTEMATIC PATERNALISM AND UNIONIZATION

Unionization as a prime agent in the development of regularized personnel practices also figures in the three other firm case studies, but only at one stage, and usually a final stage, in more complicated histories. Notable here are efforts made by strong, morally inspired owners and managers to experiment with a gamut of programs aimed at both providing better welfare and instilling greater loyalty and discipline in employees. Ultimately, these initiatives became less the work of charismatic figures and more bureaucratic and organizational in nature as successful union campaigns made them an integral part of union contracts.

The famous John B. Stetson Hat Company provides almost a perfect case in point. Stetson founded his company in 1865, and within fifty years his firm would grow to employ more than 5,000 workers and produce one-quarter of the felt hats manufactured and sold in the United States. Stetson's success was based on his deliberate strategy of using fine fur materials and marketing a varied, custom product line. To render his hats distinct, Stetson also decided to sell them in specially made boxes to be adorned with what became the famous Stetson logo and design.[48]

In the 1870s Stetson began building a large, fully integrated factory complex. On the premises all aspects of production were conducted (including the manufacture of Stetson hat labels and boxes); fur felt was prepared, cleaned, died, cut, sized, shaped, sewn, trimmed, and finished within the walls of the plant. Because Stetson aimed at a custom market, much of the work involved skilled hand labor (only in the 1930s were important processes mechanized). Generally, less-skilled female labor was employed in preparation and adornment, while skilled male labor attended to the cutting, sewing, shaping, and finishing of the hats.

Extremely high labor costs and a tradition of independence among hat makers forced Stetson to pay great attention to employee relations in the firm. His approach was basically paternalistic. By the 1920s, Stetson and his company had become world famous not only for his hats but also for his various employee programs, including a cooperative store where foodstuffs could be bought at wholesale prices, language and civic courses (especially for foreign-born employees), group life insurance plans, a quarter-century club for veteran workers, a building loan association, an employee's savings bank, a Stetson chorus (which performed on the local radio), Stetson baseball and track teams, a weekend lodge for workers, a profit-sharing plan, a Sunday school, a hospital, a host of bonus and premium systems, and turkey giveaways on holidays.[49]

The collapse of the economy in the 1930s, however, brought great changes at the firm. Hard pressed to return a profit to investors, firm managers furloughed workers, curbed special dispensations, hired time-and-motion consultants to define new tasks and piece rates, and began steps to mechanize various aspects of production. Workers responded by forming an independent union and then joining the United Hatters, Cap and Millinery Workers International. A successful strike in 1936 led to union recognition and the reaching of a contract providing for wage increases, the forty-hour work week, overtime compensation, abolition of time-and-motion studies, and the establishment of grievance procedures and seniority rights (union controlled insurance plans would come later).[50]

The company in turn abandoned all paternalistic programs, upgraded supervision and the training of supervisors, continued mechanizing production, and created an Industrial Relations Department to set labor policy and bargain with the union. Stetson Hat maintained its presence in Philadelphia through the 1960s. The firm provides a good example of the limits of corporate paternalism and the roles played by economic pressure, labor strife, and union contracts in spurring the growth of technical and bureaucratic personnel controls.

Although not a household word like Stetson, the Brown Instrument Company became an institution in the Philadelphia business world as a renowned manufacturer of precision gauge instruments. An evolving history of paternalistic and union-induced bureaucratic answers to personnel issues also marks this firm, though with slight variations on a theme from Stetson.

The company dates its founding to 1857 when Edward Brown, inventor of the first pyrometer of American design, opened a small shop to manufacture heat and liquid flow measuring devices. Within sixty years he and his son built a large-scale firm which would garner a worldwide reputation as a producer of quality, custom measuring instruments. The firm was acquired and made a division of Honeywell Incorporated in 1934.[51]

The Browns divided their growing company into departments for engineering, purchasing, production, sales and service, and finance. The largest unit was production, which was divided into specification writing, parts manufacture, subassembly, and final assembly. The firm prospered by perfecting a system of specialized small-batch production which required the employment of large numbers of skilled workers.

The Browns recruited labor primarily from the neighborhood surrounding their factory, relying on family networks and in-house training and promotion. Young men were taken on as apprentices in parts manufacture, later becoming full-time drill press and lathe operators. Young men and women were also hired for subassembly work; the males generally were then promoted to final assembly and specification writing, or to supervisory posts. In the 1920s, Richard Brown, son of the founder, also instituted a large array of corporate welfare programs, including paid vacations and medical and life insurance. The firm became identified as one sensitive to the needs of its work force.[52]

The merger with Honeywell in 1934 led to significant changes at Brown Instrument. Fearing both suspension of various benevolent personnel practices and the possible closing of the plant after the new management takeover, workers at Brown began to organize. In 1936, officials from the newly formed CIO United Electrical, Radio, and Machine Workers Union were invited to assist in establishing a local at the company. Within weeks the firm's new managers agreed to recognize the union and the first of many contracts was reached. It created fixed wage and incentive payment schedules, hours standards, apprenticeship arrangements, job classification and promotion schemes, grievance procedures, seniority rights, and fringe benefits.[53] In effect, union contracts formalized many of the procedures practiced by the paternally minded Browns. Office and supervisory staff, it should be noted, remained nonunionized, and for these workers Honeywell's management has repeatedly had to institute new perquisites to attract and keep them.[54]

Two other factors are important in understanding the work experience at Brown. The company operated in a stable, nonseasonal, well-established market; as a result, the firm never experienced financial difficulties or fluctuations and even in bad times was able to offer steady work. Second, the custom nature of the product has put a premium on skill; the firm has never operated on an assembly line basis, and workers retain substantial control over the pace of work. The company as such has offered its workers regular, protected employment with intrinsic and extrinisic rewards, and loyalty to the firm and tenure remain high.

The quality of the work experience—the dignity of labor offered and performed—also figures in the industrial relations history of the Baldwin Locomotive Works, which, like Stetson, was one of Philadelphia's most famous firms. Here too is evident the move from deliberate managerial initiatives to union-induced controls.

Matthias Baldwin established his famous Baldwin Locomotive Works in the early 1830s. His plant grew into a multiblock complex comprising nineteen acres of city space and Baldwin became one of the largest employers in Philadelphia. In the 1920s, the company moved its operations twelve miles outside the city to a 616-acre facility, and the company could then boast a worldwide work force of close to 22,000 people.[55]

Growth, however, did not change the basic way locomotives were constructed at Baldwin. From its inception, the firm always produced engines to order, following the specifications and needs of the large number of railroads that became its customers. Skill and craft characterized the whole process. Specifications were turned into blueprints; drawings were then sent to the pattern shop for models to be made, which in turn went to the foundry where they were used to make molds for iron castings. Drawings also went to forge areas where large components were shaped, to the boiler shop where copper was cut and formed into boilers, or to the machine, tinsmith, and tender shops, where metals were cut, lathed, drilled, folded, and finished into needed components. The various parts would then be gathered in the erecting shops for assembly by skilled assemblers; painters and carpenters would put on the finishing touches.[56]

The production of custom engines required skilled workers, and managers from Baldwin onward devoted great time and effort to developing and maintaining the skills of its work force. The firm never adopted automated or through-process technologies (the custom nature of the product precluded such innovations); more notably, company officials never introduced experiments with scientific management, time-and-motion studies, piece rates, or any kind of paternalistic programs.[57] During the late nineteenth and early twentieth centuries, certain production areas were operated on the basis of inside contracting. Certain skilled workers entered into agreements with management to supervise crews in filling stipulated orders. The program, however, proved unwieldly and difficult to monitor and was ultimately jettisoned.[58] Workers laboring under subcontractors at Baldwin, it should be noted, always remained compensated directly by the company according to daily wage schedules.

Assembling and maintaining a highly skilled work force represented the singular personnel problem of the firm. Matthias Baldwin personally attended to the training of the men he recruited and created a formal apprenticeship system. Upon his death the system went into eclipse but was revived in a more systematic way by Samuel Vauclain, general superintendent of the works and later president of the firm, in the early 1900s. Young recruits attended classes and on a rotating basis served in all shops of the plant for fixed periods of time before acceptance as full-time workers. In 1909 the company reported that 90 percent of its work force had been recruited and trained internally. Vauclain's particular apprenticeship program, despite a good deal of publicity and fanfare, was eventually abandoned, but apprentice training remained a feature of the works and was to come under union aegis when the company was organized in the 1930s and 1940s.[59]

The Baldwin Locomotive Works represented a mammoth industrial enterprise producing a basic capital good, but one in which skill and craft were maintained (partly because of the nature of the product but also because of deliberate company policy). Loyalty could be engendered through the work itself, and also the high wages the firm gained a reputation in the Philadelphia region for offering. Baldwin never went in for paternalistic programs, despite its very visible presence in the city and the public role many of its leading executives assumed. The company was forced to recognize various craft and industrial unions and reach contracts in the 1930s and 1940s, but unionization occurred without the great incident associated with New Deal–era labor campaigns. Written into agreements were procedures already practiced through custom.

SYSTEMATIC PATERNALISM AND ANTIUNIONISM

In the cases of Stetson, Brown, and Baldwin, deliberate interventions by managers were followed by further elaboration and articulation through unionization. Another kind of history occurred in an equally famous Philadelphia enterprise, John Wanamaker's department store. Here unionization never occurred, and significant formalization of labor relations came directly through the extraordinary initiatives of one formidable figure, John Wanamaker himself.

Wanamaker opened his first retail store in 1861 at the age of twenty-three. Believing success would lie in product diversification and horizontal expansion, he continually enlargened his store; in 1875 he moved his multidepartmental retail outlet to a large railroad depot and in 1910 to the multistory building in center city Philadelphia which remains the flagship store of the large Wanamaker chain to this day.[60]

John Wanamaker was a pioneer in departmentalized approaches to management and in advertising techniques. He also developed new strategies for organizing the work of what became an army of sales and office clerks, supervisors, and buyers. Wanamaker personally attended to the structuring, training, and rewarding of his managerial staff (management training and incentive programs were a feature in the firm by the 1890s). As early as the 1880s a centralized personnel office was also established to facilitate recruitment of sales and office help (the firm was one of the first to use personality and aptitude tests in job placement). For sales positions, women were preferred who came from respectable homes, showed grace and decorum in interviews, dressed well, and most important, spoke English. Moreover, Wanamaker developed a succession of programs to engender diligence and loyalty: he established a store school for young employees and various in-store vocational training programs; paid vacations, the ten-hour day, and the five-and-a-half-day work week were instituted in the 1880s; a medical clinic, savings and loan association, life and pension insurance plans, and numerous employee clubs and teams were features too by the first decade of the twentieth century.[61]

Wanamaker's reputation as a leader in corporate welfare initiatives is well deserved (he referred to his employees as "my store family"); so too was his reputation as a vehement opponent of trade unions.[62] Wanamaker's successors continued his basic approach to personnel matters after his death, including vigilant response to threats of unionization; his store provides a singular example of a strong personality establishing labor control through deliberate paternalistic and bureaucratic means.

The example of John Wanamaker may please advocates of Great Man explanations of historical change, but other interpretations are possible and applicable. Organizational theorists would point to the obvious complexity and size of Wanamaker's operation and note that extraordinary measures were in order; similarly, a human capital theory or technology-based approach might stress that Wanamaker was faced with the problem of molding a new kind of task force engaged in a new skill—namely, retail selling—and that special programs and initiatives were necessary. The sway of Wanamaker was so substantial that attributing developments purely to his personal agency is still compelling.

A seemingly simple answer can be found to the question of labor relations at a firm such as Wanamaker's. At the upper ends of the scale of formalization, another and last case study is to be considered that forms a most complicated story: the Philadelphia Gas Works (PGW). The City Council of Philadelphia established the Philadelphia Gas Works in 1834 to manufacture coal gas for use in street lighting and private homes. The works first existed as a private company, then became a city-run agency, was leased to a private concern in 1897, and finally became a municipal commission again in the early 1970s. Despite changes in the form of ownership, PGW has always been a major employer of Philadelphia's laboring population.[63]

Since its inception the work force at PGW has been divided into three components: production, distribution, and sales. Before 1900 the largest number of employees—common day laborers, for the most part—were occupied in the manufacture of coal gas in retort houses. Mechanization and automation at the turn of the century and eventual large-scale purchasing of natural gas from western suppliers in the late 1940s successively slashed and eliminated employment in production. A stable, fairly large percentage of workers has been engaged in distribution—the installation and repair of gas lines and meters—while vastly growing proportions of employees have been involved with sales (the latter including meter readers, clerks, billers, sales representatives, and accountants).[64]

Until 1897, when the works was leased to the privately owned United Gas Improvement Company (UGI), the management of PGW's personnel was haphazard and without deliberate initiative. Appointments at all levels were tied to political patronage, and complaints by customers of uncertain service led to calls for reform in the late nineteenth century and UGI's eventual takeover.[65]

UGI officials, trying to turn a profit, moved quickly to cut employment, fire political appointees, fully automate gas production, and mechanize the office. To gain loyalty from gas employees, hours were reduced from 60 to 50 a week, a system of paid vacations begun, a medical dispensary and dental clinic for workers built, and various company-sponsored recreational activities established.[66] Most important, a personnel department was created during World War I, during a period of labor shortage, to rationalize recruitment, testing of applicants, training, work assignments, job classification, and promotion procedures. This was followed by the initiation of a wide range of paternalistic programs and the creation of an Employee Representative Committee in 1933.[67]

PGW's employment history offers a good example of efforts to establish labor control through technical means in production and bureaucratic means in service areas. Before 1897 personal connections and political favor functioned as prime motivators; UGI then sought to motivate workers through organizational rewards. UGI's need to return a profit (general tax revenues could be counted on to cover losses when municipal authorities ran the works), the very diversity of activities at the agency, the growing white collar, relatively autonomous component of the work force, and the public nature of operations, all contributed to the deliberate personnel initiatives taken by UGI officials during the first third of the century, initiatives that affect work relations and arrangements to this very day. Of all the case histories, this is probably the most complex and stands on its own.

CONCLUSION AND IMPLICATIONS

The particularities of each of the above twenty firm-level case studies, and not just the Philadelphia Gas Works, militates against generalizations. Certainly no one framework adequately explains the varied histories of personnel practice and policy development discovered in the enterprises considered. Size and complexity, for example, certainly mattered, as did the corporate form—with one exception, the Insurance Company of North America, firms characterized by informal relations were small-to-medium in size, engaged in the production of single services or products, and family owned and operated. Still, in two small proprietorships, Perseverance Iron and H. C. Wood, personnel practices were extremely formalized. Similarly, consideration of costs and technological innovation spurred changes in some instances, but were not critical factors in most. Articulated conceptions of personal relations do not seem to have played a great role in this way, but ethical standards and values affected the work experience in firms touched by the likes of John B. Stetson and the owners of Lea & Febriger.

A few common denominators can be isolated. Unskilled work, availability of labor, and/or family ownership and management were components of unformalized situations; skilled or new kinds of work and/or labor conflict and organization marked cases noteworthy for the emergence of formal personnel policies. There is evidence in these findings to satisfy vying theories, but the total portrait offered by labor market segmentation theorists, with some major provisos, seems to best fit the layered and spectrum-like quality of the results. Growing scale of operations, the corporate form, and labor pressure required or forced management to act differently and deliberately toward labor; the persistence of firms outside this realm in turn meant the continuation of traditional, nonbureaucratic practices. Personalistic relations, however, did not preclude stable, desirable employment, as witness the kind of work experience offered in such family-operated firms as Herder Cutlery. The question of skill and the ability of organized skilled workers to force regularization of labor policies at times even unilaterally in both large- and small-scale settings necessitates further qualification, but not dismissal, of the segmentation argument.

The twenty Philadelphia case studies also raise an interrelated issue concerning timing. Students of industrial relations history point to various critical moments in the development of modern personnel practices. Taylorism and the advent of scientific management at the turn of the twentieth century represents for some the most critical development.[68] Other scholars discounting the impact of Taylor and his disciples look to the 1910s, World War I, and the work of the first generation of more liberal personnel management reformers.[69] The decade of the twenties similarly is frequently cited for the proliferation of experiments with corporate welfare programs,[70] the thirties for the impact of mass production unionism,[71] and the forties for either the role of government regulations in affecting employment policies, the growth of bureaucratic methods of labor control, or retrenchment on the part of the managerial community (if the list is taken to our own times, affirmative action rulings, innovations with so-called quality work teams, and recent antiunion initiatives could be deemed a new stage).[72] The existence in the literature of so many offered turning points, however, should raise suspicions about treating industrial relations history in such a developmental way, suspicions confirmed by the Philadelphia firms studied.

First, but on a note of less importance, the cases analyzed indicate the need to start the story of modern personnel initiatives in the 1880s. The growth of large-scale enterprises, their challenge to republican and producerist values and visions, encouraged a pioneer generation of religiously and ethically inspired enterprise-builders—the Stetsons and Wanamakers of Philadelphia and the Pullmans of Chicago, for example—to innovate with various plans to engender greater fealty and productivity among employees (the depression of the 1870s and such tumultuous events as the railroad strikes of July 1877 served as definite backdrops). Later initiatives were to follow with different means, as in the case of scientific management or recognition of unions, but with the same ends in mind.

Of greater significance than the timing is the fact that a canvas of diverse firms and not just companies famous for managerial experiments reveals no generalized or single progression; the Philadelphia story, in fact, is notable for the persistance of old forms and old methods. Moreover, rather than a linear or stage-like progression, what is critical is the continuity of efforts, of continued crisis and response; the Philadelphia case studies manifest an ongoing history, in other words.

The last point can be highlighted by a brief reference to a twenty-first case study, of a venerable employer of labor in the city, the Pennsylvania Railroad. The Pennsylvania Railroad (at least until its unholy demise) provided textbook writers with a textbook case of bureaucratic development.[73] By the turn of the twentieth century, the Pennsylvania had the most highly articulated hierarchies, flowcharts, and systems of reports, rules, and regulations developed by an American enterprise. Recognition of railroad labor brotherhoods combined with increased governmental regulation of railroad labor affairs made industrial relations on the Pennsylvania quintessentially formalized. Yet, as late as the decade of the 1950s, top managers were still bedeviled by what was deemed to be the chaotic nature of labor recruitment and placement on the road. Three years of committee investigation and suggestion led to the centralization of recruitment offices, the publishing of the carrier's first hiring manual, and the creation of new employment tests, forms, and procedures. The story thus did not terminate in 1860, 1900, or 1945. Papers in the archives of the Pennsylvania Railroad reveal the oscillating and recurring rather than evolutionary nature of industrial relations history.[74]

On the question of timing and successive if not developmental initiatives on industrial relation, some side comment on Frederick Winslow Taylor is in order. Certainly, no history of evolving personnel practices in Philadelphia is complete without mention of Taylor. Taylor in fact grew up in the Germantown section of the city, the child of wealthy and prominent parents—his mother, a Quaker, was an active abolitionist. To his parents' dismay he abandoned academic studies in his late teens and became a machinist's apprentice and later a foreman and engineer at the Midvale Steel company in the city.[75] At Midvale, Taylor began a series of experiments aimed at increasing the efficiency of the flows of goods through the productive process and the productivity of workers employed there. Although he innovated with a range of managerial reforms, Taylor is most famous for his time-and-motion studies, his effort to break work into detailed, easily supervised tasks, catalogue them, establish expected rates for finishing jobs, and structure incentive schemes to boost output. Philadelphia became an important testing ground for Taylor and his principles at such firms as Midvale Steel, Tabor Manufacturing, and the Link-Belt Company.[76]

Taylor and the disciples and competitors who surrounded him ultimately constituted a movement, dubbed scientific management, and they have been seen, as was noted, as critical agents in the history of the American workplace. They transformed work, eliminating skills and the sway of skilled craftsmen and rendering work repetitious, without intrinsic meaning, and alienating. This vision of Taylor and his co-conspirators, however, bears little relation to the historical record, and here Philadelphia case studies confirm the need to qualify the impact of scientific management. Proponents of scientific management techniques rarely succeeded in setting their innovations in place. Resistance from foremen who were threatened by these new consultants, more notable resistance from workers, and the administrative nightmare involved in cataloguing tasks and establishing rates—particularly in firms whose product lines were always changing, as was the norm in Philadelphia—doomed most Tayloristic experiments from the start.[77] Any number of case studies of the actual implementation of scientific management reforms confirms this conclusion. Had Taylor succeeded, in fact, industrial relations history would not be marked by further stages of development and initiative. But more important, an emphasis purely on the technical side of work overlooks the importance of social relations at the point of production. Time-and-motion studies do not by themselves define the nature of the work experience. For example, the same managers at a company such as Link-Belt in Philadelphia, who personally invited Taylor into the firm to reorganize production, innovated at the exact same time with an impressive and effective array of paternalistic programs (the kind of programs that Taylor detested).[78] Similarly, in firms such as Brown Instrument mentioned above, time-and-motion studies became and remained a basic part of the production process, but benevolent benefits first and unionization later had a much greater impact on the nature of labor relations at the company. Taylor is a part, and a small part at that, of a larger multifaceted, multilayered, and ever contested story.

The uneven history of personnel practices in Philadelphia can be seen in ongoing labor tensions in firms and management searches for solutions as well as the persistence of old forms of practice and old relationships. The staggered nature of change is also and finally evident in two other ways that deserve emphasis. First concerns the chief agents of change. Extraordinary personalities, organization-minded bureaucrats, craft unionists, industrial unionists, and government officials played a role in developments described in this article, and at least in Philadelphia for the period under study, no single set of actors seems more important or dominant; all contributed to this history. Second, the different kinds of personnel policies manifest within particular firms in Philadelphia add an additional element of complexity. Here, important distinctions loom between production workers and office and store staff—the former subject either to the personal authority and sway of strong plant superintendants, the technical controls embedded in mechanization, or the bureaucratic controls achieved in union contracts; the latter encouraged over the years through organizational rewards conceived and distributed from the top. Yet, further qualifications have to be drawn between clerical and sales staffs in the office and store. The histories of such diverse firms as John Gay & Sons Carpet Company, the Insurance Company of North America, and John Wanamaker's indicates that people in sales—whether salesmen and agents on the road or saleswomen behind the counter—because of their relative autonomy, direct relations with clients and customers, and handling of monies, required special interventions and inducements. In the modern, large-scale office until very recent times, managers have been less impelled to initiate programs for their work forces behind the desk.[79] In firms employing production, sales, and clerical help—as in the case of the Brown Instrument Company—the approach to all three has differed, with again office people garnering the least attention.

Firms records can reveal the oscillating, recurring, and uneven nature of personnel practices highlighted in this essay. They also reveal important details not accessible in public or private surveys or official pronouncements: the profound impact on the work experience made by an insurance company's demand for new safety measures or a government agency's call for greater information and record keeping; the importance of a particular foreman's or plant superintendent's personality and bearing, of tradition-mindedness in family-operated firms, of neighborhood and family hiring and sociability on the job, of the threat of business takeovers and closings, of the persistence of craft sensibilities and pride in work, even when mundane tasks are involved, of informal and formal protections lost and gained, of stable employment, of good jobs and bad, of the insults and injuries, personal and physical, as well as the dignities of labor. This can only be known with an eye to the point of production.[80]

3

Scientific Management and the Workplace, 1920–1935

■

DANIEL NELSON

In view of its presumed role in twentieth-century industrial management, scientific management remains one of the unaccountable enigmas of American labor history. Its origins are clear, thanks to the aggressive research of Milton Nadworny, Hugh Aitken, and others, but its post-1920 fate has attracted less attention.[1] A small but influential group of consultants and industrialists, preaching a newly humanized and psychologically sophisticated Taylorism, became the elite of the management movement in the United States and Europe in the 1920s.[2] Did they have any influence on the practice of management? A larger group of university professors drew on scientific management to create professional specialties in management and industrial engineering, with similarly unexplored consequences. The fate of Taylorism on the shop floor is no more certain. Some pioneer consultants, such as Morris L. Cooke and Lillian Gilbreth, continued their earlier work; others, such as Carl Barth, Richard Feiss, and Harrington Emerson, suffered economic and professional reversals. The 1925 expulsion of Taylorism (and Feiss) from the Joseph & Feiss Company, one of the model plants of the 1910s, was symptomatic of the uncertain climate of the postwar era. The rise of opportunistic consultants such as Charles Bedaux, the proliferation of published sources on management methods, and the appearance of university-trained middle managers who had been inculcated with the insights of the pioneers immensely complicated the lives of the original Taylor disciples and the job of the latter-day historian.

Given these problems, is it possible to measure the impact of scientific management on the workplace in the 1920s and afterward? In recent years, one group of scholars has answered with a vigorous affirmative. Since the early 1970s, radical social scientists such as Harry Braverman, Katherine Stone, Richard Edwards, Dan Clawson, and most recently, David Montgomery, have made Taylorism a central feature of their critiques of American capitalism.[3] The association is natural. The radical perspective is based on the assumption that the organization of modern industry is inherently exploitative.[4] Though some of the radicals concede a role to market forces and technology, they see management innovations as expressions of the employer's desire to claim a larger share of the product of industry at the expense of the worker. This perspective makes Taylorism an inviting target. Frederick W. Taylor's *The Principles of Scientific Management* (1911) is a treasure trove of incriminating rhetoric. The famous Hoxie report of 1915, with its predictions of deskilling and degradation, provides additional evidence from the shop floor.[5] The apparent popularity of Taylorism among employers supplies the finishing touch. Following Braverman's pioneering reinterpretation of the history of work, which accorded Taylorism a central role in the degradation of the wage earner, other radicals have focused on Taylorism. Montgomery writes:

> The essence of scientific management was systematic separation of the mental component of commodity production from the manual. The functions of thinking and deciding were what management sought to wrest from the worker, so that the manual efforts of wage earners might be directed in detail by a "superior intelligence."[6]

Although the radicals differ on particulars, they emphasize three central points. First, they argue that Taylorism remained a distinguishable entity and affected a large percentage of workers. In Braverman's words, it "dominated the world of production."[7] Second, as Montgomery stresses, Taylorism accelerated the destruction of craft skills by separating physical from mental labor and transferring production planning and management from the shop to the office. Third, Taylorism enhanced the manager's control of the worker, principally through the time study process—the study and reorganization of work, the measurement of the worker's activities via time and motion study, and either a piece rate or an incentive wage. The result was another staple of social science writing, a widespread sense of powerlessness and anomie.

The radicals' critique has great appeal. It gives the diverse and complicated history of industry a sharper focus; helps to explain the persistence of issues that have sustained social science scholarship since the 1920s; shifts attention from the work of individual consultants and engineers to the work of all consultants, engineers, and employers; emphasizes the social costs of managerial innovations; and underlines the importance of shop floor issues in business history. Finally, it invites additional work. For all their fervor, the radicals have done surprisingly little to show how and where Taylorism de-skilled individuals and decreased the possibility for individual initiative. Their work is suggestive and impressionistic. With the exception of Montgomery's recent study, the books and articles cited above rely on standard secondary sources and published materials.[8] And Montgomery's account, despite its copious documentation, relies almost exclusively on anecdotal evidence. However useful, the radical critique remains a series of provocative hypotheses rather than a description of Taylorism in the workplace.

Was scientific management in fact widely adopted? The answer obviously depends on what is measured. There is little doubt that Taylorism in the most general sense, as a conception of management that transcended narrow functional activities, won wide acceptance. In the burgeoning universities of the 1920s, Taylorism was the catalyst that produced programs in industrial engineering and, more important, in production, personnel, and marketing management in schools of business administration. Taylorism also stood for a set of broad principles—functional organization, systematic operations, standards, and managerial controls—that won wide favor among the administrators of hierarchies. Most pertinent to the radical critique, Taylorism included various prescriptions for successful industrial operations. They included purchasing and inventory control systems, cost accounting, production planning, functional foremanship, time and motion study, and an incentive wage. Though less glamorous than the broader "principles," these "details" of scientific management were not unimportant. They included the germ of modern management accounting and industrial psychology, for example.[9] If the radicals are right, they also led to a fundamental alteration in the character of industrial work and in the role of skilled workers in the factory.

The popularity of the "details" has intrigued scholars since the 1910s. Before World War I the diffusion of scientific management could be estimated by counting the consultants' clients. The rapid diffusion of management techniques during and after the war and the related developments noted earlier soon made that approach unreliable. In 1922 Horace B. Drury, an early academic expert, ventured that "there are few important factories where the influence of scientific management has not been felt, to at least a small extent," leaving the reader to distinguish between "important" and "unimportant" factories and "small" and "large" extents.[10] Gradually, sweeping generalizations gave way to an alternative approach which holds greater promise. In the 1920s and 1930s, concerns about labor problems and competition among consultants encouraged detailed studies of incentive wage plans. For the wary historian, these studies, notably the authoritative surveys of the National Industrial Conference Board, provide abundant information about the diffusion of scientific management in the postwar years. The plans themselves tell relatively little about the impact of scientific management on the character of factory work. But because the incentive was often part of a managerial package, it can be a meaningful landmark, signifying the prior use of time study, the introduction of systematic production planning, and a transfer of much of the foreman's power to the engineering, production, and personnel staffs. The incentive wage was often the visible tip of a much larger body of managerial innovation.

There are problems with this approach. The first is the problem of piece rates. Many firms that introduced other features of scientific management used piece rates rather than more complex incentive plans. Conversely, piece rates did not necessarily indicate a commitment to scientific management. This ambiguity is impossible to eliminate. Second, it was possible to introduce scientific management without an incentive wage of either type.[11] Oil and chemical companies, for example, used continuous process technologies that did not rely on human initiative and therefore did not warrant incentive plans. This did not prevent firms such as Standard Oil of New Jersey and DuPont from embracing the principles and many of the practical features of scientific management. In fact, however, there were few firms with wholly automated operations, then or later. Standard Oil and DuPont, for example, had large numbers of employees who performed more conventional duties and exercised considerable initiative. Both companies had large time study departments, used incentive wage plans, and tried to improve productivity in ways that were familiar to any machine shop owner.[12]

Third, scientific management had applications outside manufacturing, which are not reflected in the wage-system surveys. The number of such efforts is difficult to estimate. More than 90 percent of the documented applications during the pre–World War I years were in factories.[13] Bedaux's more flexible and opportunistic approach did not change the proportions in later years.[14] Other evidence from the 1920s is fragmentary or inconclusive. In short, until more information

TABLE 3.1 Distribution of Employees by Wage System

	EMPLOYEES			
System	*1923*	*1924*	*1928*	*1935*
Time Wage	55.7%	56.1%	47.3%	56.3%
Piece Rate	37.5	36.6	37.0	22.1
Premium and bonus[a]	6.8	7.3	15.7	21.6

SOURCE: National Industrial Conference Board, *Systems of Wage Payment* (New York, 1930), p. 9; NICB, *Financial Incentives, A Method for Stimulating Achievement in Industry* (New York, 1935), p. 17.

[a] Included thirteen specialized incentive plans, including group piece rates.

is available, studies of incentive wage systems in manufacturing probably provide the best available guide to the impact of Taylorism in the workplace during the 1920s and 1930s.

The Conference Board reports, based on surveys of a large, randomly selected group of manufacturing firms, are summarized in table 3.1.[15] Given the inherent ambiguity in the piece rate figures, it appears that scientific management spread slowly and fitfully. By 1924, two decades after Taylor launched his campaign to educate American industrialists, at least 7 percent of manufacturing workers, and possibly as many as 37 percent, worked under scientific management. In 1928 the respective figures were 16 percent and 37 percent. For the entire economy the figures were 5 to 17 percent of nonagricultural workers and 3 to 9 percent of the labor force.[16] The proportions for 1935 are even less certain. Many firms, such as General Motors and other auto manufacturers, retained scientific management methods but abandoned piece rates as part of union-avoidance strategies during the New Deal years. Others embraced scientific management and premium and bonus plans to increase productivity during the depression. The net change was probably a small increase in the proportion of workers in scientifically managed plants.[17]

The 1928 survey suggests a strong positive correlation between plant size and wage systems. Table 3.2 shows that the smallest firms rarely used piece rates or special incentive systems. As plant size increased, piece rates became more common; but only in medium-sized and large establishments (100 or more, and especially 350 and more employees) do bonus plans and scientific management play an obvious role.[18] In the largest plants they are clearly a significant force. Indeed, only one of the 36 plants with more than 3,500 employees did not use some sort of incentive or piece rate plan.[19] The data thus

TABLE 3.2 Plant Size and Wage Systems

Workers	No. of Plants	Time Only	Time and Piecework	Time, Piecework, and Bonus
1–50	155	68%	25%	6%
51–100	191	50	45	6
101–150	142	36	48	16
151–350	324	23	56	21
351–750	187	17	55	29
751–1,500	122	5	57	39
1,501–3,500	57	4	67	30
3,500+	36	3	42	56

SOURCE: NICB, *Systems of Wage Payment* (New York, 1930) p. 7.

strongly suggest that the decision to embrace Taylorism was not a random phenomenon dependent on personal whims, familiarity with the work of one of Taylor's famous demonstration plants, personal zeal, social conscience (as Taylor might have argued), or rapaciousness (as the radicals might counter), as it may have been during Taylor's lifetime. By the 1920s manufacturers had concluded that Taylorism was more appropriate for the types of activities that occurred in large plants than in small plants. The information on individual installations suggests an additional refinement: with few exceptions scientific management found favor among executives who had earlier introduced mass production technologies. It was an effective answer to the myriad problems that often prevented large, expensive factories from achieving their potential. Machine operations by semiskilled workers were probably the most obvious target. Yet mass production plants and their employees were a small proportion of all plants and workers. In other kinds of industry the advantages of scientific management were less compelling; at some point the costs of additional staff, clerical procedure, and disruptions of routine outweighed the benefits. The point is that as long as manufacturers responded rationally to their environments, Taylorism would never be universally applied; it would never dominate production.

Did Taylorism deskill workers? The Conference Board data underline a point that is easily overlooked: most small plants remained immune to the management movement. In these establishments there was no separation of mental and physical labor, no transfer of skill to the plant office—or at least no more than would have occurred if Taylorism had never appeared. Even if the radicals' argument holds for the rest of industry, there remained a substantial and significant safety valve.[20]

The data also indicate that most plants, regardless of size, had substantial groups of workers who remained on time rates and had little or no contact with time study and other features of Taylorism that had an immediate effect on the character of work. Who were they? Several statements about the application of piece rates provide valuable clues. The 1928 Conference Board survey concluded, for example, that piece rates have "been found unsuited in the manufacture of custom made articles, specialties and small quantities, experimental work and articles where quality is of first importance."[21] An employer volunteered that "piece work is applicable only where an operator is kept steady on one kind of machine." Another added that "it is cumbersome, ineffective and unjust to attempt to apply piece work to small jobbing businesses where the quantity of orders is small." A third concurred: "We should question the value of piece work unless the work is repetitive and that quantity of production is reasonably large."[22] The contrast, then, was between workers who made "custom made articles," "specialties," "small quantities," and high-quality goods on the one hand and those who made large quantities of standardized goods on the other. The former, clearly, are the skilled workers; the latter are semiskilled or what the radicals call deskilled workers. There is no evidence that some plants had all semiskilled workers, or, more important, that workers moved from one category to the other. Employers apparently did not introduce incentive wage plans to reduce their dependence on skilled workers. Rather they used Taylorism to improve the performance of workers who were hired as semiskilled machine tenders.[23]

Other sources confirm this distinction. In 1927 E. C. Cowdrick, secretary of the famous Special Conference Committee, conducted a private survey of wage systems in ten of the largest mass production firms. He discovered that every firm had large numbers of hourly employees. At Goodyear Tire & Rubber, for example, they were "plumbers, sheet metal workers, electricians, carpenters, painters, riggers, machinists and pattern makers."[24] The company added a bonus to their hourly rate, based on the foreman's assessment of the following: "technical or practical knowledge, initiative, neatness around the job, correcting poor work at a saving, carefulness, reliability, ability to plan work, ability to hold down waste of material, constructive criticism and loyalty."[25] Is there a better list of the positive qualities of the eighteenth or nineteenth-century artisan? Goodyear rewarded its craft employees for being versatile, creative workers, not for being automatons.

The pattern at the other firms was identical. At International Harvester, hourly workers included tool makers, die makers, and pattern makers.[26] At Westinghouse's East Pittsburgh works, they included carpenters and machine repairmen.[27] At the company's lamp works, they included all machine shop workers. At U.S. Rubber's tire plants, they included "practically all" workers in the mechanical division, which designed, manufactured, and installed machinery.[28] At Western Electric's Hawthorne works, they included "tool makers, pattern makers, inspectors and other highly skilled employees."[29]

These reports suggest a pattern at odds with the radical critique. Manufacturers selectively introduced scientific management but their selectivity was not due to the cost or power of their skilled employees. In most cases they deliberately exempted those individuals from the web of constraints and incentives they were erecting around the jobs of less skilled employees. The data suggests that they viewed their skilled workers in the same way that small firm managers (those in the Conference Board survey with less than 50 employees) viewed all production workers, as versatile individuals who could perform a range of activities, and managed them as they had always managed skilled employees, through the personal supervision of the foremen. The difference was that they, unlike the small firm managers, did not act on instinct. They were familiar with scientific management but rejected it as inappropriate for the types of functions their skilled employees performed.

These observations, based on the experiences of a relatively small number of plants, do not exhaust the possibilities of intentional deskilling.[30] However, they do suggest that in the biggest and best-managed American factories of the 1920s, scientific management had little to do with the number or functions of skilled workers. If a similar relationship was characteristic of other, lesser plants, certainly a reasonable assumption, the potential of the deskilling hypothesis is substantially diminished. It may have some value for understanding the dynamics of machine design, for example, but it appears to be irrelevant to the activities that the radicals have usually emphasized.

The Special Conference Committee firms, with one exception, used time studies and piece rates or special incentives to manage their other production employees. (The exception was Bethlehem Steel, the company where Taylor had developed the time study process.[31] Yet Bethlehem's seemingly anomalous position was consistent with the growing conservatism of the American steel industry.) Their reliance on Taylorism provides an unusual opportunity to reexamine the radicals' control argument. Did manufacturers use time study to increase their knowledge of the production process, to discover the minute details of machine operations, and to eliminate any possibility of worker influence? In short, did they use time study to master the machine and control the worker? Or, like many employers and engineers in the studies of Nadworny, Aitken, and others, did they disregard Taylor's methods and use it to improve the foreman's traditional estimates? Cowdrick's reports on time study procedures provide important clues.

Cowdrick's data reveal substantial disparities in the operation of scientific management at the plants of the Special Conference Committee firms. Western Electric, with a time study staff of 120, had one technician for every 65 employees. Goodyear, at the other extreme, had one for every 527 employees.[32] Presumably the character of the work in the plant accounted for most of the difference. Some time study departments had responsibilities other than rate setting, and some administered complex incentive pay systems. Yet the range is so great that the possibility of substantially different conceptions of time study remains. The qualifications of the technicians also varied greatly. Most companies used foremen, skilled workers, or "technical graduates." Goodyear assigned recent college graduates as part of a training program for production executives. General Electric used a similar approach.

> Time study men have been recruited in the past from various sources ... practical experience and trade knowledge being held prerequisite. At present there is a tendency to employ mechanical engineers to a greater extent than in the past. These men are given factory training and special time study instruction before being put on the job. In one of the larger plants all the ratemen are given systematic technical training on all phases of rate setting work, including time and motion study and micromotion analyses.[33]

Despite these variations, actual time study procedures were surprisingly uniform. At Western Electric, for example,

> A time study man is not responsible for the equipment or layout of the job or the method of work. These things are under the control of the manufacturing planning division, but if the time study man thinks the job is not being done by the most efficient methods, he is expected to report the facts to the manufacturing planning division. The thoroughness of a time study and the method of establishing time standards vary somewhat in accordance with the importance of the job. ... If a job is to last only a short time ... it is not considered worthwhile to make elaborate or repeated time studies.[34]

At Westinghouse's East Pittsburgh works, which also had a time study staff of 120 and set as many as 118,000[35] rates per month,

> the time study men first analyze the job itself and the conditions under which it is performed. If possible they recommend improvements in the methods and may even suggest changes in machinery or shop layout. When the method of performing the operation has been perfected, a time study is made . . . .[36]

At the company's Mansfield, Ohio, works, which had one technician for every 61 workers,

> The time study man looks over the job, including the lay-out of machinery and equipment, and endeavors in cooperation with the foreman . . . to suggest improvements that will increase efficiency. With the process finally perfected to his satisfaction, the time study man takes shop watch readings . . . .[37]

The reports for other companies, with smaller time study staffs, are similar. At Standard Oil's pump works,

> The time study man before using the stop watch consults with the foreman as to the best method of performing it. After the layout and the method have been perfected, he takes the actual time study.[38]

At U.S. Rubber's Detroit tire plant,

> When a new job is to be time studied, the time study man first watches the operation to determine whether in his opinion it is being performed by the most efficient methods. If he has changes to suggest, he makes his recommendations to the foreman of the department. . . . When the method has been perfected to the satisfaction of the time study man, he makes observations with a stop watch.[39]

At International Harvester,

> The time study man and the foreman observe the method used and suggest any improvements that occur to them. If changes are suggested, the workman is instructed to go though the operation by the new method and is given time to practice. . . . When the time study man thinks the method of doing the job has been perfected, he takes a study with the stop watch . . . .[40]

At General Motors,

> When a time study is to be taken, the observer first studies the job to determine whether the machine or equipment layout and the method of work are such as to secure maximum efficiency. If necessary he will suggest changes in machinery or equipment. . . . When the operation

has been perfected to the satisfaction of the time study man, he takes
several time studies of the man who is actually working on the job . . . .[41]

Several common themes stand out. Time study men "perfected"
the work in a casual, often perfunctory manner. In no case did they
attempt the detailed analyses that Taylor considered essential. Nor
did they make meaningful changes in machine operations; at Western
Electric and possibly other plants they did not have the authority to
do so. In most plants they had to negotiate any changes with the
foreman. Under these conditions the possibility of an accurate time
study, in the sense that Taylor and his disciples used the term, was
highly unlikely. The chances that time study would transfer skill or
control from the shop floor to the office were even more remote. Time
study narrowed options in some cases; it may have reduced the workers' leeway in others; but it did not eliminate the informal understandings and bargains that typically characterized the relationship
between supervisors and workers. Did time study subject the machine
worker to the control of the white collar bureaucracy and ultimately
the manufacturer? If these statements are accurate, the answer is
surely no.

Though Cowdrick was a knowledgeable student of contemporary time
study, he shared the values of the managers he observed and had little
contact with the workers. Conceivably, he may have overlooked features of time study that were particularly onerous to employees. Fortunately, there is a convenient check on his findings. Shortly after his
tour of the Special Conference Committee plants, another investigator
with different values and a radically different approach made a similar journey. Stanley Mathewson was a pioneer personnel manager
whose liberal perspective and identification with workers had forced
him to find a refuge in academe, as the placement director of Antioch
College's innovative cooperative work-study program.[42] His 1928 study
and the book that grew out of it, *Restriction of Output Among Unorganized Workers* (1931), were landmarks in the developing social science
of industry. The book was also a de facto progress report on the state
of scientific management. Except for the coincidence of its publication with the onset of the depression, it might have changed the public
perception of industrial management and of scientific management in
particular.[43]

The guiding force behind the Mathewson report was William M.
Leiserson, the prominent economist and arbitrator, who joined the
Antioch faculty in 1925. An acute observer of contemporary industry,

Leiserson was impressed with the potency of the managerial innovations of the preceding quarter-century. The decline of the labor movement was one convenient measure of their effectiveness.[44] He was therefore surprised and perplexed by a common theme in the reports of students who returned from jobs in industry. They noted the prevalence of informal production restrictions even in supposedly well-managed plants. He discussed the reports with Mathewson and asked the students to write detailed accounts of their experiences.

In the meantime, the new Social Science Research Council (SSRC) had authorized a series of surveys of academic research in order to determine which areas and types of projects deserved financial support. A committee on capital and labor, headed by Henry S. Dennison, an influential manufacturer, asked Leiserson to participate. Leiserson took advantage of the occasion to suggest a project of his own:

> We have been gathering a lot of material here on the subject of Restriction of Output, which I think your committee will find of interest. Our students, who work in a wide variety of industries, are writing out for us all the examples of conscious restriction of output by working people with which they have come in contact. Some of the information we get in this way is extremely valuable and we want to use it to work out plans for helping to eliminate the restriction.[45]

Leiserson continued to push his project and by early 1928 had secured the financial support of the SSRC, the assistance of the committee on capital and labor, and the cooperation of the Antioch administration. He then recruited Mathewson to work in various factories and write reports of his personal experiences. Mathewson later recalled that he gathered material in 105 establishments in 47 localities, though those totals included the students' reports. He personally held "eleven different jobs" in Pittsburgh and Detroit, including positions at the Westinghouse East Pittsburgh works and in several Ford and General Motors plants.[46]

Mathewson used a technique that the Cleveland publicist Whiting Williams had popularized earlier in the decade. He dressed in overalls and cap, worked alongside other factory employees, and frequented workers' haunts in his spare time. At the end of each day he would record his experiences and conversations in a letter to Leiserson.[47] Mathewson also interviewed more than 60 executives. He took his assignment seriously, prompting Leiserson to remind him not to let his "feelings about a particular incident or condition get into the description of it" and to "remember that you are not going out to prove that you can 'bear up' under the dirtiest job that the management can give you."[48] On another occasion Leiserson felt compelled to warn him not to argue with the men he interviewed.[49]

One reason for Mathewson's aggressiveness was his discovery that restriction of output was even more widespread than the student reports had suggested, and that executives remained oblivious to it because of a naïve confidence in scientific management. An incident at General Motors was symptomatic of his experiences:

> Two of the major executives . . . are of the sincere belief that since group-bonus has been introduced, and production standards have been set under this system, restriction of output has been practically elimi-nated in their plant. In support of this opinion the general manager stated, "One man now does in one day what it took three and one-half men to do ten years ago." Stated another way, the average output for each man has increased two hundred and fifty per cent in ten years. This executive recognizes, of course, that management, machinery, methods and material have all contributed to this increase, but he holds that increased man-hour effort has also played an important part.[50]

Mathewson then "scraped up an acquaintance with the first workman he saw near this plant." The man, a valve grinder,

> gave a detailed account of his own restrictive practice and of that of the workers about him. He belonged to a group which he estimated at about one hundred men. He named figures just as convincing as those given by the executives to show that he and all his fellow workers were restricting output. They turned in work that would show a maximum earning power of only 90 cents an hour. Even that amount made some of them nervous and was a limit recently set as an experiment, to see just how high they could go without exposing themselves to a rate cut. The grinder stated that the group could easily put their earnings up to $1.15 an hour, but did not dare invite a cut by doing so.[51]

When Mathewson inquired about the foreman's attitude, the worker insisted that his supervisor "not only approved, but had helped the workers figure out exactly how much each man should do" to avoid a rate cut.[52] Mathewson interviewed other workers at the plant and heard similar stories. He concluded that far from knowing everything about their employees' work, GM executives knew virtually nothing.[53]

In all, Mathewson collected reports of 223 instances of output re-striction. After vigorous pruning by Leiserson, Dennison, and others, he included 142 examples in his final manuscript. They are listed by industry in table 3.3. The manufacturing total is divided between those that mention time study or other features of scientific manage-ment and those that do not. The "scientific management" category

TABLE 3.3 Restriction of Output, by Industry

Construction	11
All manufacturing	100
Scientific Management	22
Non–Scientific Management	78
Services	26
Total	142

SOURCE: Stanley Mathewson, *Restriction of Output Among Unorganized Workers* (New York, 1931).

probably understates the actual number by a substantial margin. Of Mathewson's 23 examples from the auto industry, for instance, 19 fall into the nonscientific management category because they do not explicitly mention time study or an incentive wage. Yet many of the 19 are undoubtedly General Motors cases and belong in the other category. The actual total of scientific management cases may be closer to 40 percent rather than the reported 22 percent. Certainly Mathewson's summary statement is consistent with the larger proportion. He had seen, he recalled:

> foremen working at cross purposes with time-study men and showing workers how to make time studies inaccurate; workmen killing time by the hour because the day's "limit" had been reached; men afraid to let the management learn of improved methods which they had discovered for themselves; older workers teaching youngsters to keep secret from the management the amount they could comfortably produce in a day; managements trying first one "wage incentive" plan, then another, in an effort to induce men to do what we believe they really wanted to do in the first place.[54]

In the last analysis, "the situation which [Frederick A.] Halsey and Taylor discovered obtains today."[55]

In his conclusion Mathewson was even more explicit in attacking the control hypothesis. Citing charges of the "speed-up" in mass production, he wrote that "For every worker . . . who appeared overtaxed, we encountered dozens who were successfully matching wits with management in self-protective resistance against wage-incentive plans, piece-rate cuts and prospective layoffs." The "over-speeded worker" was "largely a myth."[56]

The Mathewson report created a sensation among those who read it. Dennison Manufacturing Company managers reviewed the draft with great interest.[57] Walter V. Bingham, the prominent industrial psychologist and adviser to the project, was enthusiastic about the book's prospects.[58] Though Viking Press did not release the book until early 1931, after the collapse of the economy had deflected attention from the issues of efficiency and productivity, the reviews were enthusiastic. R. W. Stone of the University of Chicago grasped the essence of Leiserson's and Mathewson's achievement when he wrote that the book "casts . . . in doubtful perspective the scientific character of managerial methods," especially "the effectiveness of wage incentive plans."[59]

How did mass production workers view scientific management in the 1920s? The workers Mathewson and the Antioch students encountered agreed that it was a threat but not the threat that the radical scholars have described. Workers feared that they would lose money or even their jobs but not their skills or their ability to influence the character and pace of their work. Their attitudes reflected the persistence of older managerial habits in an era of scientific management. Rate cutting, alienated foremen, and undetected restrictive practices were perversions of scientific management, indicators that the time study practices Cowdrick reported were indeed imperfect. The workers' statements, like Cowdrick's observations, were commentaries on the difficulty of introducing scientific management as Taylor and his immediate disciples prescribed it, on the conservatism of those on the lowest rungs of the managerial ladder, and on a tendency to disregard the gritty details of shop management, a trend that would become more insidious in the next two decades. But the workers' statements were also a commentary on the control hypothesis. In the plants of the best-managed American companies, the companies that impressed Leiserson as harbingers of a new industrial era, workers apparently had no more difficulty protecting their role in the manufacturing process than they had had in the factories of a half-century before. Control, in the radicals' sense, did not exist.

What conclusions do these surveys of industry in the 1920s suggest about the fate of scientific management at the height of its popularity? Whatever the applicability of the more general principles of scientific management, it seems clear that Taylorism had a comparatively modest effect on the workplace in the decade and a half after Taylor's death. That was not because of any inherent limitation or flaw. Employers could have taken Taylor's advice; could have tried to reduce their dependence on skilled workers; could have transferred skill from the plant to the office; could have imposed more thoroughgoing controls on their employees; in short, could have lived up to the radicals' expectations. Instead, they approached Taylorism critically and skeptically, assuming that it had limited applicability, even in manufacturing. When they did apply it, they disregarded Taylor's prescriptions and authorized (if effect) a more modest approach. Their use of time study lacked the rigor that Taylor and the other pioneers had insisted upon and consequently produced different and far less arresting results. At the same time they blithely insisted that they had been true to Taylor's ideas and had accomplished what even a casual observer like Mathewson could see was not true. Their motives may have included indifference or other factors; the documents are unhelpful on that point. But there can be little doubt that an examination of scientific management in the workplace "undermines rather severely," as one of the reviewers of the Mathewson report wrote, "the popular assumptions that have been made concerning the efficiency and cooperativeness of workers. . . ."[60]

In retrospect, then, Taylorism was interesting and historically significant not because it ushered in a new and unrewarding era for workers but because it added a dimension to mass production manufacturing that was hitherto missing. It was a capstone to the technological breakthroughs that made it possible for three or four generations of poorly educated and ill-prepared young people to work as something other than unskilled laborers—and, as the Cowdrick and Mathewson reports indicate, as something other than degraded automatons too. This was much less than Taylor had envisioned and the radical scholars have claimed. But if the record of Taylorism in industry after 1920 does not support apocalyptic views of the workers' degradation, it does explain what observers such as Drury meant when they wrote that virtually all "important factories" had felt the influence of scientific management "to at least a small extent."

4

Ford Welfare Capitalism in Its Economic Context

■

DANIEL M. G. RAFF

In this essay, I propose to view welfare capitalism services as part of a labor market strategy, as one element of the total compensation paid out to employees. I see the firms providing this sort of compensation as institutions committed to their own survival and profitability, reluctant simply to give away money but always alert to their own material interests. This suggests the somewhat unusual course of examining the incidence and history of welfare programs in terms of the economics of the firms that offered them and the markets for labor in which the firms operated. Were the firms paying out more—in cash and in the value of services—than they needed to in order to get the workers in the door? Is there a plausible explanation consistent with firms being run to maximize profits, appropriately defined? All this is relevant to the question of motive, that is, of altruism versus the requirements of (competitive) industry. There is also the question of why welfare firms made part of their payout in kind rather than in cash. Can one point to economic considerations that might have shaped the mix and changes in it?

The essay considers a single episode in the history of welfare capitalism in considerable detail. The one I have chosen is the famous set of policies implemented by the Ford Motor Company beginning in the winter of 1913–1914. I cannot, of course, dismiss the possibility that the company implemented the program solely on the basis of Henry

I AM GRATEFUL to Sanford Jacoby, Charles Conn, J. Bradford DeLong, Gerald Friedman, Howard Gitelman, Harold Levy, Peter Temin, Robert Zevin, an anonymous referee, and an audience at the 1987 annual meeting of the Social Science History Association for comments and suggestions. This work was supported generously by the Division of Research of the Harvard Business School. The usual disclaimer applies.

Ford's whims. But I will argue that the technical change and labor market conditions which were making the company very profitable also strongly suggested a set of policies of the sort it in fact deployed. I go on to draw contrasts. Other local automobile firms used a different technology. The policies they chose were different, and their attitudes towards the policies important to Ford were quite indifferent. I also consider the Ford policies as time passed. Ford's labor market changed in ways which are crucial to the calculus I describe. Ford's policies changed too.

The Ford episode is perfectly consistent with the ideas that firms are generally run to maximize profits and that their particular internal institutions and policies are designed, or at least evolve, with this larger goal in mind. I am therefore arguing that the history of particular firms' policies cannot be understood without studying the evolution of the way the firms made money by mobilizing physical and human assets to meet some market need.

This essay is intended to raise questions as much as to answer them. The background changes at Ford are well known, clear-cut, and extraordinarily well documented. They are much better known than the analogous facts for any other welfare firm. More firm-level studies of the history of welfare work and other sorts of compensation in the context of changing technology, job contents and requirements, and local labor supply conditions would be a very useful contribution to the debate about welfare capitalism.

TECHNOLOGY IN AUTOMOBILE MANUFACTURING BEFORE THE NEW POLICIES AT FORD

In the period when the Ford Motor Company first showed any signs of contemplating welfare measures or any other important departures from conventional labor market practices, major changes were going on in the process of making Ford cars. The company was the first to produce automobiles on any scale through any means other than the actions of a group of relatively autonomous, highly skilled mechanics.

Theretofore, automobile manufacturing plants had really engaged in the assembly of parts that were purchased on contract from a variety of local machine shops. Often the parts were not made to particularly high tolerances; generally they were very far from being interchangeable. Considerable craft skills were therefore required to work the metal enough to make the parts fit together. Division of labor was slight. Master mechanics were chiefly employed. Their experience and judgment were required to get the job done.

Ford began making its own parts with single-purpose machine tools and other dedicated equipment. The company made its parts to unusually and extraordinarily high tolerances. This rendered the parts genuinely interchangeable: no fitting whatever took place on the Ford factory floor. In the way Ford minimized setup times and facilitated unskilled, high-speed assembly, it exploited and developed what is known as "American system" production in a radical way.[1] The attention the engineering side of this was paid in the trade press suggests that it was a distinctive investment and production strategy.[2] And it was: in the words of the leading historian of the American system, Ford mechanics developed "fresh ideas in gauging, fixture design, machine tool design and placement, factory layout, quality control, and materials handling."[3] As the equipment in question was largely custom made, the strategy was certainly an expensive one.

Because most of the parts being produced were particular to Model T's, coordination of logistical flows became the first managerial priority. Intensive exploitation of fixed factors of production such as the single-purpose machine tools—factors whose principal costs lay in their purchase price—became the second. In all this, tasks on the shop floor were becoming more tightly integrated. In due course the enterprise became more vertically integrated as well, which tied in even more of the owners' capital.

The reliance on dedicated machine tools rather than skilled craftsmen and general-purpose tools allowed Ford to hire immigrants with little industrial experience of any description: the work the company needed done was principally machine tending and unskilled assembly. But this did not save Ford from the dangers of investing in assets which could be held hostage. The new production system and the investments behind it were generating large profits. But employees could in principle reduce those profits or possibly even prevent the company from taking any at all by disrupting the shop floor coordination, restricting output, or effectively immobilizing key machines. As the skill levels declined and the costs of disruption grew, so too grew the ease of disruption.

The first experiments with assembly lines for subassemblies at Ford started in March 1913. A line for final assembly was first tried out in the following October. By the beginning of the new year it was clear that the line could work and be synchronized. Three were put into place. All the plant—including subassembly and parts manufacturing—was being driven to the pace of final assembly demands. At precisely this juncture, when the logistical flows of the whole enterprise became tautly and inextricably interconnected, the company announced a huge wage raise and the panoply of welfare programs for which it became famous.

HOW WAS EXPENDITURE ON EMPLOYEES INCREASED, AND WHAT WERE THE UNDERLYING ECONOMIC ISSUES?

THE DETAILS WERE ANNOUNCED AT A PRESS CONFERENCE IN HENRY FORD'S OFFICE ON JANUARY 5, 1914. AN ANNOUNCEMENT WAS READ OUT TO A GROUP of local reporters. The Ford Motor Company would more than double the daily earnings paid to the great mass of its production workers. Previously these individuals had earned $2.34 per nine-hour day. Their pay was to be increased to the princely sum of $5.00 for eight hours. In this the Ford workers became both much better paid than they had been and much better paid than they would be anywhere else in the industry.

The increase took the form of a supplement labeled "profit-sharing." This was not profit-sharing in the usual economists' sense, since (as events proved) it did not respond in any systematic way to changes in company profits. It was not, strictly speaking, a wage supplement with a funny name, since workers had to pass a screening interview with a social worker to be eligible for it. But for all who passed the screening—in fact, it appears, virtually everyone who tried—it was for practical purposes a wage supplement. Each period's gross take-home pay had two components. One approximated the going rate for that grade of labor. The other was the so-called profit-share. The screening was elaborate but not very expensive.[4] The related welfare activities implemented soon thereafter do not seem to have been expensive either.[5] I will therefore begin my analysis by asking what might have made the profit-share in itself a productive expenditure.

It is implausible that this huge rise in compensation represented the workings of supply and demand in the labor market. The country in general and the Midwest in particular—both its rural and its industrial parts—were sliding into a depression. Poor relief in Detroit was at its highest levels in many years. Immense lines, on many days numbering as many as 12,000 and more, formed outside the Ford factory in the weeks following the announcement. These job seekers were prepared to wait all night during a Great Lakes winter. Fire hoses could drive them away but only long enough for a change into dry clothes. It seems inescapable that Ford jobs were thought to be an attractive proposition at the quoted wage. Ford was paying more than it had to.

Was the company then just giving away its money? An economist would immediately think of three sorts of explanations of why a profit-maximizing firm might nonetheless want to pay such high wages. They are, respectively, minimizing the costs due to lost training of high turnover, minimizing the costs of hiring relatively less-productive workers (to whom the high wages would be an especially good deal), and minimizing the costs of shirking on the job. None of the three is persuasive as a central motive, but each fails to persuade in an instructive way. It is worth going through them one by one.

The thrust of the technological changes described in the preceding section was to radically routinize all but a handful of the jobs at Ford. Work force skills that were still crucial for producing autos elsewhere became progressively less relevant to the mass of jobs making cars at Ford. Instead, Ford engineers built the skills into single-purpose machine tools making strictly interchangeable parts.

Ford had dramatically heavy turnover in the period leading up to the five-dollar day, including one twelve-month period with a rate of 412 percent. But the deskilling had been going on fast enough and long enough that this was not necessarily very costly in terms of wasted training. Documents in the Ford archives permit crude calculations of these costs. At the most resolutely optimistic, one cannot place them above 30 percent of the profit-share.[6]

Since the point of all this technical change was to allow essentially unskilled workers to do the production work, the second group of explanations appear to be nonstarters. If there were unobservable but intrinsic skills or productivity attributes which were valuable in the jobs at hand, the firm might have been willing to pay premium wages to find workers who possessed them. But there were no such skills or attributes. By and large, the work in question was either machine minding or assembly-line operations. One might be tempted to argue that ability to tolerate the pace was such an attribute. But this ability could be observed essentially instantaneously, for reasons I discuss in the next paragraph. The cost of hiring a person who did not have much of it was essentially zero.

The most obviously promising approach is the third: perhaps there were many opportunities for the exercise of discretion and so for shirking. The high wage might serve as incentive to refrain if there was some chance of getting caught, since the alternative employments were all much less well paid. The difficulty with this concerns the ease of monitoring, which got cheaper and more efficient (in the sense that the monitoring mechanisms identified shirkers and replaced them much more incisively and swiftly than before) as a part of the technical change. The shop floor was laid out systematically; and when everyone was keeping pace, the work flowed smoothly. When someone did not keep pace, work in process piled up visibly. (One might, of course, shirk by doing a job incompletely rather than slowly.[7] But I see no evidence in any company records or trade sources that this was occurring to any significant degree, never mind getting worse, at the time of the events in question.)[8] Thus the problem of monitoring was getting less rather than more severe; and though the costs of shirking were on the increase (more pieces going by each worker in each time unit), the speed with which shirkers could be caught and replaced seems to have been rising extremely quickly. Reports in the engineering and management press of the day suggest there just wasn't much scope for shirking. Ratios of supervisory staff to production workers were sharply on the rise.[9]

On the other hand, the company's means of dealing with shirkers, however effective for isolated individuals, would have been very much less efficient in dealing with groups. These might be easy to identify; but swooping down on them, plucking them out of the circuit, and instantaneously replacing them with another group that knew exactly what to do would have been another matter entirely, given that there were many fewer supervisors than jobs.

In the abstract, then, the possibility of collective action raises the question of work norms and the source of management's confidence that it could simply come in each day and unilaterally decide on the speed of the line. More concretely, it raises the specter of the sit-down strike. This was a company whose capital stock was to a first approximation completely dedicated to making black Model T Fords. The handsome stream of profits was the return on coordination involving the use of these machines. Collective action which interfered with that was a direct threat to the profits. Such collective action was very much in the air in Detroit in this period. Syndicalists had been active in the auto plants in the springtime. They had organized one major strike, and they had shown a worrying degree of interest in the Ford workers and factory.[10]

One can make detailed claims that Ford's (expected-)profit-maximizing strategy was precisely the profit-sharing approach of buying the peace.[11] The company decided to pay the handsome wage to such a large fraction of its employees because a very large fraction of its employees worked on the shop floor. It was those on the shop floor who could interfere with the action of the great machine.[12] Ford wanted to give them a stake, however ill-defined, in the present and future prosperity of the company.

WHY PAY SOME OF IT OUT IN KIND?

The home visits by the social workers and the company's main other welfare service, Americanization classes, bear examination in this context. The question is why it might have been cost-minimizing to give out these particular services rather than increasing the cash payout at the margin. Scale economies in the provision of the services come into it; but the main part of my answer is a contingent fact about the employees, namely that peculiarities of their circumstances ensured that they would place an unusually high value on the particular services offered.

I have remarked that technical change at Ford allowed the company to employ essentially unskilled laborers for the great bulk of its factory employees. But the labor force it hired had several other attributes of interest as well. They were overwhelmingly foreign born and mostly recent arrivals. (This is particularly striking in the winter of 1913–1914 because plenty of underemployed Americans were streaming into Detroit from the Michigan backcountry at the time.) Few seemed to speak English well. All seemed to feel that they had accomplished a great thing by getting to America; but almost all seemed to be living only on the margins of American life. This was not simply a matter of being poor. They were outsiders, and daily life conspired in many ways to make them feel it. There is the ring of truth in the Ford worker's letter which comments (in Serbian) that "without a knowledge of the English language I am handicapped. I want to become a citizen of the United States. Simply because I cannot talk English, I am often looked down upon. ...."[13] "There exists in the mind of the average American," the author quoting this writes, "a feeling of superiority to the immigrants. The immigrant is treated as though of a lower class due to the fact that he speaks a foreign language and has strangely different customs and often a limited experience."[14]

The immigrants had seen the rough edge of this already:

A great deal of the immigrant's good will is lost at Ellis Island. He comes here, strong in body, restless in mind, imperfectly educated, impelled by a passion for freedom and justice. Heretofore, his individuality has been subordinated in the State. He imagines that here he will be treated as an individual, as a person; that he can enter into personal relations with the country of his choice. It is an indefinite expectation, doubtless, but very real. His first contact with the country is at Ellis Island, and there he meets what to all outward appearance is precisely the kind of thing he fancied he had left behind him: the impersonal functionary, the rigid routine untempered by any semblance of personal interest or sympathy, the inquisitorial and suspicious attitude. An immigrant woman once told me, "My whole voyage over was full of anticipation. I had heard wonderful things of the land of the free. After being detained a few days at Ellis Island, I walked out of the Barge Office free at last, but utterly crushed in spirit. The good will which was ready to meet the good will of the country seemed to have died, and its place was taken by a discouragement and suspicion that was a great hindrance in adjustment to my new life."[15]

Even without such a context, the personal visit by a Sociological Department investigator would have been a great event in an immigrant tenement neighborhood. The investigator seems to have arrived by car, with a driver and, if required, an interpreter as well. He looked around the employee's home, notebook in hand. He asked his routine of questions about cleanliness, diet, and home life and then went on his way. If he was satisfied by what he saw and by the answers and assurances he obtained, theretofore unimaginable wealth followed, flowing to all those supported by the Ford employee. Bank accounts would be opened, lots purchased, larger, brighter, and cleaner houses built.[16] Living standards would improve radically. Sometimes these came as dramatic interventions, carried out with considerable panache.[17] The impressions left must have been deep ones.

These impressions can only have been deepened by the way the investigators were told to go about the day-to-day aspects of their jobs. Here is Samuel Marquis, the head of the Sociological Department and formerly one of the senior and most eminent Episcopal ministers in Detroit, addressing the assembled investigators.

> I know you men must run up against some awfully discouraging cases. You have got to be able, in spite of the things you meet, to believe in men and to keep your courage up in the face of discouragements, [for] in order to make a man trust himself you have first got to trust him. There are a lot of workmen in this world who have got a lot in them, who aren't doing their best simply because nobody has ever come to them and told them, "Here, old fellow, you've got a lot more in you than I've seen."[18]

What leaps out from the page in this address is its diction of moral uplift. It would not have been lost on Marquis's listeners that these words were not just fine words: they were to be accompanied by a handsome tender of interest and self-denominated trust. Henry Ford said he preferred to give the workers the money instead of spending it for them. Those who were not up to the responsibility might lose the privilege, but it was for them to decide whether to seize the extraordinary opportunity the company offered them to lead a respectworthy life. Were the investigators to be neutral observers? "I simply [suggest]," Marquis went on,

> that you light the fires of hope where they have gone out, that you tell men not only their faults and mistakes, but also tell them of their virtues, that you give a man a brace once in a while for making good, that you go into the business, along with the other things you are doing, of giving encouragement . . . .[19]

It was indeed, he is saying, for the workers to choose. But the investigators could help them make the choices which would "turn round" —that is, elevate—and even, in a humble and distinctly American way, enoble their lives.[20]

The second Sociological Department activity, often begun before the first, was the department's program of English and Americanization classes. These had several distinctive aspects. They were taught by company employees. They were taught on site. In both these respects, no one could mistake that this was an enterprise of the Ford Motor Company. Furthermore, they were taught from materials designed—so far as the students could make out, at the behest of the company—for use by adult immigrant workers: there was in the Ford classroom none of the subtle humiliation of grown men squeezed into tiny seats in elementary schools reading sentences about happy, singing birds and much-adored babies.[21] And the pedagogy was a species of the direct method. The instructor said "I brush my teeth," making the brushing motions, and his pupils shouted it back, brushing away just as vigorously. He also mimed washing himself before setting off for work in the morning, occasioning much hilarity as well as imitation. Once he got to work, the traces of some missing lessons suggest, he was a model of subordination on the shop floor. So, no doubt, were the students: belonging and participating, "each in his own place," seem to have been the teaching materials' theme.[22] "[A]s we adapt the machinery in the shop to turning out the kind of automobile we have in mind," said the department head in a speech to educators in 1916, "so we have constructed an educational system with a view to producing the human product in mind."[23]

The climax to which the curriculum came was systematic preparation for the naturalization exams, that is, official entry to the political nation. It must have seemed of a piece: participation, incorporation, and great gifts following on doing what you were told. The investigators were very keen on regular class attendance.

The usual interpretation of these is Samuel Levin's: Henry Ford paid men $2.34 an hour to do the work and the balance of $5.00 to live the way he wanted.[24] The investigators told the workers what they had to do; and the classes explained how they had to do it. It seems to me that this interpretation attends too much to the form of the interchange and inquires too little about the spirit. To many of the employees, these forms of life would have a meaning far more important to them than any sense of what Henry Ford desired.

Photographs from commencement exercises at the end of the Americanization courses show Sunday-go-to-meeting suits, razor creases, and a mixture of the broadest smiles imaginable and looks of fierce seriousness. The closing ceremony also bears describing.

> The "Melting Pot" exercises were dramatic in the extreme. A deckhand came down the gangplank of the ocean liner, [its hulk and deck] represented in canvas facsimile.
>
> "What cargo?" was the hail he received. "About 230 hunkies," he called back. "Send 'em along and we'll see what the melting pot will do for them," said the other and from the ship came a line of immigrants, in the poor garments of their native lands. Into the gaping pot they went. Then six instructors of the Ford School, with long ladles, started stirring. "Stir! Stir!" urged the superintendent of the school. The six bent to greater efforts. From the pot fluttered a flag, held high, then the first of the finished product of the pot appeared, waving his hat. The crowd cheered as he mounted the edge and came down the steps on the side. Many others followed him, gathering in two groups on either side of the cauldron. In contrast to the shabby rags they wore when they unloaded from the ship, all wore neat suits. They were American in looks. And ask any one of them what nationality he is and the reply will come quickly, "American!" "Polish-American?" you might ask. "No, American," would be the answer. For they are taught in the Ford School that the hyphen is a minus sign.[25]

> "Any spectator . . . saw the pride which shone from the former aliens' faces as they waved little flags on their way down the steps from the huge cauldron, symbolic of the fusing process which makes raw immigrants into loyal Americans."[26]

In its first five years of operations, some 16,000 employees graduated from this institution. They attended on their own time, and the teaching was done by volunteers. The main expenses borne by the company were lesson sheets and electricity. The loyalty engendered must have seemed cheap at the price.

WAS FORD WELFARE CAPITALISM ACTUALLY DIFFERENT?

The standard modern monograph on welfare capitalism uses as a definition of its subject "any service provided [by an employer] for the comfort or improvement of employees which was neither a necessity of the industry nor required by law."[27] The phrase originates in a Bureau of Labor Statistics survey published in 1919; and by "a necessity of the industry" the survey's authors undoubtedly meant services without which even the best-suited and most highly motivated employees could not do their job.[28] To an economist the phrase has a different set of connotations. It sounds as if it refers at least as much to competition among firms seeking to hire workers, as in the gloss "a requirement for production given the skill-, effort-, and diligence requirements of the technology and given that the firm must attract and retain its work force." It suggests that studies of welfare capitalism would focus on how firms made their products (and so their profits), what this led them to need and want from their employees, and the packages of wages and services this led them to offer employees. But the traditional literature is of a very different character.

The monograph, Stuart Brandes's *American Welfare Capitalism*, is representative of the literature it draws on. It starts out with a definition and some broadly sketched history and then gets down to the serious business of making lists. These are organized by type of activity, one chapter for each. The roster of types includes housing, education, religion, recreation, profit-sharing and stock-ownership plans, medical care, pensions, social work, and employee representation schemes. A large number of firms are cited as examples, many of them in many chapters each. But essentially nothing else is said about any of these firms other than that it paid for some particular program at some time or other.

The impression this catalogue of benevolent activities leaves on the reader is one of an incidentally variegated but fundamentally homogeneous, and static, set of activities. Firms offered services as well as wages. One infers that there were variations from place to place in demand for the services and in sources of supply other than the firm. Thus carrying out the new ideal in any particular place might not require a firm to mount the whole range of activities. But there is nothing in Brandes's account to suggest that overarching objectives would be specific to particular industries, never mind specific to particular technologies or strategies of shop floor organization. There is certainly no discussion of the history of the diffusion of technologies and ideas about organizing work. And there is nothing to say firms were offering any more than they had to in order to attract and retain their workers. The bulk of the book is a simple catalogue of facts, framed by chapters about why and how the movement started and why and how it ended. This is perfectly in keeping with earlier studies of the subject.[29]

There is one widely read revisionist response to Brandes's study and in particular to his conclusions about welfare capitalism's end. This appears in the version of an essay by David Brody reprinted (with material on the Brandes book which was not in the initial version) in Brody's *Workers in Industrial America*.[30] The essay focuses on welfare activities in the 1920s. Brody's principal quarrel with Brandes concerns why welfare capitalism's moment eventually passed.[31] He takes issue neither with the underlying characterization of welfare capitalism nor with the static vision of its history.

Brody's explanation of the rise and development (to the extent he thinks there was any) turns on the fact that in the period his essay examines, the well-known activist firms were all very large. Brody remarks that this had been characteristic of the movement all along.[32] He argues that welfare capitalism came into fashion in the aftermath of the consolidation movement of the late nineties and the antitrust legislation that followed. When he sees the activities being carried on by enterprises which were in the main very large scale, he takes the welfare firms' motives to be well summed up in the remark that "Big-business leaders anxiously cultivated national favor. That alone, Elbert Gary and George Perkins had argued during the Progressive period, might protect the vulnerable industrial giants from anti-trust action."[33] The big firms were trying to deflect the government's attention from the high levels of their profits.

The antitrust explanation raises the problem I have identified in a very direct way, for it points to economic motives as a central explanatory principle and then fails to analyze them very deeply. If such motives are in fact a central element, why take the level of profits as a given? The building blocks of an economist's explanation would be the tastes of workers and the resources and technology available to firms, not the utility levels the workers ultimately achieve and the profits the firms eventually earn. The focus here should be on technology. Might there not be important connections between the aspects of technology and competition which were inducing and sustaining the concentrated industries (and their unusually high profits) on the one hand and the motives of those who approved the welfare expenditure on the other, that is, between the details of production processes and those of what the economist would construe as compensation and motivation schemes? There surely is something to Brody's argument. But there are also microeconomic motivations for welfare capitalism that Brody and the other authors do not discuss.

These explanations might have fine detail. Consider, for example, the observation, referred to above, that certain well-known welfare firms in the 1920s were large. Even at the level of establishments firms can be large in any of several different senses; and largeness in any one can in principle be independent of largeness in the others. A factory could be physically extensive, or it could be large in the sense of producing a great deal of output, perhaps through the intensive use of elaborate and expensive capital equipment. Alternately, it could simply employ a great many people, working either in large and heterogeneous groups or in small, homogeneous ones. The incentives facing the factory owners to provide any particular welfare service— for example, English language lessons—could well be different in these different situations. If the basic motive behind providing such services was an economic one, we would expect to see different behavior. And if we followed the policies of a single firm over time, we would not be surprised to see those policies change as key aspects of the firm's demand for labor changed or as shifts occurred in the surrounding labor market and in the terms on which the firm could obtain labor.

Ford stood well ahead of its automotive competitors in deploying mass production, with all the productivity and inflexibilities that it entailed. Pay policies at Ford were uniquely generous for the industry. The preceding discussion therefore raises the question of how its welfare activities compared in scale and in variety.

Virtually throughout the teens, surveys and articles in trade journals suggest, the Ford Motor Company was distinctive in both respects: there was precious little in the way of welfare activities on the part of other automobile manufacturers. Such autobiographical memoirs of auto workers as have survived also leave the impression that for most of the decade this sort of activity was simply not common. What was reported was modest in scope and diffuse in import. In May 1914, for example, *The Automobile*, an authoritative trade journal, published an unsigned survey article entitled "Practical Welfare in Motor Factories."[34] The bulk of the examples concern athletic

leagues, fields, factory lunchrooms, and, "for those who desire rest,
. . . factory buildings . . . skirted with large trees under which there
are benches and settees where the employees may lounge during the
noon hour." There is a reference to a mutual benefit association (i.e.,
a health insurance fund), subscription to which was open to employees of a group of 15 motor factory firms in Flint, Michigan. The
contribution rates are given explicitly, and it is not at all clear that
the firms contributed anything other than some legal advice, organizational work, and bulletin board space. The description of this association begins "The vehicle workers . . . have combined. . . ." The
vehicle workers probably thought of it as their own association.

For some sense of context, the article casually characterizes the
factories whose programs it reports as "machine shops." It seems that
Ford-style production did not even begin diffusing in any serious way
until after the war.[35] General Motors began to build employee housing
in 1919; this was the same postwar epoch of ownership and management in which (not long thereafter) it hired Ford's senior production
manager to start mass-producing the Chevrolet.

Documents in the papers of the Americanization Committee of
Detroit reveal that the picture is even more stark regarding the educational work. One can trace the efforts, started formally in early
1915, of activist Detroiters to enlist the aid of local businesses in
teaching the immigrants English and some civics. Several matters are
very plain. The City of Detroit was perfectly happy to appropriate
funds to run evening sessions in the public schools.[36] The problem
was not the supply of places but the demand for them. The key to
raising demand lay in employer enthusiasm.[37] Almost all employers,
a number of prominent automobile manufacturers and suppliers
prominent among them, fell into one of two categories. Some were
willing to advertise the evening school classes.[38] Some were not.[39] (It
interfered with running a night shift.) None save Ford seem to have
seen any point in having the classes on site, let alone in a way point-
edly identified with the company.[40] But Ford really must have seen
something in the idea. It ran classes on almost as large a scale as the
public schools for the entire city did. Its numbers swamped those of
the YMCA, the only other important nongovernmental provider of
these services.[41]

It is instructive to consider the choice context in which the Ford
program came to an end. As the middle years of the decade passed,
more and more of the immigrants and the new immigrant employees
passed through the programs. The wartime inflation came to Detroit,
and the company allowed the real value of the "profit-share" to melt

down to quite a low level, though it kept adjusting the market wage component upwards.[42] This could be substitution at the margin. Ideas change slowly. In the short run, the only way to buy the peace might well have been to pay cash. But over time, ideas sink in, and ongoing behavior can reinforce them. Over time, then, it might have been less expensive to shift the weight of reliance from cash to investment in ideas. The next period of labor turmoil in Detroit and turbulence at Ford was not until after the war. Immigration had essentially ceased; and other means of work force control were cheaper. The company had very tentatively explored reaching out to the one group which might have shared the earlier susceptibility—blacks come up to Detroit from the South, living in the city's most extreme poverty and, despite their citizenship, scarcely members of the political nation. But the company did not pursue the idea with any vigor. There were too many threateningly disruptive complications. Other ways seemed easier. The company raised wages instead.

CONCLUSION

At the time of the survey of welfare practices conducted in 1913 by the Bureau of Labor Statistics, welfare policies were far more widespread than the BLS report suggests. The BLS report discusses 50 firms employing them. But in 1914, the National Civic Federation listed over 2,500.[43] The proportion of establishments in the overall economy adopting welfare policies was probably small, but those establishments tended to employ relatively large numbers of people.[44] Indeed, firms we would think of as mass production firms were prominent among the adopters.[45] This fact is given edge by the fact that crude indices of the overall pace of adoption are strongly correlated with Griffin's well-known index of industrial unrest.[46] The mass production firms had expensive physical capital and tightly coupled production processes. Unrest could cost their owners dear.

The welfare capitalism movement offered a repertoire of policies to the Ford Motor Company. But the package of policies Ford adopted was idiosyncratic, and the details of that idiosyncrasy suggest that its inspiration, like that of the five-dollar-a-day compensation scheme, derived from the company's innovative technology and production economics and from particular conditions in the labor markets in which it operated rather than from employers' simple altruism or from some popular theory of the responsibilities of employers in social life.

It would be worth exploring how widely this explanation is true. This would require coupling the detailed history of welfare capitalist institutions to the history of the evolution of production technology. But to argue that the latter was irrelevant to the former is to take a very odd position. Businessmen, after all, are famous for their relentless focus on reducing costs and making more money.

II
POLITICS AND
LABOR MARKETS
∎

After 1890, the center of gravity in American industry shifted to giant corporations serving national markets. Between 1904 and 1923, the proportion of the manufacturing work force employed in very large establishments (over 1,000 workers) doubled, rising from 12 to 25 percent. The personnel policies of these corporations often served as models for smaller companies from the same industry or region. Large mass production firms dominated the images of industry found in newspapers and books during these years. Like giant lightning rods, such firms drew the criticism and indignation of a citizenry concerned about industrial unrest and other problems associated with corporate capitalism.

It is thus understandable that much of the new historical research on American employers concentrates on large firms during the first three to four decades of this century, a time when those firms fashioned the rough outlines of the modern bureaucratic workplace. With its focus on large and professionally managed firms, the new research can be viewed as part of the historical project first identified by Louis Galambos some twenty years ago as the "organizational synthesis in modern American history." Galambos saw the core of that emerging synthesis in the transition from small-scale, informal, locally and regionally oriented groups to large-scale, national, bureaucratic organizations.

But these trends were far from inevitable or universal. Locally oriented firms did not disappear, nor was ownership uniformly displaced by professional management. Alongside the oligopolistic sector of the economy was a sizable competitive sector in which proprietary capitalism managed to hold sway, and still does. As Martin J. Sklar writes in his magisterial work *The Corporate Reconstruction of American Capitalism* (1988), "although tending toward relative decline and a permanent position of subordination, nevertheless, market relations, forms of thought, political movements, and cultural patterns associated with small-producer and proprietary enterprise remained widespread, influential, and strongly represented in party politics, Congress, and the judiciary, and at the state and local levels of politics and government." Although Sklar does not dwell on the subject, market relations in this sector were distinguished by their heavy reliance on craft workers, whose skills provided the small job shop with its economic raison d'être. Along with craft labor came a distinctive approach to workplace organization that included collective bargaining, which was rarely practiced in large mass production firms until the 1930s and 1940s. In other words, until the 1930s proprietary capitalists were more immediately and passionately concerned with containing trade unions than were managers of larger companies.

Howell Harris opens this section with an essay examining the Philadelphia Metal Manufacturers Association, an employers' association made up of small- to medium-sized, locally owned metalworking firms. His essay goes a long way toward closing what has heretofore been a wide gap in our knowledge of the industrial relations activities of small American firms. Harris points out that the Philadelphia firms were "niche" producers, who depended on their multiskilled work force to function and to compete. Various craft unions sought to turn that dependence to their advantage, and the Philadelphia employers responded by banding together to defeat strikes and maintain the open shop.

The association's chief activity was its labor bureau, which provided member firms with blacklists and strikebreakers. Employers were less interested in gaining control of the labor process than they were in holding down the cost of an existing, skill-based labor process. Moreover, with their small size and constantly changing product lines, these firms were unable to or unconcerned with establishing internal labor markets. Instead, the labor bureau assisted them with the more pressing task of regulating supply levels in the external labor market, which was the main arena of union-management conflict in Philadelphia.

In other parts of the nation and other industries, employer rejection of unionism stemmed from more than "the calculations of self-interest," as Daniel Ernst phrases it in his essay on proprietary capitalists and the law. After all, unionism potentially could have served as a device to stabilize labor and product markets, as it did in such competitive industries as apparel, construction, and coal. American employers' rejection of this approach had as much to do with ideology as with economics, what Ernst calls the "passion" of the "strong-minded businessmen who identified themselves closely with their enterprises." But like their counterparts in Philadelphia, the proprietary capitalists analyzed by Ernst usually chose not to fight unionism on their own. Lacking the resources of the large employer, these small businessmen turned to each other or to local politics and the courts in their effort to defeat unions. Workplace programs—such as scientific management or welfare work—were less common among proprietary capitalists than were activities oriented to the world outside the firm.

For most of the past sixty years, legal scholars—from Felix Frankfurter to Morton Horwitz—have portrayed the courts of nineteenth-century America as being exceedingly hostile to social reform and trade unionism. Considerable evidence has been brought forth to support the change that the courts reinterpreted contract and constitutional law to fit the employer's changing needs. It comes as little surprise, then, that proprietary capitalists battling unions during the early twentieth century turned to the courts in search of injunctions, damages, and bans on the closed shop. These they often received, but Ernst convincingly makes the point that during the Progressive era the courts became more pragmatic, more supportive of reform, and more reluctant to do the employer's bidding than traditional legal historiography would have it. Especially in urban jurisdictions such as Chicago and New York, judges were far from predictable or consistent in their antiunionism. In an ironic twist, Ernst attributes the shift in judicial attitudes to the rise of corporate capitalism. Like other members of the middle class, judges began to perceive unionism as a counterbalance to growing concentrations of economic power. They "believed that fair play and social welfare required greater tolerance of combination on the part of labor," even when the plaintiffs were themselves neither large nor powerful.

5

Getting It Together: The Metal Manufacturers' Association of Philadelphia, c. 1900–1930

■

HOWELL JOHN HARRIS

In her presidential address at a recent conference of business historians, Mira Wilkins asserted: "In dealing with modern business history from the late nineteenth century . . . the significant actors are not the small, single product, single plant, single function, local market enterprises run by one entrepreneur, but rather . . . the multiproduct, multiplant, multifunctional, multidivisional, multinational enterprises administered by a managerial hierarchy."[1]

This is Chandleresque business history speaking with all the confidence properly belonging to a representative of an intellectual orientation which determines the conventional scholarly wisdom and which seems to do little more than conform to common sense. After all, big corporate institutions matter more than small ones. If they endure for several generations and provide key building blocks in the economies of not just the United States but the whole nonsocialist world, surely they deserve all the attention lavished on them?

Institutionally minded labor and social historians who have opened up the study of industrial relations policy and practice in the United States have been just as preoccupied with managerial thinking and behavior within the core of America's "dual economy." And the (somewhat overlapping) group of scholars who have added to our knowledge of the development of productioin, employment, and personnel management have similarly worked, or been capable of being fitted, quite comfortably within the dominant Chandler paradigm.[2]

Readers may detect a note of *mea culpa* at this point. My own *Right to Manage* argued that what was fundamental to business responses

111

to the challenge of labor under the "New Deal dispensation" in the late 1930s and 1940s was the thoroughgoing implementation of corporate industrial relations "strategies and structures"—a pregnant phrase, if ever there was one—congruent with the main drift of managerial behavior within the center firm. Similarly, Jacoby's *Employing Bureaucracy* concentrated on the development of bureaucratic structures—employment, personnel, or industrial relations departments—within firms which had already strengthened and extended management's span of control in other areas by similar means, involving the assignment of responsibility for new and traditional tasks to staff specialists. The policies those professionals pursued eventually contributed toward the formation of "internal labor markets"— a process comparable to the internalization of decisions and transactions hitherto accomplished in and by an unregulated external marketplace, and their subjection to a degree of proactive managerial control, which is at the heart of Alfred Chandler's account of the rise of the American corporate commonwealth.[3]

What, if anything, is wrong with this body of scholarship? It is not what we have done but what we have neglected. We have helped integrate the history of corporate industrial relations policy within the Chandler paradigm. But we have done so while the sufficiency of the conventional wisdom—as a key to the past and, implicitly, a guide to the present and likely future—has been called to account and found wanting.

The most visible assault on the classic story of industrial development, as a matter of progressive bureaucratization and the emergence of Weberian "rationality" as the measure of good practice in business administration, has come from the prolific pens of Michael Piore and Charles Sabel. Contemporary crises in the competitiveness of industries committed to a "Fordist" production regime, particularly in the United States and the United Kingdom, have stimulated Piore and Sabel to search out explanations for, and viable alternatives to, what they see as the excessively rigid, hierarchical structures and bureaucratized practices of the great capitalist behemoths.

Piore and Sabel, and the latter's collaborator Jonathan Zeitlin, have been principally responsible for sketching in a usable past for the "flexible firms" which they depict as offering the older industrial nations a path toward a revitalized, perhaps more humane and cooperative, post-Fordist future. This exercise has involved a certain amount of creative wishful thinking.[4]

The family-owned, personally or informally managed, undercapitalized, skill-dependent firm turns in their account from an anachronism, or at best a quaint survival in the byways of the business system, into a building block for the future. The business historian is advised to scrap his presentist assumptions and teleological interpretive framework—what Philip Scranton has called the ever-upwards "From Lowell to General Motors by way of the Railroads" view of corporate development. After all, we can see that past's future in the Anglo-American present, and it no longer works especially well.

The quest for "Historical Alternatives to Mass Production" has become a major transatlantic academic enterprise. Scholars engaged in it do not deny the twentieth-century triumph of the Chandleresque corporation with its Fordist production strategy. What they question is its inevitability and universality, and they ask us to see its limitations.

Not all product markets are broad, homogeneous, and satisfied with standardized goods. Not all consumers are undiscriminating and merely price sensitive. There is a place, even—perhaps especially— in the modern industrial economy for the "niche producer" of goods made in small batches or to order, sold on the quality of their workmanship or design, commanding a price premium, and having to be made according to a production regime in which "economies of scale" and "deskilling" have no place.

The "niche producer" depends on a multiskilled work force to function and to compete. Unlike the Chandleresque corporation, it cannot build an internal labor market. It does not have the size, the resources, or the relatively stable demand for fairly homogeneous labor, or skills which are company-specific, to underpin such an institution. Its workers are autonomous. They move from firm to firm, taking their human capital with them and acquiring more as they gain varied experience.

Such firms are not integrated operations; they specialize according to function or process, and produce finished goods as a result of their ability to interrelate with one another. Chandler's history is a paean to the advantages of integration and the internalization of transactions; Piore et al. write instead in praise of loose ties. A mass of transactions external to the firm itself give small enterprises, embedded in an industrial region, access to a wide range of resources on which they depend but which they cannot command by themselves. "Relational contracting" underpins the small firm's production system and competitive strategy.[5]

Advantages accruing from localization also turned such firms into viable competitors with, or substitutes for, mass production enterprises in the past—and implicitly in Piore's text, might do so in the future. Firms themselves, or in concert with local governments, established joint research and training programs serving a mass of small firms in distinct industrial city-regions. Such "public-private" partnerships gave small firms the ability collectively to invest in their industry's future—in the new products, processes, and designs which saved them from the fate of obsolescence and in the versatile human capital essential to exploit innovations and respond quickly to shifts in consumer preferences.

A major exercise in historiographical revisionism is under way. But, thus far, most of the published work of the Historical Alternatives school consists of programmatic essays using history as a quarry from which to hew supporting evidence. Most notably, the policy orientation and didactic purpose of Piore and Sabel's *Second Industrial Divide* are unmistakable. The lessons are intended for Americans, but few of the supporting examples are homegrown.

The only substantial research-based monographs which chart the rise, maturity, and eventual decline of an industrial region characterized by "flexible specialization" within the United States are Philip Scranton's *Proprietary Capitalism* and *Figured Tapestry*, on the Philadelphia textile industry in the nineteenth and twentieth centuries. Scranton does not offer his readers policy lessons. What he does provide is a fuller understanding of how things were, how they came to be, and why they changed; he gives them a sense of the variety and openness of the past—of the many worlds of American business which cannot be encompassed within the Chandler paradigm.[6]

The purpose of this essay is to suggest ways in which a comparable reorientation of research into the history of employment management may be accomplished by paying attention to "combined and uneven development" within the American economy. The aim of any such exercise in revision will be not to discard the story we have written so far but to supplement it.

First, we know a fair amount about industrial relations policy and practice in larger or notably well-managed smaller firms since about 1900, but what about the rest, about small- to middle-sized run-of-the-mill enterprises? Granovetter's recent research has alerted us to the enduring quantitative importance of such firms; *pace* Mira Wilkins, it seems rather arbitrary to deem them insignificant before we have actually looked into them.[7]

Second, the existing literature gives us a reasonable grasp of the main drift of labor-management relations in American manufacturing through the same period. But we are short of detailed studies of the *variety* of practices and accommodations managers and workers developed. In their absence, we make assumptions about what was representative or typical which may not be justified.

For example, we know something about the "open shop" policy in the metal trades in the early decades of this century, particularly as it affected firms employing large numbers of semiskilled machine tenders. But what of the small-batch and custom manufacturers who had little choice but to depend on skilled workers, unionized or not? How did such firms behave toward their work forces?[8]

Third, we have a good knowledge of what (some) large firms did with their own managerial and other resources to extend their control over their work forces. The "administrative capacity" of the Chandleresque firm to establish its own internal labor market and "unitary corporatist" industrial relations system was sufficient to the task, particularly in the context of the weak, fragmented state and feeble labor movement of early twentieth-century America. But what of those firms lacking market power and elaborate management structures? How did they cope with their employment management problems? Did they not, in tune with similarly situated enterprises in other industrial societies at the same time, find ways of acting together?

The research on which this article is based concerns a group of small- to middle-sized firms in the periphery of the dual economy: single-function or single-process businesses which rarely operated more than one plant; which were generally owned and managed by families or partnerships; whose management structures were underdeveloped and informal; which did not develop internal labor markets; which did not pursue "deskilling" of their labor forces; and which were about as far from the Chandlerite mainstream as one could hope to find.

These firms were members of the Metal Manufacturers Association of Philadelphia (MMA), an employers' association they set up in 1903 to look after their collective interests in their battles with skilled trades unionism and which did so very effectively for the next three decades.[9]

EMPLOYERS' ASSOCIATIONS AND "AMERICAN EXCEPTIONALISM"

Employers' associations are almost as neglected by business and industrial relations historians as the kinds of firm that joined them. They are unimportant in contemporary American labor relations except in industries such as coal mining, clothing, construction, printing, and trucking. Such industries have a large number of weak and vulnerable firms dealing with powerful, often quasicraft unions—or at least, they had such characteristics in the era when lasting, though fading, patterns of organized union-employer relations were being established.

But if we look at most industrial sectors in the post–New Deal or "collective bargaining" era we cannot fail to be impressed by the propensity of American manufacturing firms to go it alone in developing their labor relations policies. In international comparisons between the industrial relations systems of the advanced liberal-capitalist nations, the United States stands out as having the least collectivist employer behavior. The essential unit for the conduct of labor relations—or, increasingly, union avoidance—is the firm itself, or even the single plant. There are numerous explanations for this—notably, that by the 1930s American firms possessed the managerial resources to enable them to cope with the challenge of labor by themselves; and that since then federal law on union recognition and collective bargaining has underwritten this degree of decentralization.[10]

The splendid isolation of the American employer is not, of course, total. Firms do draw on outside assistance. They use labor lawyers, compensation consultants, advisers on corporate communications, industrial psychologists, and a wide range of other purveyors of special applied expertise. Those firms which are members of employers' associations can secure similar services from association staff.

But these "external" sources of information and advice *support* the fundamental decision making and executive autonomy of the American manufacturing firm. They do not begin to compare with the limitations on that freedom where labor relations are carried on by an employers' association on its members' behalf. Other nations' capitalists have depended on employers' associations with very significant functions to help them meet the challenge of labor; not so those of the United States during the collective-bargaining era.

What, then, is the point of studying the history of employers' associations in the United States when their roles have been so circumscribed as compared with, for example, those of the Scandinavian nations? Three arguments can be offered for taking an interest in organizations of marginal importance to the development of American industrial relations since the 1930s.

First, and most basically, 'twas *not* ever thus. In the "open shop" era, c. 1900–1935, employers' associations were important actors in their own right, and played a variety of supporting roles in relation to their members' successful union-busting and union-avoidance strategies. Contemplation of such organizations' present unimportance should not blind us to their past, when they counted for more.

Second, there is little research on them. Most of what there is, is more than 60 years old and near contemporaneous with the antiunion or "open shop" associations it examines; or 25 to 40 years old and confined to those comparatively few industrial sectors characterized by bargaining employers' associations in the postwar heyday of the American labor movement.[11]

Third, studying such associations offers us a way of extending our knowledge of the development of the American industrial relations system beyond those sectors and subjects comparatively well served by recent historiography. The open-shop employers' association provides us with a combination lens and lantern for peering into the world of the little businessman, at best a "provincial influential," in the early part of this century when such associations were most important in speaking for him and furthering his interests.

Employers' associations came in different shapes and sizes—"peak associations" like the National Association of Manufacturers (NAM) or the National Industrial Conference Board (NICB), which concentrated on lobbying, propaganda, and research; national associations confining their activities to one industry or sector of an industry, such as the National Metal Trades Association (NMTA) or National Founders Association (NFA); state and local general associations, such as the Illinois Manufacturers' Association or the Employers' Association of Detroit; and local specialized associations, of which the Metal Manufacturers Association of Philadelphia (MMA) is representative.[12]

Most of the American associations in all these different categories which were active in the pre–New Deal era had their origins in the two great bursts of union growth and employer reaction, 1898–1904 and 1916–1921. To get employers to advance beyond Adam Smith's "tacit, but constant and uniform combination" to found, join, and maintain functional associations took some external stimulus. Throughout the period in question, the presence or threat of unionization was that essential provocation.

Union-busting was the employers' association's raison d'être and greatest achievement. But it was not the whole story. Member firms had a wide range of employment problems apart from those directly connected with labor relations. Their associations existed as service providers, having to cater to the many needs of a voluntary membership. This article will examine the resulting diverse activities in which employers' associations participated, activities which had to do with the undramatic, everyday management of the employment relationship, not with those episodic breakdowns in managerial control which required firms and their associations to deploy the familiar techniques of labor replacement and employer belligerency.

THE MMA: ORIGINS AND DEVELOPMENT

The MMA was unusual in that it included both foundries and general machine shops within the same local association, but in other respects it was like metal trades employers' associations then proliferating in cities across America's industrial heartland. Its originators, like theirs, belonged to the two great national associations, the NFA and NMTA, which looked after the labor relations problems of middle-sized metal manufacturing concerns.

Those associations had been formed in 1898 and 1899 to confront and contain the growing strength of the Iron Molders' Union (IMU) and the International Association of Machinists (IAM). IMU membership rose from less than 12,000 in 1897 to more than 52,000 in 1903, representing about half of the skilled metal-molding work force in the United States. The IAM grew from about 18,000 members in 1899 to almost 56,000 in 1904, but machinists were about three times as numerous as molders; so the density of union organization in the country's machine shops was only about a third that in its foundries.[13]

Philadelphia was America's oldest manufacturing city, with a notably broad and heterogeneous industrial base. The textile sector was Philadelphia's largest, but metal products came a close second. The foundry and machine shop "industry" was the city's single largest, by product value, with 370 establishments employing almost 20,000 men. In metal products—as in manufacturing in general—Philadelphia ranked third in the country after New York and Chicago.[14]

The MMA recruited from a particular subdivision within this local manufacturing community. Philadelphia's metalworking industry comprised a few very large concerns at one end of the size spectrum —J. G. Brill (streetcars), William Cramp (ships), Midvale Steel (ordnance), Henry Disston (saws), with between 1,000 and 5,000 employees, and above all Baldwin Locomotive with more than 10,000—and a mass of small workshops at the other. The MMA recruited from the middle: until the mid-1920s, with rare exceptions, from among single-plant, locally owned and managed firms with less than 500 employees. More precisely, between 1916 and 1922, firms with between 50 and 250 employees made up about half of the membership, and employed between a half and about a third of the association's total blue collar work force. Throughout the whole period, the average number of "operatives" reported by member firms fluctuated between 100 and 150, only getting outside those bounds at the peaks or troughs of business cycles. The size distribution of MMA member firms was quite broad, including (by the late 1920s) everything from small machine repairers to giant radio and turbine manufacturers, but in terms of membership (if not employment) the middle-sized proprietary firm remained the stable core of the association.[15]

Evidence on the industrial distribution of MMA membership complements the above picture of selective recruitment. There were whole subsectors of the metal trades where the MMA did not recruit at all, while membership clustered in a comparatively few areas where its presence was substantial or dominant, representing as it did the larger-than-average firms. In 1924, for example, though MMA members were only one-tenth of the total number of firms in the city's metal trades (83 of 829), they employed about a quarter of the industry's work force (18,386 of 71,760). Among machine shop operators and machine tool makers, they included 29 (19 percent) of the city's 151 firms among their number, and employed 5,793 or 58 percent of the total of 10,016 workers. A similarly high density prevailed in the city's ferrous and nonferrous foundries.

Brass and bronze products, electrical apparatus and supplies, gas and electric fixtures, hardware, iron and steel castings, machine shops, machine tool makers and machine repairers, plumbers' supplies and steam fittings, professional and scientific instruments were the census categories comprising four-fifths of member firms between 1916 and 1930. This situation had obtained, in broad outline, from the organization's beginnings. Obviously, these categories are so broad as to be of limited use: firms within them occupied a variety of different product markets, giving them different problems, interests, and outlooks. In their labor market situations, however, they were more uniformly placed, which explains much of the nature and purposes of the association they supported.

They had the same few union adversaries—molders, machinists, pattern makers, platers, polishers, and buffers. And they were highly sensitive to the impact successful unionization might have on labor costs and productivity because they were labor intensive. Direct labor costs made up a large proportion of firms' value added by manufacture in these sectors: in 1899, more than half in foundry and machine shop products, plumbers' supplies and steam fittings, professional and scientific instruments, and hardware. There was little change in these figures over the next twenty years.[16]

Direct labor costs might not be firms' largest: raw materials, fuel, and power generally took a bigger share of the total income in heat-using industries like the foundry trade. But MMA members were characteristically price takers with respect to the often oligopolistic suppliers of these essential commodities. What was distinctive about labor costs, besides how large they bulked in firms' value added out of which all other costs and profit had to be won, was that they were in some measure *controllable* by the firm itself. Or at least, they might be made so.[17]

The antiunion employers' association helped with that task by opposing unions' attempts to set higher, more inelastic, and standardized supply prices for the most expensive and productive grades of labor; to limit the supply of that labor; to oppose employers' efforts to find partial substitutes for it or to make the limited supply stretch further; and to limit employers' flexibility in maximizing its utilization. In this context, the establishment and maintenance of a "union-free environment" was both an article of faith and a competitive necessity for employers.[18]

So much for the MMA's objective. How did it go about attaining it? Here too there was substantial continuity from the 1900s until the 1920s. The MMA existed, first and foremost, for strikebreaking. And it rapidly acquired the strength to justify its boast about never losing a strike for any member with the guts for a fight to the finish. It won the isolated strikes which occurred in most years before the 1920s, and two major campaigns in which it faced down the molders and machinists, respectively.

In 1904–1906 most MMA members operatiing foundries were involved in a succession of strikes and lockouts when they sought to deny formal recognition to the IMU, and to enforce nonunion conditions (longer hours, lower piece rates, more piecework, more "apprentices" and handymen, more mechanization). In 1916, the peak year for strikes involving MMA members in this period, two-thirds of member firms were involved in strikes. This time the MMA was on the defensive, and the IAM was the chief antagonist as its members unsuccessfully fought for union recognition and the eight-hour day.

The MMA won these victories without using the heavier weapons wielded by belligerent employers at the same time, including the big local firms involved in the mass battless between Baldwin Locomotive, Midvale Steel and Ordnance, and Cramp's Shipyard and their metal trades employees, which provided violent punctuation marks in Philadelphia labor relations throughout the Progressive era. The MMA's big neighbors used espionage and blacklisting, and sometimes invoked state and judicial repression of their employees; Midvale

Steel resorted to company unionism. The MMA did none of these things. Its record was not spotless, but it was surprisingly clean, surviving close scrutiny by investigators from the U.S. Commission on Industrial Relations in 1914.[19]

It did not deal with commercial strikebreaking agencies or private detective firms. It paid for information only once, but it received some free from dissident union members and friendly national employers' associations. MMA members did not seek injunctions against strikers. They had no need to. Only once did the MMA hire guards to protect strikebreakers at its members' shops, and even then nothing dramatic occurred. Three guards covered eleven chandelier manufacturers whose 400 workers struck for thirteen weeks in 1910–1911 in the second-biggest strike the MMA confronted before the war. Metal manufacturers normally relied on the city police to maintain order during strikes, protection which the association's lobbying helped secure from successive Republican local administrations.

One of the most surprising aspects of the MMA's history to a researcher who expected to find plentiful blood and gore resulting from employer belligerency during the "Age of Industrial Violence," and juicy examples of unsavory employer practices, is how little of any of these things there is to report. One single compensation payment to one strikebreaker in a thirty-year period, for damage done by pickets to his dentures, is all the evidence MMA records offer.

So what did the MMA do that was so effective? Defeating unions required that it be able to provide struck member firms with replacement workers, allowing them to resume operations and demoralize the strikers. This was a relatively peaceful, straightforward process. Even at the height of organized labor's strength in prewar Philadelphia, the MMA was able to recruit ample numbers of skilled and unskilled strikebreakers, overwhelmingly from within the city, to get them into its members' plants, and to persuade them to stay on the job at least until the strike was lost.

Philadelphia metalworkers do not appear to have displayed a deep, principled commitment to the methods and goals of collective action. Rather, they accommodated themselves as individuals to the results of their employers' successful counterorganization.[20]

Metal manufacturers used the rhetoric of employer class consciousness to try to cement the often fragile solidarity of their own association, but there is little evidence that they were any less pragmatic about collective action than their employees. Members' attachment to the association was largely instrumental. Its quickly established and carefully maintained reputation as a successful strikebreaking agency helped guarantee their support. But in most years few firms were seriously threatened by strikes—the best reminder of their need for an employers' association as an insurance policy; and in years of depression, when firms were particularly inclined to cut out optional expenditures, a slack labor market put workers and unions on the defensive, and strikes were very rare.

The association maintained itself in this context by rendering a worthwhile service to its members on a shoestring budget. For two decades, dues were fixed at 10¢ per blue collar worker per month, i.e., in real terms they declined. In the worst recessions dues were waived altogether by an executive committee which preferred to lose income rather than influence and members. As a result, even in years of depression such as 1907–1909 and 1912–1915, the association's rate of resignations (which most frequently resulted from bankruptcy, retrenchment, or firms closing down) rarely exceeded 6 percent per annum.

What other facilities than strikebreaking were members getting for their dues? First, a businessmen's club, whose regular banquets were quite lavish occasions at which members ate, drank, entertained one another, and listened to uplifting or interesting speeches. As much as a fifth of the association's annual income was, literally, consumed in sociability—about the same proportion as was directly spent on strikebreaking in a busy year, and usually a far greater amount.

Members used the social gatherings as opportunities to reward subordinates, or treat customers, by taking them as guests, partly at association expense. These meetings were useful occasions for making or renewing business contacts—highly important for firms which typically did not make completed goods for a consumer market but instead supplied semifinished products, equipment, and services to other manufacturers. Philadelphia firms were linked together by complex networks of subcontracting. Close and frequent contacts between businessmen oiled the wheels of commerce. Institutions such as the Union League, Manufacturers', Engineers', and Foundrymen's Clubs, or the Philadelphia Bourse, provided other meeting grounds for local businessmen. The MMA plugged into this established framework for purposeful sociability which reinforced the employer solidarity the association encouraged.

More expensive than the banquets, and much more important in bringing members into regular and frequent contact with the MMA as an institution and the services it had to offer, was the work of the association's labor bureau, which absorbed well over half the annual budget. The secretary, who ran it, was the association's only employee for its first decade and the head of a small but effective team by the late 1920s. The secretary was the MMA's strikebreaker-in-chief in times of crisis, recruiting scabs inside and outside the city, and maintaining liaison with the NFA and NMTA. But most of the time he was engaged in a rather different routine activity.

THE LABOR BUREAU AND THE LABOR MARKET

The MMA modeled its labor bureau on those of the local NMTA branches in Worcester, Massachusetts, and Cincinnati, Ohio, which were the pioneers in this line of activity. It hired an NMTA organizer as its first secretary. The MMA was not eligible to become an NMTA branch, because its members straddled the jurisdictional boundaries between the NMTA and the NFA. Nevertheless, the MMA and its secretary maintained close contact with the NMTA, followed its lead, and implemented in Philadelphia strategies to enhance employers' collective control of the labor market which the NMTA promoted.[21]

The labor bureau was a key feature of the NMTA's program for eliminating the IAM and other skilled trades unions, which the association developed after the breakdown of its short-lived experiment with national collective bargaining in 1900–1901. The NMTA required its branches to establish labor bureaus; and it devolved responsibility for the recruitment of strikebreakers on them. Discussions about improving bureau management and meetings between branch secretaries and national officers were major features of annual NMTA conventions.

Strikebreaking and blacklisting were important NMTA labor bureau functions. But the bureaus' routine behavior is less well known and barely understood. The labor bureau was a particular kind of employment and placement agency, dedicated to making the labor market work better, in employers' *and* employees' interests. An examination of the MMA bureau's behavior illustrates the sort of employment management problems to which many middle-sized employers could make only a collective response.

How could employers find workers in turn-of-the-century America? By personal contact, personal recommendation through existing workers, or workers' personal application at the plant doorway. These were the informal mechanisms by which most workers found jobs and employers found "help." But they did not always work satisfactorily.[22]

MMA members had particular problems of recruitment. Their skilled work forces did not live in the immediate locality of their small, scattered plants. Firms were able to hire common labor at the factory gate. Men of proven competence and particular skills were harder to find. And one of the special and enduring features of the Philadelphia labor market was that there was a rather large proportion of such small plants and of skilled labor well into the twentieth century. The two depended on one another.[23]

Throughout the open-shop era, MMA strategy and behavior were powerfully affected by the nature of member firms' products, labor markets, and labor processes. MMA member firms' labor policies were dedicated not to "deskilling" in any meaningful sense but to trying to maintain an ample supply of skilled workers, while rigging the market, depressing wages, and suppressing workers' collective attempts to share in determining the rules under which they worked.[24]

Typical MMA members had little alternative to continued reliance on cheap, skilled, flexible labor. This was especially true of those producing small batches or specially commissioned single units of relatively expensive capital goods. They won orders by promising prompt delivery and quality manufacture, as well as a competitive price. They had to be able to meet highly specific customer requirements and to adjust to wide fluctuations in demand. They did so by trimming overhead and fixed costs, and not tying up capital in special-purpose machinery which, however technically "efficient," was of limited utility. Skilled men were functional substitutes for the equipment and managerial resources such firms lacked. An all-around machinist could turn a general-purpose machine tool to a variety of uses; a trained molder could produce almost anything in cast metal weighing from ounces to tons. And you could hire the man when you needed him, and let him go when you did not.[25]

But when there was work pouring into the shops, as in 1898–1902, or the first part of 1907, or 1916–1919, you had to be able to find your man, on pain of losing business. Where could you go? You could poach skilled men from other local firms, thereby increasing wage rates and turnover; you could rely on your foreman—generally a skilled man himself—with his contacts in the craft community; or you could turn to the unions' business agents and their offices, which served as informal employment exchanges, telling unemployed local skilled men, or sojourners and tramping artisans, where they could find work in "fair" shops, i.e., under union conditions. This placement service was a valued one—a selling point of a union such as the IMU to the employers with whom it dealt, and even more of an advantage to skilled men over their unskilled brethren, who had no such assistance in the task of finding their way around the labor market.

If the MMA was to break the union "stranglehold" on the loyalties of its skilled workers, it had to offer member firms an alternative, and better, source of "help," and skilled workers a better way of getting in touch with job opportunities. This was what the labor bureau provided—a centrally located office for one-stop job shopping for skilled metal tradesmen; a courteous reception; no fees to either side; no obligation—the bureau only recommended a man to a firm, the foreman, superintendent, or proprietor still did the actual hiring; and no inflexible opposition to the employment of union members.

Other labor bureaus might maintain a blacklist, but in a formal sense Philadelphia's never did. This was largely because the MMA included both nonunion shops, where no activist was tolerated, and shops granting unions informal recognition. The MMA had to cater for a membership diverse not just in the range of skilled men they employed, but in their ability to minimize or ignore the union presence in their work forces.

It would warn firms who wanted to maintain nonunion conditions not to hire too many "card men," i.e., passive unionists who retained their membership even though they were willing to accept work in nonunion shops; it would attempt to send "card men" to union shops, and "independent workmen" to the rest; it would warn firms not to hire named activists and make it clear that if they found themselves in trouble because they ignored the warning, they would have to look after themselves. But this warning would not guarantee that the "agitator" would be fired.

Thus the MMA was not absolutely antiunion. It aimed to maintain its members' independence in labor relations matters, and that degree of employer autonomy could result in a pragmatic decision to get along with the union at the workshop level. What the MMA would not tolerate was its members' entering into any formal agreement and accepting "union dictation"—if they did, they were expelled; and it was equally determined to atomize labor relations and steer clear of centralized recognition and bargaining. Its ideal was the individual employer dealing with independent workmen, but if he chose to deal with them through a shop committee or business agent that was more or less his affair. However, despite repeated union approaches and entreaties, it would neither recognize nor negotiate with unions itself.

So in the case of the Philadelphia MMA, it seems that the common rhetoric of the open-shop employer—that his workers were free to join or not to join a union, as they saw fit, but he would take no notice of that decision when he hired them and would not let his employment practices be governed by them—better reflected reality than it did in other contemporary settings. The larger Philadelphia metal trades firms which claimed to be open shops fitted the realistic contemporary definition—they were open only to nonunionists or to undiscovered and inactive unionists. The MMA's membership's behavior was more moderate than that. Their aim was to alter the balance in their relations with skilled workers, not necessarily to eliminate unions entirely.

The labor bureau's usefulness went beyond its undermining of unions. Association members were protected, to some degree, even against the harmful consequences of the resulting "free" labor market. To the extent that they hired through the bureau, they were inhibited from hiring skilled men from one another, a practice which, in rush times, gave scarce manpower a real advantage. When they let a man go—as an adjustment to changing demand rather than as a disciplinary measure—they had somewhere to send him, some hope that his skills would not be lost to the local labor market. When they needed men, they could call both on informal enterprise-specific labor pools and if that failed on the association's central register. They were creating an association-wide approximation to an internal labor market for the benefit of members who could not possibly have built their own at the level of the individual firm.

With the breakdown of traditional apprenticeship, and given the inadequacy of formal training provision, this imperfect labor market for skilled men even served as a way of organizing the process of "picking up a trade." Foremen encouraged purposeful movement from one shop to another, until men acquired the all-around experience local metal trades employers valued. A man's employment record with the MMA turned into a sort of certificate of competence, or at least proof of experience. An employer did not have to rely entirely on trying the man out—an expensive, chancy business.

The success of the MMA's open-shop campaign depended not on crude belligerency but on the labor bureau's routine activity of compiling an ever-growing cardfile with details of men who worked, or had at any time worked, for its member firms. It knew their track records; knew what work they could do; cultivated their good will by helping them find regular jobs, and so could turn to them when an emergency occurred.

The labor bureau's ability to recruit local "independent workmen" as strikebreakers depended on its success in helping make the MMA's rhetoric of the mutuality of interests between masters and men credible to the latter. All that skilled men were offered by the bureau was some reduction in the costs and hassle of job search, and perhaps in frictional unemployment too, but in early twentieth-century Philadelphia no other institution, public or private, offered anything better.[26]

Philadelphia's skilled workmen had it demonstrated to them that the costs of union membership were high, and might include local unemployability for activists; and that the benefits were few. They seem to have become reconciled, to would-be organizers' distress, to the new regime of employer sovereignty.

That sovereignty did not necessarily entail revolutions in the experience of labor within the workshop. Philadelphia was the home of Frederick W. Taylor, and there were some notable "scientifically managed" firms within the MMA's membership; but for the most part they were traditional, undynamic enterprises, content or constrained to continue to depend on skilled men paid by daywork or simple piecework, and paid rather less than their fellows in other large cities, well into the 1920s.

GETTING IT TOGETHER: A SUMMING-UP

Running the labor bureau was not the whole of the MMA's secretary's job; occasional strikebreaking and routine recruitment were not the only services the MMA rendered its members, particularly after the near elimination of skilled trades unionism from the Philadelphia metal trades in the 1920s removed the MMA's original raison d'être.

From 1910 on, in response to an increased flow of "progressive" laws from the state legislature which had the potential to increase members' labor costs and restrict their cherished "freedom of employment," the MMA collaborated with the newly formed Pennsylvania Manufacturers' Association (PMA) to develop an effective businessmen's lobby in Harrisburg. One law that the PMA got amended, but was unable to block, provided for workmen's compensation. The MMA bought its members their insurance protection against this new liability at a group discount rate from the same supplier as it relied on for its political protection.[27]

During the war, the MMA added to its more directly employment-related functions. Its secretary began to collect regular, detailed statistics on wages paid to, and hours worked by, the workmen its members employed. Its aim was to provide members with accurate, up-to-date labor market data, so that they could discover whether their rates were out of line, understand some of the reasons underlying difficulties in recruiting or retaining workers, and, if they chose, adjust their rates to deal with the problem. The MMA eschewed collective bargaining, but it was not averse to encouraging its members to use labor market data as the basis for coordinated wage movements and intelligent employment decisions. The wage-and-hour surveys grew in coverage and sophistication through the twenties, as nonmembers began to supply data on their own metal trades work forces. Access to this data was one of the reasons large firms abandoned their reluctance to join the MMA in the mid- to late 1920s: it was precisely the sort of information they needed to operate their own wage policies, so that they could establish themselves as market leaders with a preferential call on the local skilled labor pool.

As the turbulence of Philadelphia-area labor relations in the teens was succeeded by the quietude of the twenties, the research role of the MMA grew as its strikebreaking machinery rusted with disuse. In collaboration with the Industrial Research Department of the University of Pennsylvania's Wharton School of Finance and Commerce, the MMA sponsored joint research into, for example, the future needs of the local foundry industry for skilled labor and how they might be met. The major focus of this research, however, was that central preoccupation of the new breed of personnel managers, turnover—its definition, measurement, and control.[28]

The MMA also aimed to resupply, as well as understand the dynamics of, the local skilled labor market through its cooperative training programs for foremen and machinists' apprentices launched in response to a growing skilled labor shortage in the mid- to late 1920s. This had been caused by the sharp reduction of a traditional source of manpower—immigrants from northern and western Europe. Here again we can see how member firms' skill-dependent labor processes gave them sufficient reason for continuing collaborative effort, even in the absence of any credible strike threat. "Getting it together" enabled them to take steps to resupply the local skilled labor market without being inhibited by the usual considerations limiting firms' own training activities. Much of the cost was borne, thanks to the MMA's lobbying, by the city, state, and even federal vocational education budgets; in principle, the benefits were available to the whole of the local metal-manufacturing community, of which the MMA by 1929 constituted about one-eighth of the firms, employing more than a third of the total metal trades work force.

The MMA grew to its largest membership during the 1920s on the basis of these "progressive" joint personnel programs. It served the needs of its members and of the distinctive Philadelphia industrial district. It included both traditional proprietary firms, and a number of larger "managerial" firms such as General Electric and Westinghouse, whose Philadelphia capital-goods manufacturing plants were as skill-dependent as many smaller operators'.

An examination of the MMA's history serves this essay's purpose of introducing readers of this book to the neglected worlds of labor relations and employment management in regions and sectors which do not seem to fit within either the Chandler paradigm of business history or the more diffuse "labor process" orientation of much recent labor history.

But how well does this case serve those who might wish to discover a "usable past" for cooperative programs serving "flexible-specialized" firms in the new manufacturing districts of a revived industrial America?

In short, badly. This may seem rather churlish and ungrateful: my efforts at discovery and interpretation have been mightily assisted by the insights of the "Historical Alternatives to Mass Production" school, which suggested that middle-sized firms, interfirm organizations, and manufacturing districts were all objects worthy of study. But what does this case study actually show?

Fundamentally, it shows that in Philadelphia, at least, proprietary "niche producers" were scarcely interested in, or capable of, cooperating on any project which did not have the immediate object of sustaining their dominant position in the labor market and maintaining the short-term viability of their labor process. The MMA that they established was a voluntary body with a minimal hold over the loyalties of its members and a strictly limited ability to infringe on their entrepreneurial sovereignty. All it could do, as the creature of a parochial membership, was to provide services, information, and advice.

It could not compel a member to pursue a particular labor relations strategy—it could simply withhold support if a strike were the consequence of his unwise actions, or in extreme cases expel him if he failed to toe the line. It might persuade members to cooperate with the labor bureau, to supply it with information and to hire through it, but it could not require these departures from informal and decentralized man-management as a condition of membership. It could encourage members to adjust wages and hours in the light of inflation and labor market conditions, but it could not eliminate the wide gulf between high- and low-wage firms in its membership, and did not try to. In short, it could lead its members' horses to the waters of enlightened manpower management, but it could not make them drink.

Its members operated in a variety of different product markets, so that where no basis for unity of action was provided by their common interests as employers of skilled labor, it was even less successful in developing joint activities and affecting their behavior. For example, there were occasional desultory discussions about encouraging member firms to give preference to one another in their business dealings, by trading and contracting with one another if possible, but nothing came of these proposals for the reduction of competition.

Equally unsuccessful were the rather more serious attempts the MMA made in the twenties to get local foundry operators—members of a stagnant or declining industry plagued by technological and managerial backwardness—to adopt common cost-accounting techniques. The idea was that less-efficient firms should not, out of ignorance, undercut the bids of their more efficient neighbors and lower the whole local foundry trade's profitability by being prepared to take on work at prices that covered immediate costs but yielded no return on investment. Such a program made sense to the "progressive" foundrymen who were its sponsors, but their more backward neighbors were understandably reluctant to volunteer to go out of business, which was the program's logic.

Outside the areas of labor relations and employment management, therefore, the MMA's efforts to serve as a joint research and development agency to its diverse and self-interested membership were infrequent, insubstantial, and unproductive. Within those regions it was continuously active, and rather effective. Entrepreneurial collectivism depended for its success on proprietors' and managers' perceived class interests as employers: no other purposes had the necessary centripetal, action-producing effects within a business community like Philadelphia's.

So this research does not seem to contribute much positive to the search for a "usable past" à la Sabel and Piore. Middle-sized Philadelphia metal trades firms look to have been as mired in proprietary independence as their regional neighbors studied by James Soltow.[29] At best they displayed a strictly limited commitment to the virtues of collectivism. Most of the time, they refused to have any truck with proposals for combined action by businessmen in any area unrelated to labor market management.

When they did consider such joint programs, they were no less individualistic and shortsighted. They were just looking for ways to maintain the short-run viability of an existing productive and commercial regime, which did not include any that were likely to save them from progressive marginalization within an increasingly concentrated manufacturing economy. They were investigating programs —such as restrictive trading, or price maintenance—where anything they might have tried to achieve would have been undermined both by the limited commitment of members to the association's goals, the weak disciplinary sanctions available to it, and by the consequences of their being such a large unorganized sector even within those areas of the Philadelphia metal trades where the MMA was strongest.

In the areas of job training and cooperative research, the MMA could be adventurous in part because other bodies (the University of Pennsylvania, the Rockefeller Foundation, the educational authorities) provided resources, and the activities were of unquestionable legitimacy. Had the MMA enjoyed any success in encouraging anticompetitive behavior among its members—in product rather than labor markets, that is—it would have run the risk of falling foul of the antitrust laws. At the very least, it would have been operating in a legal gray area where it could gain none of the external support from state agencies—before the NRA experiment in 1933–1935, that is—essential to make such collectivist behavior work.

As a contribution to the literature of business historical revisionism, therefore, this essay offers little. Philadelphia was not like Lyons, Solingen, or Emilia-Romagna. Its proprietary firms could not build the multifunctional interfirm and public-private organizations which flourished in other entrepreneurial cultures and under other laws.

However, as an account of a union-free, interfirm, industrial relations system characterized by skill-dependent labor processes, careful attention to labor market management, low levels of overt conflict, and a degree of mutuality of interests between proprietors and their craft employees, the case study has more to recommend it.

Without suggesting that all the world, or at least all of manufacturing America, was like Philadelphia in the open-shop era, it may at least be reasonable for me to suggest to other interested scholars that, before they dismiss this as just an aberrant, albeit substantial, case, they should examine associational labor relations systems in other mixed manufacturing cities at the same time. Too little is known about such places and their characteristic middle-sized firms. Rather than rushing to judgment on this matter, historians should run to the archives, the trade press, and businessmen's convention proceedings. Until then, the jury must remain out.

6

The Closed Shop, the Proprietary Capitalist, and the Law, 1897–1915

■

DANIEL R. ERNST

At least since John R. Commons and his associates exhumed the labor conspiracy cases of antebellum America, it has been hard to imagine a time when an employer faced with an industrial dispute did not consider the law a stalwart ally. The thin stream of criminal prosecutions Commons uncovered widened after the Civil War, as labor unrest in 1877 and the mid-1880s prompted judges and legislators to specify the grounds upon which labor activism could be attacked. The substantive law of labor disputes worked out in these cases served as the platform for an explosion of employer-initiated suits against unions after 1895. Although criminal prosecutions and damage suits formed an important part of the caseload, the bulk of the increase consisted of suits in which employers asked judges to issue injunctions which restrained workers and union leaders from injuring the property rights of employers.[1]

Thanks to the efforts of generations of labor historians, we know much about how this burst of labor litigation looked from the perspective of union leaders and rank-and-file workers. They saw employers and courts formed into a united front, bent on violating the rights of workers and frustrating the legitimate aspirations of the labor movement. The view from the perspective of the employers is much less clear. We still have no systematic understanding of what led some employers but not others to turn to the courts for assistance in breaking a strike or boycott; the relative advantages to an employer of labor injunctions, damage suits, and simple criminal prosecutions for assault or trespass; and why legal action sometimes altered the course of a labor dispute and sometimes had no effect.

The privileging of organized labor's perspective has also obscured our understanding of how judges resolved the labor disputes which came before them during the Progressive era. All too often, judges are presumed to have willingly abetted the employers in their efforts to obtain a tractable work force. From this perspective, the passage of the National Labor Relations Act (NLRA) in 1935 worked an epochal change by substituting enlightened administrative statesmanship for the pro-employer partisanship of the judiciary. The revolution has long seemed so successful and the old regime so lamentable that few historians have thought studying the labor law of the earlier period would repay the effort.

Of late, this interpretation of twentieth-century labor law has been battered but not broken. The work of left-leaning labor historians and legal academics has cast the New Deal collective-bargaining regime in an unfavorable light by showing how this liberal reform frustrated the radical aspirations of rank-and-file workers. But if their emphasis on the political trade-offs of our national labor policy has made the NLRA look less enlightened, they have yet to revise the conventional account of the benighted common-law regime it ousted.[2] Instead, right-minded historians and legal academics have attempted that task. Their rehabilitation of the injunction judges and the common law of labor disputes has shown that the prevailing interpretation has preserved only one side of a wide-open debate about the law of work in industrial America. Yet too often these revisionists have merely reargued the case for the courts and employers when a nonadversarial approach would have better advanced our understanding.[3]

Although none of us can completely escape our political commitments as we approach the past, even historians of so controversial a subject as the law of labor relations can hold in abeyance preconceived notions of villains and victims long enough to investigate complexities overlooked by conventional interpreters and the revisionists. For if the American Federation of Labor denounced judges as "the pliant tools of corporate wealth," many employers accused them of timidity or worse. And if the courts outlawed some of the means and ends of labor activism, they also ringingly endorsed labor agitation for the improvement of wages, hours, and working conditions. Once we put out from the safe harbor of schematic understandings of the history of the law of work, we will discover a complicated, intractable past that can suggest ways of dealing with the complicated, intractable problems of the present.

One extremely revealing guide for this undertaking is suggested by this collection of essays. The common law of labor relations can profitably be studied as a chapter in the history of employers' labor policies and strategies. In this spirit, then, this essay surveys a portion of the very large terrain of early twentieth-century labor law which needs to be recharted by historians willing to check the guidance offered by unionists against that of employers, judges, middle-class consumers, and other social groups. It describes an organized attempt by employers and their lawyers to outlaw a fundamental tenet of national trade unionism in the early twentieth century. This attempt failed when judges proved to be more responsive to the interests and values of their fellow members of the middle class than to the wants or needs of the proprietary capitalists who sought their aid.

THE PLIGHT OF THE PROPRIETARY CAPITALISTS

The leaders in the legal campaign against the closed-shop contract were the owner-managers of small firms in competitive industries, such as metal fabricating, hatting, clothing manufacture, and textiles. In general, they conducted their businesses as sole proprietors or as one of a small number of partners, who were often their relatives. As a rule, their firms were not the sprawling, multiunit enterprises founded during a great wave of mergers between 1895 and 1904, which revolutionized the organization of many industries as more than 1,800 individual firms disappeared into larger combines.[4] The proprietary capitalists identified themselves closely with their businesses, which they viewed as the product of their own or their ancestors' tireless efforts and calculations.

At the turn of the twentieth century a surge in trade union membership challenged the proprietary capitalist for control over his business. The total membership of American trade unions more than doubled in the three years after 1899. By 1902, union membership totaled almost 1.4 million; in 1903 it stood at just under 2 million. Unions in the mining, construction, metalworking, garment, and textile industries registered the most dramatic increases. Accompanying the jump in trade union membership was a new militancy, as labor leaders demanded more than higher wages or shorter hours. Strikes for "the recognition of the union and of union rules" increased five hundred percent between 1898 and 1901, accounting for over 36 percent of all strikes in the latter year.[5]

Recognizing the union limited employers' authority in two respects. First, employers agreed to hire only union members in good standing. In contrast, the nonunion employer could hire whom he wished and fire them at will. By running a "closed shop" the employer thus compromised his exclusive control over personnel decisions. But the second and "gravest phase" of recognition was its consequences for determining the pace and methods of production. The employer agreed to abide by the union's work rules, as policed by a shop steward in his midst. For many employers, this perversely violated the basic tenets of the work ethic by granting control over their property to irresponsible union officials. The "walking delegate" lost nothing if the business failed; the employer lost the accumulated product of his own or his ancestors' efforts.[6]

In part, the employers rejected recognition from narrow calculations of economic self-interest: the union wages and work rules made production more costly and hampered the unionized employer's ability to compete with the employers of cheaper, nonunion labor. These calculations could be altered if all employers in a given industry recognized the union and successfully passed the increased labor costs on to consumers. The prospect of such arrangements between employers' organizations and labor unions led to a brief golden age of national trade agreements around the turn of the century. When these experiments failed to bring the promised relief, usually because of the persistence of unorganized sectors, the employers gave up their conciliatory policy and belligerently opposed the unions.[7]

The calculations of economic self-interest, however, are only a partial explanation of the employers' response to these industrial constraints, for they do not account for the passion and self-righteousness of the employers' objections. These strong-minded businessmen identified themselves closely with their enterprises. A threat to the full control of their companies jeopardized not simply their profits but also, as Robert Wiebe writes, their "pride and habits," their "way of life." By following (or simulating) the precepts of the work ethic they had conserved a business patrimony or created one for their descendants; now industrial and labor combinations threatened their legacy. Moreover, so accustomed were they to identifying their own virtues with the sources of America's prosperity that they readily believed their loss of control jeopardized the welfare of the entire nation.[8]

THE OPEN SHOP MOVEMENT AND THE LAW

The anxieties of the proprietary capitalists boiled over after 1900. Across the industrial North, employers rallied in local associations to defend the "open shop," the principle that employers should hire without regard to membership in labor unions. The National Association of Manufacturers (NAM), originally founded to promote international trade, became a leading advocate of the open shop in 1903, and other national employers' associations joined the movement, including the National Metal Trades Association (NMTA), the United Typothetae of America, the National Founders' Association (NFA), and the National Erectors' Association (NEA).

These groups offered their members an array of services, as Howell Harris's contribution to this volume demonstrates. One facet of their work was apprising the rank and file of legal remedies at annual conventions and in official publications, such as *American Industries* and the *Bulletin of the NMTA*. Several associations went further and hired legal counsel to advise members in their suits against labor unions. These lawyers, the heralds of a full-blown promanagement labor bar, included Alexander C. Allen, Dudley Taylor, and James Wilkerson, who represented the Chicago Employers' Association; Levy Mayer, counsel to the Illinois Manufacturers' Association; James A. Emery of the Citizens' Industrial Alliance of San Francisco, the Citizen's Industrial Association of America (CIAA), and the NAM; Walter Drew of the Citizens' Alliance of Grand Rapids and the NEA; and Chester Culver and George Monaghan of the Employers' Association of Detroit and the NFA. A more dramatic development was the founding in 1903 of the American Anti-Boycott Association (AABA) for the sole purpose of litigating and lobbying on behalf of employers. Led first by Daniel Davenport and later by Walter Gordon Merritt, the AABA sponsored some of the era's most important labor cases.[9]

Much more research is needed before we will have a thorough understanding of the circumstances which led employers to turn to the law and the effect of their litigation on the course of labor disputes. Episodic evidence, the testimony of contemporary observers, and other sources permit a few provisional conclusions, however. First, lawyers often advised employers to use the criminal law before resorting to an injunction. The Chicago lawyer Dudley Taylor told the labor researcher Edwin Witte that it was "vastly more cumbersome and expensive to prosecute for contempt of court" than for the "average run of criminal cases." Contempt proceedings required the preparation of affidavits; in Chicago at least, they almost invariably required the examination of witnesses; and they resulted in sentences which were no more severe than in criminal cases.[10]

Taylor thought injunctions were useful chiefly when employers sought to regulate or abolish picketing during a strike. Police had wide discretion in determining whether a given picket constituted disorderly conduct, obstructing traffic, or disturbing the peace, and employers charged that they often failed to exercise it properly. "We had inadequate police protection, with the result that finally we decided the only way we could get relief was through injunction," explained the vice-president of a picketed company.[11] As Witte reported, many employers' attorneys insisted "that injunctions have a distinct value in setting a standard for peace officers and the police courts, and in giving them backbone to enforce the criminal law." In many cases judges specified the number and location of pickets; in violent disputes they often banned all picketing near a targeted plant.[12]

In other circumstances the effectiveness of injunctions is by no means clear. If the threat of lawsuits sharply curtailed nationally conducted campaigns against the distributors of the goods of "unfair" firms, injunctions against other forms of secondary pressure were much less promising. In the construction industry, for example, the need to complete a project by a guaranteed date made it "utter ruin" (in Dudley Taylor's words) for a contractor to complain about labor activism. Even when injunctions were obtained against a strong, self-confident union—such as the United Brotherhood of Carpenters—the effects could be minimal. Thus, between 1910 and 1912 manufacturers of wood trim boycotted by New York City carpenters obtained no less than five different injunctions, without effect. "The lawyers in New York cannot do anything," a distributor complained to a boycotted manufacturer. "It seems that the temporary injunction you got out is of no use as these people pay no attention to same."[13]

Damage actions were at least as problematic for employers, as they rarely recovered enough money to cover legal fees, much less the business losses incurred during a labor dispute. In part the barrier to successful damage suits was procedural. In several jurisdictions employers could not sue voluntary associations. In these states, the coffers of unions that refused to incorporate were beyond reach, leaving the employer to pursue a remedy against individual workers. Where, as in Connecticut's hatting industry, workers were relatively prosperous and settled and state law permitted the prejudgment attachment of real estate and bank accounts, employers still might proceed; where, as in the structural iron construction industry, workers were penurious and transient, a damage suit seemed a waste of time.[14]

Even in the most favorable circumstance, damage suits were lengthy and costly. Their successful prosecution often required unusual fortitude and additional financial support. Perhaps the most famous damage suit of the era was the Danbury Hatters' case *(Loewe v. Lawlor)*, in which the hat manufacturer Dietrich Loewe sued some 250 members of the United Hatters of North America over a boycott of his goods. Loewe ultimately received over $250,000 from the hatters' union and the AFL after almost fifteen years in the courts, but in the interim his firm went into receivership, and he lived out his years on an annuity contributed by his fellow employers. The costs of the litigation had been assumed by the AABA, which saw the case through to its conclusion. Most employers were forced to make their own, individual calculations of cost and benefits. For them, a damage suit could serve as a harrying tactic—a way of forcing a labor union to commit scarce funds to a legal defense in the midst of a labor dispute—but it rarely paid to pursue the case to trial, much less through lengthy appeals.[15]

Left to the varying resolve of individual employers, the policies of the open-shop movement had little chance of being written into law. Policymaking through litigation required that individual plaintiffs receive independent financial support and that the campaign be coordinated by a central authority.[16] The AABA was established to perform this role, and under Daniel Davenport it set out to convince the courts throughout the country to outlaw strikes for the closed shop.

CONSPIRACY DOCTRINE AND THE CLOSED SHOP

The legal doctrine which Davenport hoped to turn against the closed-shop contract was the common law of conspiracy. Under this doctrine, a combination was unlawful if it employed unlawful means or sought an unlawful purpose—one which tended to "prejudice the public or oppress individuals." Since the 1880s, judges had been nearly unanimous in denouncing labor combinations which sought to force the discharge of nonunion workers. Such combinations, they held, violated the "unlawful purpose" branch of the conspiracy doctrine by infringing the individual rights of employers and nonunion workers.[17]

Strikes to force employers to sign agreements recognizing the union, like strikes to oust nonunion employees, limited the hiring decisions of manufacturers. Yet these strikes differed from the older form of labor activism in two important respects. First, signing a closed-shop agreement did not necessarily require an employer to discharge any of his workers, so long as the union accepted all his employees into its ranks. The "openness" of unions became the subject of a fierce debate between antiunion employers, who considered unions closed, monopolistic factions, and labor leaders, who claimed (in Samuel Gompers's words) that "the whole world is invited to come in and join the ranks of labor."[18]

Second, closed-shop agreements formally obligated employers to abide by uniform work rules and standards. The leaders of national labor unions understood that their rules and wage rates could hamper the ability of union manufacturers to compete with nonunion firms. By organizing an entire industry, the union could remove this disparity, but, as holdout firms or new entrants charged, it could also raise the cost consumers paid for goods. Thus, strikes for union recognition implicated a "public interest"—of mass consumers—much more directly than did earlier forms of labor activism.

The legality of the closed-shop contract first came before a leading state supreme court in an indirect fashion. *Curran v. Galen* (1897) was a suit by an engineer against members of a local union of brewery workers in Rochester, New York, who forced the engineer's discharge when he refused to join the union. The unionists pleaded as a defense that they had acted in accordance with a closed-shop agreement with the local Ale and Brewers' Association. A unanimous New York Court of Appeals rejected this defense and generally condemned closed-shop contracts as tending toward the "repression of individual freedom" and establishing "monopolies and exclusive privileges."[19]

Were *Curran*'s condemnation of the closed-shop contract limited by the facts of the case, it would have worked no great change in the calculations of employers and unions. Labor unions had long been found liable for the discharge of nonunion workers. The court's sweeping denunciation of the closed-shop contract, however, led some legal commentators to doubt the legality of the contracts in all circumstances, and this raised the prospect that the employer who entered into such an agreement might face a court suit.[20] To see how unsettling this was for a union employer, consider a lawyer's opinion letter, written in 1900, on an agreement between the Mason Builders' Association and the bricklayers' unions of New York City. Just entering into the contract would not be unlawful, the lawyer wrote. So long as both parties complied with the contract, all would be well. Trouble loomed, however, should a master mason employ a nonunion worker and then comply with the union's demand that the worker be discharged. Such an employer would tread "dangerously near the border line" of liability under *Curran*.[21]

The antiunion warriors of the open-shop movement saw *Curran* as a stepping stone to the creation of a legal precedent holding that open-shop contracts were unlawful in all circumstances. The *Curran* court's dictum that closed-shop agreements interfered with the private rights of workers and employers and the public interest in free competition suggested that another court might find the signing of such an agreement to be an unlawful purpose under the conspiracy doctrine. Armed with such a precedent, a lawyer for an employer could obtain an injunction against even a peacefully conducted strike if it aimed at the establishment of a closed shop.

When the AABA officially commenced operation in the summer of 1903, the search for a test case was high on its agenda. As Daniel Davenport later recalled, "we looked around for a case where we could bring up this question about the illegality of a combination to compel a person to unionize his shop, and . . . fortunately for the people of this country, the opportunity arose in Chicago."[22]

THE *CHRISTENSEN* CASE

The case involved the Kellogg Switchboard and Supply Company. In the spring of 1903 Kellogg employed between 500 and 600 workers, 90 percent of whom belonged to one of fourteen different unions. In May, the overwhelming majority of the work force struck to obtain contracts which granted the closed shop, limited the use of apprentices, and permitted sympathetic strikes. For three weeks the strike continued without incident, but when the plant began operating with nonunion workers, isolated assaults occurred. On May 25, Judge Jesse Holdom of the Cook County Superior Court granted a sweeping injunction drafted by Kellogg's attorney, Alexander C. Allen. The injunction banned "any act whatever" (including peaceful persuasion) that furthered the unions' conspiracy to obstruct Kellogg's "free, uninterrupted and unhindered control and direction of its business and affairs."[23]

The strike escalated dramatically in June and early July when Chicago's teamsters struck in sympathy with Kellogg's workers. In the first years of the century the teamsters had made themselves (as a journalist put it) "the arrogant overlords of a great community's business" through a combination of organization, sympathetic strikes, violence, and graft.[24] Their support of the strike kept freight from moving in or out of Kellogg's plant. Violence against nonunion workers stepped up, and wild riots erupted when nonunion teamsters, accompanied by a guard of 400 policemen, moved several shipments to and from the plant. In retaliation, the teamsters' union threatened to halt coal deliveries to the city's power plants. The Chicago Federation of Labor promised funds to fight Holdom's injunction; the Chicago Employers' Association, the Illinois Manufacturers' Association and the AABA endorsed Kellogg's side of the fight.

On July 20, Attorney Allen (now financed by the AABA) convinced Judge Holdom to extend the injunction to include the teamsters. No teamster was ever held in contempt of the injunction, yet, as an observer wrote, the order helped convince "that large neutral element which is not permanently enlisted on either side of the labor-capital struggle" that the unions were in the wrong.[25] This certainly was the lesson that the employers drew for the public: as Daniel Davenport told the Chicago press, "If it has come to this that either the law or the labor unions must go, the latter might as well get ready to leave." The public outcry led conservative leaders in Chicago's labor movement to withdraw their support, and on the evening of July 23, the teamster's union formally ended its sympathetic activities. The strike dragged on for months, but in the end Kellogg succeeded in maintaining open-shop conditions.[26]

Holdom's original injunction was a model of aggressive judicial intervention in labor disputes. Its sweeping terms were premised on the theory that once the purpose of a strike was found to be unlawful, *any* means to advance the strike were forbidden, no matter how innocuous or constitutionally protected in other circumstances. Peaceful picketing, other forms of persuasion, and the payment of strike dues all fell afoul of its prohibition.[27]

Clarence Darrow, attorney for the defendants, contested the injunction in an interlocutory appeal to Illinois's intermediate appellate court in July 1903. Arguing while strike-related rioting was at its height, Darrow conceded that some injunction should issue but insisted that it should prohibit only violent conduct. Alexander Allen and James H. Wilkerson, another Chicago attorney, rejected Darrow's framing of the case as turning on the means used by the strikers. "The right of men to speak and to walk the streets is not assailed," they told the court. The real issue in the case was the strikers' *purpose*—to compel Kellogg to enter into "unlawful agreements," which violated public policy, the employer's right to manage, and the rights of nonunion workers.[28]

The appellate court disapproved of the closed shop but stopped short of declaring it an unlawful aim of labor agitation. "We are not to be understood as holding that a request to appellee [Kellogg] to enter into an agreement to employ none but union men was in itself unlawful," it cautioned. Instead, the court held unlawful the strikers' methods—"so-called persuasion, backed up by acts of violence." Although the appellate court refused to modify Holdom's injunction, it did suggest that peaceful picketing should not be enjoined, and it did not endorse Allen's and Wilkerson's reasoning that the unlawful purpose of the strikers made all of their acts enjoinable.[29]

In the wake of this decision, however, the AABA's lawyers stuck to their original theory of the case. Every contract which excluded a nonunion man from "the free opportunity to earn his living" was criminal, Davenport insisted. "Every proposition to that effect by union men to their employers is criminal. Every act done to carry out such a contract to the exclusion of the non-union men is criminal." But Darrow and the strikers continued to interpret the litigation as turning on the means used by the strikers. As long as they used peaceful means of persuasion, they maintained, they could exercise their constitutional rights to walk the streets near the plant and to speak to any replacement worker, Judge Holdom's injunction notwithstanding.[30]

Holdom thought otherwise and found several strikers in contempt of court. The strikers appealed, and in May 1904, Judge Francis Adams of the intermediate appellate court affirmed the contempt citations in *Christensen v. People.* Issued during the flood tide of the open-shop movement, Adams's opinion quickly became the subject of considerable debate and conflicting interpretations.

Adams offered two independent bases for his decision. First, after reviewing the strikers' menacing comments, threats, assaults, and mass picketing, he condemned the strike under the "unlawful means" branch of the conspiracy doctrine. This was, given the case law of the time, a quite unremarkable ruling. If the case stood only for the proposition that violent picketing was unlawful, it posed no new threat to the labor movement.[31]

Adams went on, however, to declare the strikers' *purpose* unlawful for two reasons. First, the closed-shop agreements they sought would, if executed, "tend to create a monopoly in favor of the members of the different unions, to the exclusion of workmen not members of such unions." Second, they violated criminal statutes prohibiting combinations to deprive owners of the lawful use and management of their property and to prevent persons from obtaining employment.[32] Adams's reasoning along this branch of conspiracy doctrine paralleled the statements of the *Curran* court and seemed to realize the earlier case's promise for the open-shop movement.

The opinion delighted the lawyers for antiunion employers. "It is impossible to exaggerate the importance of this decision," declared Horace K. Tenney, an associate of Wilkerson. The issue of the closed shop was squarely presented to the court, Tenney maintained, and

Adams declared it in violation of both civil and criminal law. Adams's holding that the contract violated the criminal law was especially significant in that it permitted employers to invoke the doctrine of solicitation against labor leaders. "It will even be a crime to submit a closed-shop agreement in the future to an employer for his signature," another lawyer predicted, and the enthusiastic editor of the NMTA's journal concurred. "It certainly would not be safe for a walking delegate or other labor leader to be caught with a supply of them in his pockets," the editor gloated.[33]

The open-shop advocates hoped *Christensen* would have an even more important deterrent effect on employers. Thus Levy Mayer, counsel for the Illinois Manufacturers' Association, prophesied, "When the employer of labor in this state awakes to the situation that he is a party to a criminal conspiracy, the floodgates will open and non-union labor will . . . receive the protection that all the injunctions and processes of the courts have hitherto been unable to give them." No wonder the NMTA editor believed that *Christensen* had sounded the "death knell of the closed shop."[34]

Samuel Gompers, always ready to expect the worst from the courts, shared the employers' interpretation of the case, although of course he denounced what they praised. The agents of secret antiunion societies had long sought to obtain from some "subservient" court a decision holding the closed shop unlawful, Gompers charged. "At last they have succeeded."[35] But a different, more lawyerly reading of the case was possible, one which minimized its significance as an anti-union precedent. Under this reading, the true basis for Adams's decision was his holding that the strikers used unlawful means in pursuit of their goals. His remark that the closed shop was an unlawful purpose was superfluous and did not bind others judges.

The strongest advocate of this position, and the most thoroughgoing critic of *Christensen*, was Louis D. Brandeis. In his contribution to a symposium sponsored by the National Civic Federation, Brandeis argued that the case merely applied "the well established and sound rule that picketing attended by intimidation and coercion is unlawful and will be enjoined." Adam's apparent holding about the closed shop was therefore but "an elaborate dictum."[36]

JUDICIAL ACCOMMODATION

In the years after *Christensen* was decided, the AABA worked to establish the open-shop reading of the case. "Our idea has been to get, in

as many States of the Union as we can, test cases where some application may be made of the immortal principles recognized in that
decision," Davenport told a convention of open-shop employers in
November 1905.[37] Already he could point to three cases which endorsed *Christensen*'s general condemnation of closed-shop contracts.
Two months after Adams's decision, a Milwaukee judge cited the case
in dissolving a temporary injunction which a tailor's union had obtained to enforce a closed-shop agreement against an employer. In
Jacobs v. Cohen, decided in December 1904, an intermediate appellate
court in New York rejected a labor union's suit to collect a bond given
to enforce a closed-shop contract. And in June 1905, the Massachusetts Supreme Judicial court upheld a verdict awarding $1,500 to a
worker who had been discharged pursuant to a closed-shop agreement. If the closed shop were treated as a legitimate object of trade
unionism, Chief Judge Knowlton warned, "every employer would be
forced into membership in a union, and the unions, by a combination
of these different trades and occupations, would have complete and
absolute control of all the industries in the country."[38]

Viewed for their cultural significance, these decisions were modest
successes for the open-shop employers, for each court gave the impri-
matur of law to their antimonopoly critique of the closed shop. Viewed
instrumentally, however, the Milwaukee, *Jacobs*, and Massachusetts
cases were much less satisfying. None of them added to the stockpile
of legal weaponry along the lines suggested by *Christensen*. In none
did an employer win an injunction against a purely peaceful attempt
to establish a closed shop. None were criminal prosecutions at the
behest of nonunion employers to break up closed-shop arrangements.
As a rule, public prosecutors showed no interest in prosecuting the
"labor trusts" as conspiracies in restraint of trade, no matter how
passionately they were urged to do so by employers' groups.[39] Indeed,
the campaign to criminalize the closed shop suffered an outright
setback in 1904 when Connecticut's highest court announced that
closed-shop agreements in themselves did not violate the criminal
laws of that state.[40]

An even clearer break from *Christensen* came in November 1905
when the New York Court of Appeals reversed the intermediate court's
decision in *Jacobs*. The contract was "but a private agreement between an employer and his employees," voluntarily entered into by
the former, Judge John C. Gray wrote for the court. "It would seem as
though an employer should be, unquestionably, free to enter into such
a contract with his workmen for the conduct of his business, without
its being deemed obnoxious upon any ground of public policy." In

Curran the Court of Appeals had denounced closed-shop contracts for repressing the freedom of the nonunion worker. In *Jacobs* it decided that the incidental discharge of nonunion workers pursuant to such a contract was nothing "with which public policy is concerned."[41]

Jacobs and a 1912 decision of the Illinois Supreme Court (which interpreted *Christensen* as Brandeis had) finally ended the AABA's search for a precedent. In 1908, Walter Gordon Merritt, the AABA's Associate Counsel, could still insist that the burden of the decided cases held strikes for the closed shop unlawful, although even he conceded that judges differed on the issue. For several years, legal commentators frankly confessed that the law was uncertain and offered no firm rule on the subject. In 1913 an influential treatise writer finally resolved the confusion in favor of the closed shop, stating as "the better view" the rule that strikes to obtain closed-shop agreements were lawful.[42]

The most convincing attempt to reconcile the cases took as its point of departure the reasoning given by the *Jacobs* majority in distinguishing that case from *Curran*. The closed-shop agreement in *Curran*, the *Jacobs* majority observed, covered all the breweries in Rochester. The brewery worker who fell afoul of the union would be prevented from "prosecuting his trade and earning a livelihood" anywhere in the city. The agreement in *Jacobs*, in contrast, covered only a single employer. A treatise writer adopted this distinction in 1910, and in 1913 it was followed in another AABA-sponsored case, *Connors v. Connolly*.[43]

Dominick Connors was one of several Danbury, Connecticut, hatters who fell afoul of the union when it had closed-shop agreements with all the manufacturers of stiff hats in the vicinity. Banned from Danbury's firms, Connors and the others secretly called on Walter Gordon Merritt, whom they knew from his work in the Danbury Hatters' case. Merritt brought suit in 1910, trying the case in a courtroom packed with angry union hatters. When a generous jury instruction permitted the jurors to find for the defendants, Merritt appealed to Connecticut's supreme court.[44]

Chief Justice Samuel O. Prentice, writing for a unanimous court, ordered a new trial. Prentice condemned the closed shop of the Danbury firms as a serious menace to the nonunion worker and an "especially intolerable" monopoly, yet he refused to condemn all agreements in which employers promised to hire only union workers. Instead, he adopted the narrower holding suggested by *Jacobs* and condemned only those closed-shop agreements which took in "an entire industry of any considerable proportions in a community."[45]

Merritt hailed *Connors* as "the most forceful and far-reaching decision upon this subject which has ever been rendered in the English-speaking countries." But the *Connors* court stopped well short of the original antimonopoly critique of the closed shop, which asked judges to find every contract for the exclusive employment of union workers a threat to free competition. The lawyers for open-shop employers had pressed upon the courts the analogy between these contracts and businessmen's conspiracies in restraint of trade, confident that it would argue in their favor. Yet as antitrust policy moderated and courts tolerated businessmen's "reasonable" restraints of trade, the analogy could be turned against the open-shop cause.[46]

Thus, the treatise writer Frederick Hale Cooke observed that if courts upheld restraints on competition which were "the natural incident or outgrowth" of a legitimate relationship between two businessmen, they should judge agreements between employers and workers by the same standard. Given the unequal bargaining power between the individual worker and his or her employer, Cooke considered a promise to hire union workers exclusively a reasonable restraint on competition. Following this reasoning, he condemned *Curran* and *Christensen*. Yet Cooke objected to closed-shop agreements which covered "so substantial a portion of those furnishing the supply of labor" as to tend to disrupt the rate of wages fixed by "the forces of competition." Such agreements, Cooke conceded, would produce a monopoly of labor exactly like monopolies of sugar and oil created by business trusts.[47]

By May 1915, even Daniel Davenport had given up the fight for a precedent against all strikes for the closed shop. Testifying before the United States Commission on Industrial Relations, Davenport surprised Chairman Frank P. Walsh by insisting that, "apart from all questions of monopoly," the closed shop was not only legal but constitutionally guaranteed. As a general proposition, Davenport explained, an employer could insist on hiring only union workers, just as he could insist on hiring only nonunion workers. The closed shop was unlawful only when it created a monopoly of an industry within a community or otherwise interfered with the rights of third parties or the general public. Otherwise, he declared, "the right of the closed shop entered into freely between the employer and the employee was as secure as the Government itself."[48]

THE CLOSED SHOP AND CONSUMER CULTURE

At the start of the twentieth century, proprietary capitalists asked the courts to grant injunctions against strikes for the closed shop. In *Christensen* Judge Adams came closest to granting their request, but the ambiguity of his reasoning fatally limited its value to the employers. Although some later courts had harsh words for the closed shop, others endorsed it, and none brought the employers closer to their goal. By the end of the Progressive era, judges were willing to commit public power against only those agreements which covered large portions of a particular industry and which threatened to raise prices for consumers.

In this corner of the common law of labor relations, at least, judges were not the mere agents of the proprietary employers who came before them, and we must look beyond the manufacturers' complaints to understand the law on the subject. The starting place for understanding the decision making of the judges is their dependence on national or regional markets for the goods they consumed. Although the relationship of judges to the dominant mode of production was— and remains—ambiguous, the judges' interest as consumers was straightforward. And because their interest was shared by many others in the Progressive era, they could quite plausibly equate the needs of consumers with the public good.[49]

If the judges shared an economic interest with other mass consumers, they also shared a wide range of values, assumptions, and beliefs with other members of the middle class. This common culture competed with their calculations of economic interest. Of particular importance was a shift in popular understanding of the scale of organization of American industry. At the start of the century, the proprietary capitalist still seemed the normal unit of American business enterprises, and that small and worthy businessman's complaints against the giant corporations and national trade unions—against business trusts and the "labor trust"—still made sense to many members of the American middle class. But as industrial combination proceeded apace and large corporations became a normal part of the industrial landscape, many believed that fair play and social welfare required greater tolerance of combination on the part of labor.

The law of the closed shop as it stood in 1915 was the product of these competing understandings of consumer interest, industrial organization, and fair play. Just as the jurists revised the law of antitrust to permit businessmen to limit competition through reasonable restraints of trade, so too did they revise the law of labor conspiracies to permit workers to limit competition through closed-shop agreements. But the jurists refused to give free rein to either capital or labor, for this would have violated what the legal historian James Willard Hurst has called "the constitutional ideal—that there be no major center of power over men's wills which was not subject to substantial accountability to centers of power outside itself."[50]

Since the Progressive era, the means by which public power is exercised over labor unions has changed dramatically. The Wagner Act of 1935 created an administrative agency which ousted the courts as the principal regulator of the affairs of labor unions. As amended by the Taft-Hartley Act of 1947, our federal labor law abolishes the most coercive form of the closed shop and permits the states to enact "right-to-work" laws, which forbid all agreements requiring membership in a union as a condition of employment. Yet it also sanctions milder forms of compulsory unionism, such as contracts requiring workers to join a union after they are hired or to pay the same initiation fees, dues, and assessments as union employees.

Similarly, if in recent years employers have learned from a new breed of antiunion experts—labor consultants—how to use the Wagner Act to frustrate organizational campaigns, they have also seen new challenges placed on their authority in the form of a startling extension of governmental intervention into the employment relationship. Thus, employers have altered their personnel practices in order to escape liability for "wrongfully discharging" their workers, and this check on their ability to fire their employees "at will" has come notwithstanding their complaints that it threatens to hamper severely their ability to compete in world markets.[51] Such seeming inconsistencies suggests that the competing understandings of the Progressive-era judges have continued to guide the formation of our labor policy and therefore the decision making of employers. The present state of those understandings, and not simply the needs of the dominant business enterprises of our day, remain our surest guide to comprehending future developments in the law of labor relations.

III
COMPARATIVE
PERSPECTIVES
■

The final section of this book contains two essays that combine historical and comparative analysis, a blend that permits us to get a better sense of what was and was not unique about American employers. The existing literature on the subject tends to stress the diversity, rather than the similarity, of national industrial relations and employment systems, although there is a divergence of opinion when it comes to explaining the origins of national diversity.

One strand, beginning with Reinhard Bendix and finding its most recent expression in the work of Ronald Dore and Charles Sabel, looks to economic development as the key to understanding variations in national industrial relations and employment systems. Among the factors considered here are the date—in world historical time—at which a nation began its industrialization process (Britain early, Japan late, and the United States somewhere in the middle) and the structure—atomistic or relatively concentrated—of its industrial organization. The two factors are related: early developers were more likely to have small proprietary firms with craft-based production systems; late developers had a greater number of large mass production firms under professional management. From these economic differences flowed variations in trade union structure, employer ideology, and employment policy. Entrepreneurial ideologies and market-oriented employment policies were more prevalent in early developing nations such as Britain, with its legacy of craft unions and proprietary capitalism, than they were in nations such as the United States or Japan, where the industrial landscape was dominated by large firms, organization-oriented employment practices, and bureaucratic ideologies of management.

150

Another strand emphasizes cultural and political differences—how the state was organized, the presence or absence of burgeois revolutions, whether social norms emphasize solidarity or individualism, how industry's objectives mesh with those of other interest groups, and so forth. Sometimes these differences are traced to economic or other structural factors such as a nation's size, although usually they are seen as having a high degree of autonomy. As applied to employer-employee relations, this strand is associated with scholars such as Seymour Martin Lipset and Barrington Moore, or more recent exponents such as Theda Skocpol and Charles Tilly. In their view, the United States is distinctive because of a relative freedom from constraint—whether emanating from below or from above—experienced by American employers. Mass unionism and welfare legislation did not take hold in the United States until the 1930s and 1940s. Before those years, the nation had comparatively low levels of union density and of government involvement in private industrial relations. Unlike employers in Edwardian England or Republican France, American employers felt neither subtle nor more overt forms of government pressure to restrain their opposition to unions or to reform their workplace and employment practices.

The opposition that unionism elicited from American employers was not unique, but it was more violent and sustained than the reaction it drew from European employers. A possible exception here was France, whose employers were (and are) renowned for the vehemence of their antiunion attitudes. But as Gerald Friedman observes in his essay, there were important differences between French and American employers of the late nineteenth and early twentieth centuries. In these years, says Friedman, the French government of the Third Republic decisively exercised its powers on behalf of organized labor. Legislation was passed that legalized unions, required conciliation of strikes, and gave labor an official role to play in the state-subsidized *bourses du travail*. State support for unions led to a rapid growth in the size of the labor movement and in the number of strikes. As a result of these threats, employers felt compelled to join together in associations intended to bolster their bargaining power and, more important, their influence within government. But this response came too late to check the growth of unionism. In contrast to their American counterparts, French employers were "too slow to mobilize and hampered by a strong state committed to republican values." Friedman concludes that they "missed their chance to crush an incipient radical labor movement, leaving them with a much more powerful class enemy."

The final essay, by Sanford Jacoby, takes up the long-debated question of American exceptionalism: why unionism and socialism were so much weaker in the United States than elsewhere. He finds an answer in the exceptional hostility to unionism of American employers, perhaps based on characteristically American business values such as individualism and a distrust of government and other forms of "outside" intervention. But, says Jacoby, a more compelling explanation would acknowledge that, although American employers may not have been innately more hostile to unions, they did have greater incentives to be hostile and a wider range of resources to effectuate their hostility than employers in other industrial nations. Incentives came from the low density rates and decentralized approach of American unions. Resources came from the comparatively large size of American firms; the willingness of the state—especially at local levels—to make available to employers its repressive and judicial apparatus; and the prevalence in American culture of values and norms that employers could mobilize against unions.

In reaction to this constellation of employer power, American union leaders chose a decentralized, conservative form of unionism, one that stood the greatest chance of making headway in a hostile environment. But their choice had the paradoxical effect of reinforcing employer opposition. It closed off the European option of getting employers to accept collective bargaining as a preferred alternative to more radical outcomes, and it raised the cost to individual employers of union recognition. As a result, says Jacoby, "a sort of feedback loop was created—the adversarial American system—in which employer hostility and conservative job control unionism sustained one another."

7

The Decline of Paternalism and the Making of the Employer Class: France, 1870–1914

■

GERALD FRIEDMAN

Employers are the missing link in labor history. For over a century, class formation has been a central concern of historical studies. Labor historians have studied the growth of class consciousness among workers in a variety of settings to explore whether a sense of common interest and a readiness to sacrifice for others is produced in the course of capitalist industrialization. An extensive literature chronicles working-class organization, describing the development of new forms of collective action, such as strikes, and new institutions, such as labor unions and radical political parties.[1] By contrast, little attention has been paid to the development of capitalist class consciousness and capitalist organizations, or even to the impact of these on the development of a working class.[2] Notwithstanding the many studies of individual capitalists and changing forms of business organization, the bourgeoisie as a class has attracted few historians.[3]

An exclusive focus on workers in the study of class formation might be appropriate where employers have no influence on the working class or where their impact never changes. Since employers obviously do affect the opportunities available for working-class action, one could conclude that scholars have assumed that employers always know and act in accord with their class interest, exhibiting a class awareness untroubled by the "false consciousness" often said to hinder the development of the working class.[4] This was Friedrich Engels'

THE AUTHOR IS grateful to the University of Massachusetts for a Faculty Research Grant, to Lynn Dugan and Pierre LaLiberté for their research assistance, to Sanford Jacoby, Sam Cohn, Debra Jacobson, Herman Lebovics, Donald Reid, and an anonymous referee for their comments; and to Rosa Rachel for her patience.

justification for ignoring capitalist class formation when he said that "capitalists are always organized. . . . their small number, the fact that they constitute a particular class, their social and commercial relations make formal organization superfluous."[5]

By discounting variations in employer behavior, Engels attributes all differences in the form or outcome of worker militancy to the workers themselves. Workers alone are "subjects" in the historical process, the only autonomous actors in a one-sided class struggle.[6] By assumption, historians have been led to conclude that differences— such as those between radical French unions and conservative American ones—were due to differences in the level of worker class consciousness. Differences in the level of capitalist class awareness are assumed away.[7]

In emphasizing close social relations and small numbers, however, Engels did not consider French employers. Certainly if size determines the ease of class organization then French employers were at a serious disadvantage. As late as 1906 there were over 10 million employers and self-employed persons in France, a number surpassing that of wage earners by nearly 200,000.[8] Nor should one casually assume that commercial and social contacts facilitated cooperation among French employers. French employers, in particular, were suspicious of outside interference in their businesses; used to managing their own affairs; and order givers rather than takers. "Individualism" for them "was not a vain word. The head of an enterprise considered himself a free man. . . . He made his own decisions."[9] Nor did employers all have common interests. They were divided by competition in product markets as well as by differing social backgrounds and economic positions: conflicts—between large and small employers *(les grands* et *les petits)*, producers of intermediate and final products, and flourishing and failing employers—regularly thwarted attempts at class alliance.[10] Fiercely competitive, some employers even sought advantage over their rivals by supporting labor unions and subsidizing strikers in hopes of bankrupting their weaker competitors.[11]

Divided as they were, French employers were rarely so class conscious as they appeared to their opponents. Employer-class institutions were created only after 1900 as a belated response by employers to worker militancy and government hostility. Until then, most employers preferred to rely on individual paternalism and state intervention to contain labor militancy. During the early Third Republic, however, state officials undermined paternalist employers, allowing a radical labor movement to develop. To stem growing labor militancy, French employers were forced to unite to change state policy. The belated development of employer-class institutions in France limited the further development of radical labor unions. In contrast with the United States, however, where employers mobilized quickly to smash a militant labor movement, France's mobilized employers faced a radical labor movement already entrenched in many workplaces and allied with a powerful political movement. France's subsequent condition as a "stalemate society" reflected the employers' inability to crush a radical labor movement that emerged before the creation of an employer class.[12]

FRENCH EMPLOYERS: THE PATERNALIST EXPERIMENT

There is an image of the traditional French employer: "Maître chez lui," master of his own house, as unwilling to tolerate interference in his business as in the direction of his family. In Val Lorwin's words, "the heads of family concerns carried with them into industry the values and habits of a tight-fisted peasantry and a cautious commercial middle class."[13] These employers could be extremely conservative in business, more concerned to maintain control over the enterprise than to seek out potential gains from new markets or technological innovations.[14] They would go to great lengths—and expense—to avoid outside interference in their business, even abstaining from borrowing to avoid giving bankers entry into their business. And they fiercely resisted interference from government officials or labor unions.

As capitalists and employers, however, French entrepreneurs after the industrial revolution of the early nineteenth century could not avoid one form of outside interference in their businesses: wage laborers. Like capitalists ever since, they faced the problem of maintaining an orderly exchange of labor for wages, ensuring that their employees worked sufficiently hard that profits could be made from their labor. They wanted disciplined workers who would arrive at work on time and perform their tasks promptly and as instructed. Both to maximize profits and to ensure their own sense of control over their workplaces, they needed obedience: "the maintenance of authority . . . the dictatorship of the *patron* is a fundamental principle . . . The *patron* is the boss, the director, he has the right to be obeyed."[15] "In the shop," one employer told his workers, "I am your boss, you are my soldiers. I order, you must obey."[16]

This demand for systematic compliance to regimented tasks challenged the traditional independence of French workers accustomed to the more relaxed work routine of artisanal shops, family farms, and rural industry. By preserving alternatives to regimented factory labor, the wide distribution of private property in nineteenth-century France and the persistence of these traditional forms of production complicated French capitalists' task further. Shortages of wage laborers for factory work led some capitalists to pay high wages. In addition to encroaching on profits, however, a high wage strategy could undermine discipline if workers spent their higher wages on drink and leisure. As Donald Reid observes, employers complained that:

> Raising wages . . . had immoral effects in and out of the workplace . . . high wages created by market competition (rather than as part of a managerial strategy) spread 'discouragement' amongst workers. What was needed was managerial leadership which gave workers 'courage' by implementing new forms of industrial relations which transcended the cash nexus to create heroes of labor who would feel attachment to the firm and who would work with more than their wages in mind.[17]

French capitalists in the early nineteenth century developed their own strategy to maintain control of the production process, a strategy that combined paternalism and private regulation of labor relations with state repression of labor militancy. Rather than adapting their payment and workplace regimes to the workers' preferences, capitalists sought to win their workers' hearts by "reforming" their preferences. Extending their domination beyond the workplace, paternalist employers established a network of social institutions all linked to the enterprise and restricted to employees in good standing. Pension and savings plans, low-rent housing, medical care, stores, schools, churches: paternalist employers provided all these in exchange for obedience. "The *patron*," one advocate of paternalism wrote:

> should be the protector of the poor and of his family, not abandoning him when he leaves the workplace but enquiring after his health, that of his wife, and his children; with an indispensable firmness, extending a generous hand. . . . Especially, he must moralize the workers . . . he must not neglect to give them an edifying example of religious belief and of an irreproachable life. . . . The worker will no longer see in the *patron* a tyrant but a beneficent master; he will then render a voluntary submission without believing that he thus compromises his dignity or his liberty.[18]

By entwining the employee in a web of company institutions, paternalist employers raised the cost of disobedience beyond the loss of a day's pay or even a job. But paternalists aspired for more: they wanted to change the way workers saw their relationship with the company. They wanted "company men" who would "identify totally with the objectives of the enterprise. For the [paternalist] *patron*, there must be no autonomous life among the subordinates, nothing separate from the workplace."[19]

The paternalists sought to conceal the wage-labor relationship behind a cloak of familial associations, insisting that they alone should govern their shops because they, like good fathers, alone knew how to care for their worker-children.[20] In exchange for the right to command the workers' labors, paternalists promised that they would attend directly to their workers' needs with their welfare programs. The alliance many paternalist employers (including Protestants) made with the Roman Catholic Church was, therefore, a natural one not because both upheld traditional values—since many capitalists did not—but because both sought to regulate the workers' mores from above. Clergy and employers, both authoritarians, promised together to care for the worker in exchange for supervising his entire life, from early upbringing to schooling, from adult church attendance to burial of the dead.[21]

With its focus on the *patron*'s unmediated domination over his work force, paternalism promised order and profitability seemingly without recourse to the support of outsiders, either other employers or the state. This made paternalism particularly attractive to French employers; they could maintain unchallenged control over the workplace. And they could do so even while proclaiming their dedication to liberal values and to laissez-faire.

Such proclamations notwithstanding, French paternalism could serve as an effective instrument of labor control only if supported by an active and repressive state apparatus. Paternalism could pacify labor only because the French state effectively repressed labor militancy, preventing workers from advancing their group interests through collective action. By itself, even the most thorough internal control could not guarantee labor discipline because even the best-indoctrinated labor force could never be fully isolated from outside influences.[22] Employers depended on the state to contain these outside influences despite their claims to self-sufficiency, paternalist firms depended on the state, not only to leave them free to manage their internal affairs but also to repress organized labor.[23]

By themselves, however, French employers lacked the political power to ensure state protection of their common interests against those of wage labor. Except for the short-lived Second Republic, France's political structure limited the influence that middle-class employers could exert over a state apparatus dominated by landed aristocrats. Divisions among employers and their failure to form class-wide institutions further limited their political influence. Some employers tried to mobilize to influence state policy, by forming, for example, the Comité des filateurs de Lille in 1824, the Comité des industriels de l'Est in 1835, and the Comité des forges in 1864.[24] Intended to promote tariff protection or to restrict the market activities of other entrepreneurs, however, early nineteenth-century employer associations never gained a wide following or influence. Indeed, their activities often exacerbated splits within the incipient employer class. A focus on tariff protection, for example, while popular in some industries (textiles, mining, and metalworking, for example), alienated employers in others (such as transportation or silk production). In short, the French *patronat* was divided and unorganized.

French employers were fortunate, however, because although they were unable to attain political power, the French government had its own reasons for repressing labor militancy. With revolutions occurring once a generation from 1789 to 1870, nineteenth-century French governments closely monitored potential threats to public order so as to crush incipient revolutionary challenges. Fearing the escalation of employment disputes, state officials designed labor legislation to reinforce employers' control over their workers. The mobility of dissatisfied or disobedient workers, for example, was restricted by Napoleonic legislation requiring that workers carry a *livret* signed by their previous employers, which reported on their employment history.[25] Other legislation, enacted in 1806, established *conseils de prud'-hommes* to arbitrate disputes between employers and their workers. These councils, whose members until 1880 were chosen by employers, were empowered to fine or even to imprison workers for violations of contract.[26]

Legislation and police action were even more restrictive of collective action. Socialist or other radical political activity was usually outlawed before 1870.[27] Strikes were illegal before 1864, and they were tightly regulated after that, while labor unions were banned under the revolutionary *Loi LeChapelier*. While not always enforced, these last prohibitions discouraged collective action by providing public officials with the authority to monitor and repress such action as they chose.

Until the 1870s, this combination of private paternalism and public repression effectively checked labor militancy in France. Employers remained vulnerable, however, because they themselves were not responsible for public repression; they depended for this essential prop of their private authority on their interests' coinciding with those of state officials. Soon after the Third Republic was established in the 1870s, however, a new group of officials with different interests assumed power. The loss of state support provoked the collapse of paternalism in what Michelle Perrot calls "the crisis of discipline" in pre–World War I France.[28]

While some historians have characterized the early French Third Republic as a "bourgeois republic" dominated by businessmen and their spokesmen, most employers would have been surprised to hear of their political power.[29] At first, business interests did wield considerable influence during the governments of the "moral order" in the early 1870s. These governments did their part to quell labor militancy by crushing the Paris Commune, exiling thousands of labor activists, and banning membership in some revolutionary organizations. The share of strikers arrested for strike-related activity, for example, was even higher during the early years of the Republic (1871–1875) than in the last years of the Empire (1864–1869), and higher than it would be again in the 1880s and 1890s.[30]

After the mid-1870s, however, business interests were no longer so well served. While emphasizing the political power of business in earlier years, Jean Lhomme notes that "in the course of the years 1871–79, a growing separation came between wealth . . . and political functions which more and more escaped [the large bourgeoisie]." "The Republic" he observes "became the symbol of opposition to the large bourgeoisie."[31] Ideological commitment, experience, and political interest all made the republicans who took control of government after 1876 unsympathetic to business. Drawn from what Gambetta labeled the "new levels"—the professional and independent middle classes rather than the business classes or the aristocracy—the republican leaders were by inclination part of what Katherine Auspitz has called the "radical bourgeoisie." Rarely employers of labor, republican politicians had devoted their youth to the political and social struggle against the imperial government of Louis Napoleon.[32] These activities placed them in an alliance with organized labor but often in direct opposition to business leaders who supported the Empire almost until the end.[33] Once in power, furthermore, they continued to depend on working-class votes against the Republic's right-wing opposition, which was supported by many business leaders.[34]

Republican ideology further reinforced the alienation of republicans from paternalist businessmen. Developed during the struggle against Louis Napoleon, the Republican program preached devotion to the French Revolution and the principles of 1789: liberty, equality, and fraternity.[35] Republicans instinctively opposed hierarchy and were committed to equality of rights, universal male suffrage, and social reform designed to elevate the status of all citizens through cooperative action and association.[36] These principles placed republicans in direct conflict with paternalist employers who, as the French syndicalist Paul Faure observed, was "a divine right *patron*" extending to the business world precisely the principles of hierarchy overthrown by the French Revolution.[37] Paternalist companies were attacked as islands "of financial and Royalist feudalism organized against the democratic party," and as "oppressive regimes" operated by royalist companies "struggling against the Republic . . . to conserve their dictatorship [over the workers] . . . to prove that the Republic is powerless to protect them . . . [and] to maintain their economic and political tutelage over the region."[38] Republicans contrasted these "oppressive companies" with strikers and union activists, "modest workers of simple faith in the Republic."[39] Addressing strikers in Decazeville in 1886, a republican deputy drew the contrast simply: "The company embodies the Orleanists [royalists], you embody the Republic. Your strike is the struggle of universal suffrage against the monarchy."[40]

Sympathetic to labor while deeply committed to private property, republicans sought to conciliate rather than repress labor unrest. They hoped thereby to channel workers away from socialism and revolutionary militancy.[41] Organization and fraternal self-help were their preferred solutions to the problems of French labor. Instead of arresting strikers, state officials sought to defuse strikes and to encourage moderation by pressuring employers to settle strikes and by supporting labor unions capable of restraining rank-and-file militancy. Republican legislation was designed to integrate organized labor into the republican order on an equal standing with business. Legislation in 1880, for example, established parity between worker and employer representatives on the *conseils de prud'hommes*. This was quickly followed by the legalization of trade unions in 1884 and by the establishment in many cities after 1887 of municipally subsidized *bourses du travail*, or trade union centers. In response to the strike wave of 1890 (with France's first May Day), republicans enacted laws on miners' safety and establishing a system of miners' delegates to represent miners before employers and government officials. Then, in 1892, laws were enacted organizing state conciliation of labor disputes and a reformed system of industrial safety and health inspection.[42]

This labor legislation tacitly allied the French state with militant labor against employers. Dominated by revolutionary syndicalists, state-subsidized *bourses du travail* served as centers for the diffusion of revolutionary action and propaganda throughout France.[43] Following the instructions of the then-Socialist Minister of Commerce, Alexandre Millerand, the reformed labor inspectors worked closely with unions and *bourses* to collect reports of possible infractions of state labor laws. Elected by the miners themselves, the new miners' delegates were largely drawn from the unions' leadership, so that the system, in effect, subsidized the establishment of a full-time, professional mine workers' union leadership.[44] State mediation of labor disputes also directly pitted state officials against employers when mediating officials pressured employers to make concessions to settle disputes. Highly advantageous to strikers, state mediation was conducted in over 20 percent of labor disputes between 1893 and 1914. Since it was as unpopular with employers as it was popular with labor, employers almost never requested it.[45] Paternalist firms were especially subject to intervention by state officials suspicious of their authoritarian claims. Premier René Waldeck-Rousseau's mediation in the 1899 strike at the Schneider steel works at Le Creusot—mediation carried out on Millerand's advice—served notice to all that the state would support the demands of organized labor against even the largest and wealthiest paternalists.[46] Standing alone, even France's strongest firms could not resist the combination of organized labor and the state.[47]

Rather than dampening labor unrest or channeling militancy away from revolutionary socialism, republican legislation sparked a surge in strike activity and membership in militant labor organizations. Starting from a few trades in the largest cities, unions spread to include workers in virtually every industry in every French department. Membership grew from 72,300 in 1884 to 1,026,000 by 1913, increasing by nearly 9.5 percent a year (table 7.1).[48] Contrary to republican hopes, unionization did not restrain other forms of labor militancy. The number of strikers increased by nearly 7.0 percent a year in 1884–1913, punctuated by strike waves that in some years involved over 10 percent of nonagricultural wage earners.[49] Some paternalists, in LeCreusot, Decazeville, and the Nord textile mills, for example, were particularly threatened by growing worker militancy because their firms had created dense networks of workplace-related social institutions that now backfired by facilitating their workers' collective action.[50] Perhaps even more threatening to both businessmen and republican activists was the continued growth of radical political organizations. Despite splits and internal difficulties, the Socialist party increased its share of the vote from under 1 percent in

TABLE 7.1 Union Membership, Strike Involvement, and
Membership in Employer Associations, France, 1884–1913

	Labor Union Membership	Strikers[a]	Employer Association Membership[b]
1884	72,300	39,500	9,128
1890	232,000	82,960	93,411
1900	588,800	159,500	158,300
1913	1,026,300	241,767	421,566

Source: Union membership and the number of strikers are from Edward Shorter and Charles Tilly, *Strikes in France* (Cambridge, Eng., 1974), pp. 371–72, 361–62. Employer association membership is from France, *Statistique Annuaire, 1913–1914* (Paris, 1915), p. 41*.

[a] Average number of strikers for five years centered on year given for 1884, 1890, and 1900. The 1913 figure is a 3-year average of 1911–1913.

[b] Membership in associations of employers *(patrons)* registered according to 1884 law on professional associations.

late-1880s to nearly 17 percent in 1914, electing about one-fifth of the Chamber.[51]

MAKING AN EMPLOYER CLASS

The collapse of paternalism amid growing state support for organized labor was a collective problem for all employers. Frightened by the growing strength of radical labor, employers were acutely conscious of their isolation from a government sympathetic to labor organization. Business leaders complained that while the governments of France's foreign competitors were attentive to the needs of capital, republican France was governed by a small clique of doctors, professors, and lawyers ignorant of economic realities and hostile to business.[52] While republican officials complained of powerful employers who "confound their particular interests with the public interest and demand that state authorities be in every case defenders of their companies against their own workers," businessmen demanded support against militant labor and called for a "government of order, a government of authority which alone can stop the internal and external decline of France."[53] Some even preached that employers should abandon their traditional individualism for cooperation in defense of their common interests as owners of property and employers of wage labor: "Neither wool, nor cotton, nor linen can be in disagreement," one textile capitalist said in 1899, "they all have the same interests to defend against the workers."[54] France, a delegate to a business convention in 1901 declared, needed a party of business "to counter the Parti ouvrier of M. Guesde."[55]

Such calls were well received by employers alarmed by growing labor unrest. Between 1884 and 1913, membership in employers' unions grew by nearly 14 percent a year. In addition to growing numbers of local employers associations, new national associations were established including the Confédération des groupes commerciaux et industriels and the Union des industries métallurgiques et minières, both formed in 1901, and the Association de défense des classes moyennes, founded in 1907.[56] As late as 1899, French employers could be described as "scattered, disoriented, discouraged, lacking the vigor to be compared with the aggressive and organized working class." By 1914, however, "the tables had changed; while the workers' unions were practically stationary, those of employers were advancing."[57]

Employer association membership increased in direct response to rising labor militancy; "The workers' growing strength and that of their unions," one advocate of employers' associations wrote, "their abusive strikes . . . require that the employers unite in defense of their interests. To the workers' unions respond unions of the employers."[58] Employer association membership in 1910 was concentrated among employers in large cities and establishments, the centers of labor union organization, strike activity, and socialist political activity (see table 7.2). Membership in employer associations was nearly seven times higher among employers struck than for those not struck, with the striker rate nearly three times higher for members than for nonmembers. Employer organization was also most common where there was a labor union. The unionization rate among employees of association members was nearly four times higher in 1910 than for nonmembers. While only 26 percent of industry by department cells without unions in 1898, 1905, or 1910 had an employer association in 1910, over 60 percent of those with a union in one of those years had an association.[59] Similarly, the departmental socialist voting share was three times higher in the 1890s and nearly two times higher in 1910 for members of employer associations than for nonmembers.[60]

Labor activists had no doubt about why employers formed associations. Alphonse Merrheim, the great French syndicalist and student of employer organization, wrote in 1909:

Never has the hour been graver for the working class. The great employer associations, directed first against the consumer, now turn their force against the CGT [Confédération générale du travail], against the proletariat . . . they hope to thus break our efforts at emancipation and

TABLE 7.2 Characteristics of Members of Employer Associations
and Employer Nonmembers, France, 1910[a]

Characteristic	Members	Nonmembers
Department percentage voting socialist		
1893	22.9	7.8
1910	19.6	11.5
Unionization rate within department and industry		
1898	9.0	1.2
1905	17.5	3.1
1910	15.3	4.1
Share of workers within department and industry striking: annual average		
1895–1899	0.95	0.31
1900–1909	0.76	0.30
Population of largest city in department		
1911	1,254,977	213,182
Average establishment size[b]		
1906	5.82	2.82
Share of employers within department and industry belonging to employer association in 1910	43.8	2.3
N (approximate)	342,700	9,622,600

SOURCE: Membership in employer associations is from France, Office du travail, *Annuaire des syndicats professionnels, 1910* (Paris, 1911). Socialist voting is from Georges LaChapelle, *Elections législatives de . . . 1893* (Paris, 1895), and Georges LaChapelle and P. G. LaChesnais, *Tableau des élections législatives de . . . 1910* (Paris, 1910). The unionization rate within the industry in the department is from France, Office du travail, *Annuaire des syndicats professionnels* for 1898, 1905, and 1910; the coding is described in Gerald Friedman, *Politics and Unions* (Ph.D. diss., Harvard University, 1986). The number of strikers is from France, Office du travail, *Statistique des grèves* for 1895–1910; the coding is described in Edward Shorter and Charles Tilly, *Strikes in France* (Cambridge, Eng., 1974). The number of employers and wage earners within the industry in the department, the average size of an establishment within the industry in the department, and the size of the department's largest city are all from France, Statistique générale, *Résultats statistique de dénombrement* for 1896, 1906, or 1911.

[a]This table shows estimates of characteristics of association members and nonmembers. These estimates were calculated as the weighted average of department and industry characteristics for 2,270 department and industry cells where the weights are the number of association members and nonmembers in the department and industry in 1910.

[b]Average number of wage earners per establishment with at least one wage earner.

stop all wage increases. . . . Less egoistic than the workers, because they understood their interests, [the employers] did not hesitate for a minute to develop union organizations as needed . . . a power to neutralize worker organization.[61]

Employers, Merrheim claimed, formed associations to defeat unions in strikes. Seeing them as organizations for combat, he emphasized their strike activities: providing financial assistance to struck members, recruiting strikebreakers, and organizing lockouts.[62] Head of the French metalworkers' union, Merrheim's main concern was with the Comité des forges and the other relatively well-financed associations of French metal manufacturers. Other employers were still much less organized to resist strikes; comparatively few belonged to associations, and the associations themselves lacked resources, permanent offices, or paid staff. Even in 1909, when Merrheim wrote, a conservative deputy wrote that "employer unionism does not exist" in France, and an activist complained that most associations were little more than "an impressive facade, . . . performing no function beyond arranging an annual banquet followed by the distribution of awards."[63]

For employers as for workers effective strike management required the resources to sustain a long conflict and the central control to prevent defections. Both were limited by what Pierre Laroque called "the fundamental individualism of the employers," and their lack "of any real collective discipline."[64] Instead of charging high dues to build up strike funds, the associations kept dues low to avoid alienating potential members. They tried to attract members with social activities, such as the annual banquets criticized above. Low dues prevented most associations from accumulating significant financial reserves; in 1910 over 80 percent had no beneficiary features at all, while another 6 percent had none beyond a journal.[65] Only 12 percent of associations had any programs involving any cash benefits to members, such as strike assistance, and even these funds were often small.[66] Lacking resources to support struck firms or to reward firms that held the line against aggressive strikers, the leaders of an association had little leverage to restrain members from action not in the collective interest.

Perhaps reflecting their lack of resources was the fact that employer associations had little direct effect on the outcome of strikes. After other strike characteristics are controlled, including the involvement of a labor union representing the strikers, the presence of an employer association lowers the probability of strikers' gaining at least some of their demands by 9.3 percent, barely a third of the absolute effect of labor unions (see table 7.3).[67] The associations' gen-

TABLE 7.3 Determinants of Strike Success, Logit Regressions for
French Strikes 1895–1899 and 1910–1914[a]

Variable	Coefficient (T-ratio)
Intercept	0.43 (2.78)
Labor union strike	0.55 (9.31)
Employer association involved	−0.20 (−1.53)
Association · log (establishment size)	0.01 (0.51)
Log (establishment size)	−0.13 (−6.13)
Striker rate in industry and department	0.09 (1.52)
Percent voting socialist in department	−0.92 (−4.34)
Urban locality	−0.51 (−8.41)
N dummy variables	
Industries	4
Years	9
Issues	4
N	7,502
Share successful:	53.81
Chi-square statistic	563.86

SOURCE: Shorter-Tilly strike data file. See Edward Shorter and Charles Tilly, *Strikes in France* (Cambridge, Eng., 1974); Gerald Friedman, "Strike Success and Union Ideology," *Journal of Economic History* (March 1988), 1-28.

[a]This table reports the results of logit regressions for the results of 7,502 individual strikes where the dependent variable equals 0 for strikes where the strikers gain none of their demands and 1 for those where the strikers gain at least some of their demands.

eral lack of resources is reflected in their inability to support employers through long strikes. While labor unions double the duration of a strike, employer associations increase strike duration by less than 10 percent.[68] The ability of some powerful employer associations to sustain extended strikes frightened prominent syndicalists, but these associations were unusual; the average French employer association was too small and too weak to have much direct impact on strike outcomes.

Employer associations may have had other, more important, functions than direct strike support; they influenced the government. Employers fought on two fronts, against labor unions and against government intervention; the greatest danger they faced "was worker pressure for government intervention, which could combine these two perils."[69] While concerned about strikes, employer associations' greater fear was "the growing intervention of the state in the area of labor relations."[70] Associations were effective in battling this intervention. Employer associations' national leaders would visit from Paris to

TABLE 7.4 Determinants of Government Mediation of French
Strikes, 1895–1899 and 1910–1914[a]

Variable	Coefficient (T-ratio)
Intercept	−2.48 (−10.20)
Labor union strike	0.36 (2.76)
Labor union strike 1910–1914	−0.38 (−0.06)
Employer association involved	−0.46 (−2.77)
Association · log (establishment size)	−0.01 (−0.23)
Log (establishment size)	−0.29 (−8.60)
Striker rate in industry and department	0.01 (0.13)
Percent voting socialist in department	−2.61 (−8.96)
Urban locality	−1.57 (−14.15)
Strikers/workers in establishment	−0.09 (−0.73)
Log (number of strikers)	0.51 (14.54)
Log (strike duration)	0.55 (18.71)
N dummy variables:	
Industries	4
Years	9
Issues	4
N	7,502
Share with intervention	20.83
Chi-square statistic	1,781.1

SOURCE: See table 7.3.

[a]This table reports the results of logit regressions for the results of 7,502 individual strikes where the dependent variable equals 0 for strikes where there is no government mediation and equals 1 where there is mediation.

encourage struck employers and to urge local officials to oppose the strike.[71] The combined influence of organized local employers and these visits was apparently effective since the presence of an employer association reduced significantly the probability that state officials would mediate a strike, lowering the probability of this intervention by even more (in absolute terms) than labor unions raised it (see table 7.4).[72]

The employer associations' effect on the behavior of state officials in strikes may have reflected the associations' electoral impact. Employer associations had political clout because they had the resources to mobilize large numbers of employers throughout the country. As head of the Comité des forges, for example, Robert Pinot was involved in all pre–World War I labor legislation in the Chamber of Deputies because he alone could furnish deputies with arguments and materials based on the *Comité*'s privileged access to employer records.

Associations were formidable lobbyists because their journals, mailing lists, and contacts throughout the country could be used to pressure recalcitrant deputies. Pinot, for example, would write members of the Comité des forges in opposition to proposed legislation and would arrange for members to write their deputies, to distribute petitions, and to visit Paris to pursuade deputies of both the justice and the political prudence of supporting the employers' view on an issue.[73]

Employers' associations also used their influence to mobilize voters for the political right and against the left. Beginning in the 1890s, even employer associations previously allied with the left, such as those of small Parisian shopkeepers, shifted to the right out of fear of socialism. Led for many years by a leading Radical, the Comité de l'alimentation, for example, moved so far to the right at the end of the 1890s that it was accused in the 1900 municipal elections of serving as "an agency of nationalist propaganda." With employer support, the new, nationalist right captured the Paris city council in those elections, reversing over a century of leftist domination of Parisian politics.[74]

By 1910, France had a resurgent right buttressed by an increasingly united business community organized in employer associations. Facing a common socialist threat to their property and economic power, employers mobilized politically without regard for their traditional individualism or their past divisions. Associations were the vehicle for this mobilization, combatting leftist ideas through their literature, rallies, and public meetings addressed by prominent right-wing politicians and activists. Preparing for the 1910 Chamber of Deputies elections, for example, an alliance of leading employer associations, including the Confédération des groupes commerciaux et industriels, the Union des industries métallurgiques et miniéres, and the Association de défense des classes moyennes, prepared an "economic charter" that they publicized prominently and presented to candidates for endorsement. This statement "summarized the determination of employers to preserve the sacred character of private property, oppose state intervention, and resist social reforms." It condemned an income tax, expanded worker pensions, and state interference in labor relations, particularly legislation for shorter hours and a weekly day off.[75]

Employer associations publicized candidates' responses to the "economic charter," endorsing those sympathetic to its program and condemning the others. The combination of employer anxiety over worker militancy and the efforts of the employer associations had a dramatic effect. In the 1910 Chamber of Deputies elections, the presence of employer associations was associated with significantly increased support for the candidates of the far right and reduced support for the socialist left. After various characteristics of an electoral district are controlled, every percentage point of increase in the share of employers belonging to associations is associated with a 2.5 percent increase in electoral support for right-wing candidates. Similarly, every percentage point of increase in the share of employers belonging to associations is associated with a 4.7 percent reduction in the Socialist (SFIO) share of the vote (see table 7.5).[76]

Although even greater in absolute size, the electoral impact of employer associations directly mirrors that of labor unions. Labor unions and employer associations together polarized the French electorate by increasing support for candidates of the extreme left and right. By the end of the "Belle Époque," labor unions and employer associations competed for influence in the French state by affecting the composition of the Chamber of Deputies, to reward their friends and to punish their class enemies.

CONCLUSION: EMPLOYER CLASS FORMATION AND THE DEVELOPMENT OF THE MODERN LABOR MOVEMENT

French employers were slow to mobilize, and their failure was costly. By the early twentieth century, when employers began to behave as an organized group, French workers had already formed strong class institutions and political alliances to advance their collective interests. French employers mobilized too late to crush France's radical labor movement, too late to reverse the impact of over two decades of republican labor policy sheltering the growth of a radical labor movement. By balancing the pressure from the left, however, mobilization allowed employers to restrain further state concessions to the organized working class. Rarely since 1914 has either organized labor or organized employers been strong enough in France to gain significant changes in social policy. As a result, both have remained mobilized, and France has maintained a lasting political stalemate.[77]

French class formation was a dialectical process where growing working-class militancy led employers to mobilize as a class. When challenges were raised to basic interests common to all, employers eventually abandoned their preference for extreme individualism and

TABLE 7.5 Effect of Organization on Voting: First Round of Elections to the French Chamber of Deputies, April 1910[a]

Variable	SOCIALISTS (SFIO) Coefficient (T-ratio)	RIGHTIST Coefficient (T-ratio)
Intercept	−1.94 (−4.72)	−0.12 (−0.51)
Share of department's employers		4.58
in associations, 1910	−6.51 (−2.83)	(2.88)
Share of department's wage		
earners in labor unions, 1910	3.41 (2.97)	−2.29 (−2.93)
Share of department's wage		
earners striking, 1910	−2.11 (−2.17)	1.28 (2.26)
Percent arrondissement labor force		
in manufacturing	−1.06 (1.06)	1.81 (−0.39)
in mining	3.98 (4.87)	−2.24 (−2.71)
Wage laborers[b]	−1.39 (0.57)	0.70 (−0.60)
Agricultural wage laborers	0.05 (0.06)	0.49 (0.98)
Log (population of largest city in		
department, in thousands)	0.004 (0.09)	0.06 (1.75)
Percent in viticulture · southern		
department	0.85 (4.47)	−0.44 (−2.39)
N	341	431
Mean of dependent variable	−0.97	−0.18
F-value	7.94	3.74
R-square	.18	.07

SOURCE: Coding of 1910 election returns matched with data on arrondissement and department characteristics; see Friedman, "French Republicanism in Theory and Decline" (unpublished paper, University of Massachusetts, March 1987).

[a] Results of regressions for the log-odds of the share of votes cast for Socialist and for rightist candidates in the first round of the 1910 Chamber of Deputies elections. The log-odds ratio is the logarithm of $(P/1 - P)$, where P is the share of votes cast for a side. The coefficients from these regressions are equivalent to those estimated by logit regressions; see Friedman, "French Republicanism."

The weights used are: VOTERS · (%SFIO) · (1 − %SFIO) and VOTERS · (%RIGHT) · (1 − %RIGHT) where VOTERS is the number of votes cast, %SFIO and %RIGHT are the percentage of votes cast for SFIO candidates and the percentage cast for rightist candidates, respectively.

[b] Only data for the total labor force in each industry are available on the arrondissement level. The number of wage laborers in an arrondissement has been estimated by multiplying the share of wage laborers of the total labor force for the department in each industry by the labor force in the industry within the arrondissement.

mobilized for collective action by forming institutions of class defense. Protected for much of the nineteenth century by a state hostile to worker collective action, French employers had been able to indulge their preference for individualism, limiting themselves to private paternalism to restrain worker militancy. The establishment of republican government removed this outside shelter and allowed a radical labor movement to flourish. Facing this challenge, French employers did mobilize to protect their common interests, although they did so long after the workers.

A dialectical framework emphasizing conflict and the impact of the state on class formation also accounts for the relative weakness of both radical labor organizations and employer associations in the United States since the late nineteenth century.[78] Like their French counterparts, American employers were extraordinarily hostile to outside interference in their business affairs, preferring, like a New York cigar manufacturer in 1885, to "reserve to ourselves . . . the right to adjust our difficulties in our own way."[79] This did not prevent American employers, however, from working together to crush radical labor as soon as it appeared. Employers responded quickly to the growth of the Knights of Labor in the early 1880s with a "war of capital against labor organization" where "the organization of capitalists" worked intently to "break up organizations of laborers."[80] Founded at the Knights' peak in 1886, the Stove Founders' National Defense Association, for example, united employers of nearly half of America's molders. The association supplied funds and strikebreakers to struck firms, and its members committed themselves to complete work ordered from a struck firm. Other associations also provided armed guards, spies, and thugs as needed to defeat unions, while pressuring government officials to supply public repression when needed.[81] In the late 1880s and again after 1900 union growth, especially the growth of radical unions, was checked by organized capital in associations whose policy was "directed . . . toward preventing strikes and disintegrating unions."[82] Powerful aids of antiunion firms, some associations could even boast, as did the Employers Association of Dayton, that "it has not yet lost a strike."[83]

The rapid and efficient mobilization of the American capitalist class intimidated American labor. Samuel Gompers justified his cautious, conservative policy as head of the American Federation of Labor by saying that he had seen "how professions of radicalism and sensationalism concentrated all the forces of organized society against a labor movement."[84] Conducted promptly and thoroughly, employer repression limited the growth of the American labor movement, preventing almost completely the development of labor's more radical wing. Left without a strong rival after each crisis, American employers could then revert, as many have in the twentieth century, to their preferred indifference to collective action.[85]

French employers could only look with envy and regret on the success of their American counterparts. Too slow to mobilize and hampered by a strong state committed to republican values, the French missed their chance to crush an incipient radical labor movement, leaving them with a much more powerful class enemy. Relatively free from organized employer resistance, French workers were able in the early years of the Third Republic to develop a particularly broad program for revolutionary social change as well as militant institutions to articulate it. Even after backing down from its most militant positions in the face of growing employer opposition and the consequent state repression after 1906, the organized French working class remained one of Europe's most militant labor movements, a continuing challenge to their employers' authority and power.[86]

8

American Exceptionalism Revisited: The Importance of Management

■

SANFORD M. JACOBY

It has been over eighty years since Werner Sombart wrote his essay "Why is There No Socialism in America?" yet the topic of American exceptionalism continues to be of great interest to social scientists and historians. The United States is held to be unique among industrial democracies not only for failing to produce a mass socialist movement but also for having relatively low unionization rates throughout the twentieth century. In 1914, shortly after Sombart published his essay, the American unionization rate was not the lowest in the world, but when adjusted for per capita income (which varied widely at the time), it was about 20 percent less than those of European nations with similar income levels. Although America's industrial unions emerged and grew dramatically during the 1930s and 1940s, those events occurred at a relatively late date in world historical time, and the density levels established in those years failed to maintain themselves. Today, even the unadjusted unionization rate is lower than that of any other advanced industrial nation, and the present trend is toward a widening of the differential. Between 1970 and 1985 the proportion of the American labor force represented by unions dropped more rapidly than in any advanced nation.[1]

Explanations for exceptionalism typically adduce a variety of factors that might account for the American worker's relatively weak interest in socialism and unionism: the absence of feudalism in the

THE AUTHOR IS grateful for comments received from Henry Phelps Brown, Samuel Cohn, Howell Harris, George Strauss, Peter Temin, Michael Wallerstein, John Windmuller, and Gavin Wright as well as from participants in presentations at Stanford University, the UCLA Institute of Industrial Relations, and the Social Science History Association meetings in New Orleans.

United States, early mass enfranchisement, working-class heterogeneity and resultant cleavages among workers, fluid class boundaries, high rates of social mobility, high earnings levels, the frontier pressure valve, and a dominant value system that stresses individualism and personal achievement.[2] In recent years, however, these traditional explanations have become the target of various criticisms. One critical approach rejects the assumption of labor exceptionalism, and claims that, despite the absence of a mass party on the left, radical and socialist ideologies did sink deep roots in the American working class.[3] Another approach argues that there is no standard pattern of working-class development: each national trajectory was unique.[4] Finally, a third approach accepts the premise of exceptionalism—that America's workers were different from those in Europe—but claims that the traditional literature has given too much emphasis to the labor side of the picture and ignored other, more structural determinants such as the nation's size and the activities of its employers and government.[5]

The present essay is most closely related to this last approach, and argues that exceptionalism could as easily be applied to American employers as to American labor, whose hostility toward unions has always been more extreme than that of employers in other nations. The essay first examines why American employers were so hostile and violent in their response to unions and then shows that this hostility goes a long way toward explaining low union density and the lack of labor radicalism in the United States. Although recognizing that American workers and unions *were* different, the essay stresses that these differences cannot be understood without taking into account the intransigence of American employers. The concept is somewhat akin to a simultaneous-equations system, in which worker and employer orientations are mutually determined, and both, in turn, contribute to exceptional American outcomes. Hence it is meaningless to say that "labor factors" mattered more than "employer factors"; both need to be considered.

WERE AMERICAN EMPLOYERS DIFFERENT?

A convenient jumping-off point is Lloyd Ulman's recent presidential address to the Industrial Relations Research Association. Ulman conjectures that national variations in union density can best be explained not in terms of worker propensities to join unions but in terms of varying national levels of employer hostility to unionism.

Although, says Ulman, all employers seek to maximize profits and so would prefer not to deal with unions, some "might choose collective bargaining even if it costs more than union avoidance but less than the most radical alternative on the current political scene."[6] That is, if faced with a choice between collective bargaining and collective expropriation, employers will always opt for the former, unless the latter is not a plausible threat. Ulman offers three examples. First, in Scandinavia, the Netherlands, and Germany, employers confronted powerful socialist union movements that posed serious threats to the economic order. In a form of buyout, employers in these nations defused such threats by proffering collective bargaining and state welfare benefits in return for union support of basic property rights. Although the exchange was not always as explicit as the Stinnes-Legien agreement of 1918, bargaining and benefits had the effect of incorporating union members into a modified but still fundamentally capitalist system. Second, in France and Italy, although the unions espoused radical ideologies, these were of a syndicalist, rather than socialist, variety. Less interested in bargaining and more politically utopian than their northern counterparts, French and Italian unions could be countered by employer political activity rather than by offers of collective bargaining. Finally, in the United States employers faced a union movement quite interested in bargaining but averse to and even contemptuous of socialist and radical doctrines. For American employers, then, there was no need to buy workers out (there was nothing to be bought), and bargaining was accepted only when workers were able to impose unavoidable strike costs on employers.

Ulman's argument is sharp and parsimonious, and his emphasis on employers as a critical determinant of union density levels is a welcome change from the usual litany of labor exceptionalism. But, paradoxically, on closer examination his model is seen to be a version of labor exceptionalism, because it is workers' "relative preferences for alternative institutional regimes" that shape dominant employer policies toward unionism. That is, American employers have been so consistently hostile to unions because American workers have been so consistently conservative. In this view, there was and is nothing distinctive about American employers. Like employers everywhere, they seek to maximize profits; the only thing unusual about them are the constraints they are (or in this case are not) subject to. As Ulman said elsewhere, "It need not be assumed . . . that unorganized American employers are a breed apart from unionized employers either at home or abroad."[7] Here, however, Ulman veers too closely to the approach taken by neoclassical economics, which abstracts from national differences in employer characteristics and assumes that all are alike everywhere, maximizing subject to constraints. Instead, the argument can be made that, when it came to labor relations, American employers *were* (and are) different.

As David Granick pointed out in a comparative study of management in developed countries, economists are perplexed when told that managers do not behave similarly when facing similar constraints. After all, do not all managers act to maximize the present discounted worth of their companies? Perhaps they think that they do, says Granick, but even in an area that one would expect to be devoid of cultural influences, namely investment strategy, Granick found startling differences between French, British, and American companies in their approach to long-range investment decisions. These he attributed to national differences in managements' education, lawfulness with respect to taxation, attitudes toward risk, and career structures.[8] In light of the recent spate of books on Japanese management, it is hardly suprising that, when we move to a less bloodless realm of the firm, such as the employment relationship, studies have discovered significant cross-national differences in managements' work-related values. Hofstede, for example, found that American managers scored more highly than others on traits such as individualism and need for recognition.[9] And, as Bendix showed in his comparative study of managerial ideologies, individualism has had a strong hold on American managements since the turn of the century, despite the subsequent development of alternative ideologies stressing teamwork and cooperation. It seems reasonable to presume, although we do not know for certain, that a deep belief in the virtues of individualism and personal achievement made American managers less willing to accept collective bargaining and other goals of unionism than managers in other nations.[10]

Although individualism is shared to a varying extent by all social classes in the United States, American managers are outliers on this dimension, both nationally and internationally. Their extreme individualism and market orientation have roots in the nation's unique pattern of economic development. Before the New Deal, the United States had the weakest government in the Western world: it was relatively small, lacked cohesion as a result of the federal system, and exercised little or no directive power over the nation's economic and social development. This can be traced to the lack of feudalism and the corresponding absence of a strong monarchical state. Moreover, because its industrial revolution started at a relatively early date, the United States had less need for the kind of state-led "catch-up" industrialization that took place in continental Europe and Japan. Consequently, "for most of the history of capitalism, the large business corporation in the United States effectively enjoyed a monopoly of political and institutional power without parallel in the capitalist world."[11] Late nineteenth- and early twentieth-century American employers did not have to make alliances with other social groups— such as a landed gentry—to achieve their goals, and rarely had to share the levers of industrial power with "outsiders" like the government. Hence they developed an especially strong belief in the virtues of free enterprise and apotheosized themselves as self-made men.[12] Being unused to coexistence or cooperation with other groups, they reacted with particular vehemence when unions sought to jointly determine various aspects of corporate management. The link between antistatism and antiunionism can be seen in the doctrine of the "freedom to control"—the right of management to control every aspect of business—which employers at the turn of the century repeatedly invoked in opposition both to antitrust legislation and to collective bargaining.[13] The fact that American employers long enjoyed virtual freedom from state direction and regulation helps to explain the vehemence of their opposition to the New Deal reforms, in particular to the Wagner Act. Had industry not come to maturity before the state assumed a regulative role, it is likely that employers would have been less suspicious of, and less hostile to, the act. Or to put it another way, the fact that the government was partially responsible for the New Deal spurt in unionization only served to heighten employer hostility; that is, the association with government had the effect of further tainting unionism.

INCENTIVES AND RESOURCES

Thus, there is a case to be made that American managers had different values and preferences which led them to be more hostile to unionism than managers in other nations. Admittedly, however, this is a speculative argument. We lack historical and contemporary survey data that would allow us to compare managerial attitudes toward unions in different nations. But even if one rejects the cultural claim that American managers were different in kind, an argument can still be constructed along the lines suggested by Ulman: *American managers, although not innately more hostile to unions than other managers, have been considerably less constrained in expressing their hostility.* Ulman suggests a negative constraint—the absence of labor radicalism—as the key factor here. But there was far more to managerial antiunionism in the United States than that. As the preceding discussion of the state suggests, American employers were situated in a uniquely favorable political situation, drew on a different set of social values, and faced economic incentives to fight unions that went far beyond the absence of worker radicalism. That is, not only did American managers have greater *incentives* to be hostile, but they had available to them a wider range of political and ideological *resources* to effectuate that hostility. Even had American labor been more radical than it was, or as radical as Wilentz and others claim it to have been, it still would have had a much harder time achieving employer recognition than labor in other nations.

Economics

As textbooks on comparative industrial relations usually note, American unions are distinctive in several respects. First, their approach to collective bargaining is highly decentralized. Bargaining is typically centered on the individual enterprise and, although industrywide contracts exist, they are far less prevalent than single-firm agreements. In Europe, by contrast, industrywide bargaining is the norm, and many countries, including even Japan, have legislation providing for the automatic extension of contract terms to unorganized firms within the industry. Second, American unions are highly job conscious, in that they concern themselves with a variety of detailed aspects of working conditions at the plant level, ranging from incentive wages, dismissals, and layoffs to conditions in the employee lunchroom. Industry or national bargaining is unsuitable for these issues and does not usually deal with them, or they are preempted in other countries by government labor codes and regulations that are more extensive than those found in the United States. Third, union density levels in the United States are lower than those in other nations.

Taken together, these characteristics provide American employers with relatively strong economic incentives to resist unions. If organized, an employer is likely to have higher labor costs than those of numerous competing domestic firms that are unorganized. In other countries, this outcome is far less likely, due to higher density levels, industrywide bargaining, and contract extension. Should an American employer resist union demands, he faces the possibility of a strike that may cause his firm to lose market share relative to domestic competitors. This threat gives American unions a bargaining edge over their foreign counterparts, allowing them to penetrate more deeply into management's plant prerogatives; but that only heightens management's resolve to try and shed its labor unions. All these factors combined will lead unorganized American managers to resist unionization: it drives up relative labor costs, entails potential strike costs, and threatens the loss of managerial prerogatives. These resistance incentives are mitigated in situations of industrywide bargaining. But it is difficult to get American employers to form bargaining coalitions because of the great variation in the size of their firms, the existence of antitrust laws, the absence of facilitative arrangements like contract extension, and, since the 1930s, the legal requirement that recognition occur via firm-by-firm elections. That requirement heightens the degree of tension in the American industrial relations system by making recognition a perpetual source of contention. In Europe and even Japan, recognition is less of an issue, both because of extension and because of laws making recognition a relatively automatic process.[14]

Not only have American employers had greater incentives to resist unions, but they also have had greater economic resources to carry out antiunion campaigns. Although the size structure of American industry has not changed greatly since the 1920s, on average American firms and plants have been larger and more dispersed than their counterparts in most other industrial nations owing to the early development of mass production in the United States and the great size of the American market. With size went considerable financial resources to fight wars of attrition against unions as well as the option of relocating production from organized to unorganized establishments in other locations. Because European firms tended to be smaller, they were more likely to band together in employer associations to coordinate resistance and raise their bargaining power relative to the unions. Once associations were formed, any bargaining that took place had the effect of standardizing wages within the industry and stabilizing competition by removing labor costs as a competitive factor. As was noted, this reduced the incentive for employer resistance, both because of wage uniformity and because managerial prerogatives were less likely to be threatened by association bargaining. This is not to say that the European associations were timid or that similar conditions were absent from the American scene. As Daniel Ernst and Howell Harris show in their essays for this volume, American firms formed employer associations for bargaining purposes in industries such as coal, apparel, transportation, construction, and even metalworking. But the bulk of the American work force was employed by firms large enough to go it alone, *mano a mano*, in a fight to remain unorganized.[15]

In addition to size, there were other reasons that European employers were more likely than their American counterparts to form associations. Geographical propinquity and more concentrated industries served to reduce the transaction costs to European employers of forming associations. Also, being more dependent on exports, European firms had a common interest in ensuring that labor costs did not get out of line with world competitive levels, especially at firms that had less bargaining power or were protected from international competition.[16] Too, in some European countries, there was a tradition of employer coalition going back to the guild masters' associations, such as those found in Denmark.[17] Finally, industrial employers outside the United States were more conscious of their class interests because they had to struggle for political recognition against other organized interests that predated the rise of industry, including landed aristocracies, petty producers, and shopkeepers. Labor exceptionalists might add that this employer class consciousness was a reaction to threats from below that were less vague than in the United States, but the claim is icing on the causal cake.

Politics

As we have seen, the relationship between business and government in the United States was unlike that found in other countries, whose states played a more directive and decisive role in the modernization process. Because of this, and because they were less dominated by business interests than in the United States, foreign governments not only pushed their employers harder to accommodate to unions, but they did so far earlier than in the United States. Although employers in other countries were far from pleased when their governments sought to channel social conflict in this fashion, their objections were relatively muted because they were accustomed to the state intervening as a broker and coordinator for competing interests. Before World War I, Germany (a late developer) stood at one end of the interventionist pole and Great Britain (the first industrial nation) at the other. But even the British state became involved in industrial relations and took actions far more favorable to unions than was the case in America, from the 1894 Royal Commission that sanctioned collective bargaining to the 1906 Trade Disputes Act that restrained the courts. Sweden, a country not usually discussed in this regard, had a government that encouraged employers to avoid violence and to negotiate with unions during the critical labor confrontation of 1905, which resulted in a mediation law and in a compromise agreement under which employers agreed to recognize the right of organization.[18] Since World War II, all European governments have moved much farther in interventionist, corporatist directions than in the United States.[19] To get a better sense of the role of state intervention, it is worth having a brief look at French and German experiences during the prewar period.

In his article for this book and elsewhere, Gerald Friedman shows that in republican France between the 1870s and World War I (when French unionization rates were comparatively higher than today), the state was ubiquitous and heavily involved in economic development and regulation. Though French industry was not powerless, it had to compete for political favors with other economic groups, including shopkeepers, large landowners, peasants, and labor. Given the strength of the state apparatus, its partial dependence on labor support, and the failure of any single group to control it, the Third Republic could function with relative autonomy in labor affairs. Hence, "state officials rarely acted simply on the behest of employers in labor disputes; instead they were guided by their own interest in maintaining social harmony and restoring order."[20] This meant that the government took various steps favoring collective bargaining, including laws explicitly legalizing unions, government mediation of labor disputes, financial aid to the union *bourses,* and a preference for conciliation rather than repression of labor disputes. French employers were far from friendly to unions, but their hostility was tempered by an interventionist state which they were unable to control, a situation rather different from that in the United States. As a result,

> American workers had to fight bloodier political battles than the French for the right of unions to exist and function . . . the rail strikes of 1877, the pitched battle of Homestead, the Ludlow massacre were bloodier than Fourmies and Draveil and Villeneuve-Sainte-Georges. The 1919 steel strike was more brutally suppressed than the French general strike of 1920. "Bloody Harlan" had no rival in the coal country of France. France had nothing like the private armies, factory arsenals, and industrial espionage services exposed by the La Follette Committee.[21]

In Wilhelmine Germany, employers tended to be exceptionally autocratic in their treatment of labor. Yet with the exception of the Ruhr coal and steel magnates, German employers in the great mass of small and medium-sized firms and those in the large new electrochemical industries gradually came to "recognize the inevitability of unions and accepted the right to strike" in the two decades before World War I.[22] An important factor in this development was the German state, which proposed a series of laws—not all of them enacted—intended to give greater influence to employee interests at the workplace and in society. These included mandatory worker committee laws (1891, 1904, 1908), laws giving special legal status to collective agreements (1910), and other legislation that stopped just short of mandatory union recognition. The inspiration for this legislation came from an influential group of nationalist intellectuals belonging to the Verein für Sozialpolitik, who held key posts in the universities and in government. These moderate advocates of social reform sought to ensure that German's rapid transition to a world economic power would occur smoothly and with a minimum of social unrest. Taking a page out of a rival's book, men such as Lujo Brentano and Max Weber thought that collective bargaining along English lines would help in achieving that smooth transition.[23] Many employers took issue with state policy in this area, though others were willing to go along, in part because of a tradition of respect for governmental and academic authority. With the onset of World War I, the patriotic stance of the unions led to the passage of a variety of laws encouraging union recognition. Again it was state authority—this time the military's—that "did much to erode employer resistance to recognition of the unions," even before the Stinnes-Legien agreement of 1918.[24]

To get a sense of how different this was from the situation in the United States, imagine that in 1900 or 1910 the federal government had owned or directed parts of heavy industry; rejected laissez-faire and promoted oligopolies; counseled employer restraint; hired John R. Commons and his associates to write national labor legislation; and did all this with the cooperation or grudging acceptance of employers. Indeed, that is hard to imagine. Although there were incidents in which the U.S. government took positive steps to shape the industrial relations system, these were limited either to key industries —principally the railroads (the Erdman and Railway Labor Acts of 1898 and 1926) and coal (the Anthracite Strike Commission of 1903) —or to temporary measures taken during the first World War. Not until the 1930s did the American government go so far as the British in muzzling the courts and giving official approval to collective bargaining. In fact, what made the United States notable was not only its lack of positive industrial relations policy but its willingness to stand to one side during violent labor disputes or to put the state's repressive apparatus at the disposal of employers. The German state was willing to use force against strikers, but by and large it restrained itself as well as German employers, and this goes a long way to explaining why, "in prewar America, management's struggle against organized labor was accompanied by greater turbulence and violence ... than in the Ruhr."[25]

According to Taft and Ross, the United States "has had the bloodiest and most violent labor history of any industrial nation in the world."[26] Although Taft and Ross presented little supporting evidence, other scholars have affirmed their judgement in comparisons between the United States on the one hand and England, Canada, Germany, and France on the other.[27] Some have attributed this high degree of violence to a strain of aggression in the national character, or to ethnic and racial cleavages in the labor force that made it easier for American employers to recruit strikebreakers—a tactic that often touched off violence.[28] But industrial violence can be traced more directly to an exceptionally high degree of employer resistance to unionism combined with the weakness of government authorities and their willingness to sanction and support employer resistance through force.

American employers had considerable resources of their own to wage battles against unions—including company guards and railway police, armed men supplied by agencies like Pinkerton, and arsenals of the sort described in the La Follette hearings. Nothing of this magnitude existed in Europe, where central governments restricted the use of repression to their own regular forces.[29] But not only did the American government allow the private use of force by employers (several states had laws specifically permitting the deputization of privately paid police); it also regularly provided direct assistance to employers during labor disputes, and did so to a much greater extent than in Europe. This assistance came in different forms, including local police and county sheriff's deputies, state militias (later known as the National Guard), and, on special occasions, the regular national army. There are no aggregate data on the use of local police in labor disputes, although this was the most common form of repression. But we do know that the state militias, which were reactivated after the Civil War primarily to police labor disputes, were on active duty in at least 150 labor disputes between 1877 and 1900, and in an equally large number between 1900 and 1935. Though federal troops less commonly intervened, they participated in the suppression of several critical strikes, including the 1877 railroad strike (the first nationwide strike) and two major pre-1933 attempts to form industrial unions— at Pullman in 1894 and in the steel strike of 1919.[30]

Why was state power so often used in support of employer resistance to unionism? The first place to look is to the peculiar dispersion of power that obtained under the federal system: each city, county, and state had its own police forces. Disputes often were local affairs, and local employers had an easier time swaying state and local units to act on their behalf than did European employers confronted with a more independent and distant state. Not only did this dispersion favor the employer; it also weakened and fragmented the labor movement.[31] Second, one must not forget the important role played by an independent judiciary with its "constitutional supremacy over labor legislation."[32] In the absence of a state willing to formulate definitive public policy for industrial relations, the task fell by default to the courts, which were exceedingly hostile to unionism—as evidenced by a steady stream of decisions enjoining strikes, boycotts, and picketing; a refusal to enforce collective bargaining agreements; and findings of unconstitutionality on what little substantive law the states developed to regulate industrial relations and inhibit violence, such as statutes banning yellow-dog contracts and blacklisting. Though the courts never touched the only other substantive form of public policy —the various state laws providing for public mediation and conciliation services—they had no need to, as "these laws were of no consequence."[33]

Finally, what underlay these factors was the unusually high degree of political power enjoyed by American employers. There was no landed aristocracy or military or monarchical traditions of a strong, relatively autonomous central state. After the Civil War growth was so rapid that large firms quickly came to dominate the economic landscape, and as a result, "American business really confronted no effective economic or political competitors to its expansion or prestige."[34] This was in sharp contrast to the situation in France, Sweden, Germany, or England, where employers were unable to control a relatively autonomous, multiparty state. Although there were notable instances in America in which local, state, and even federal governments favored labor's interests—as during World War I or in the coal, railroad, and blacklisting cases previously mentioned—these were exceptions that proved the exceptional political power of American business. That power held in check the federal government's interventionist tendencies, and that, in turn, bolstered the courts' authority and the dispersion of political power.

Ideology

It is worthwhile noting the prevalence in American culture of particular values and norms that employers have found useful in mobilizing public opinion against unions, and not just the opinions of respectable society but of the working class as well. As Lipset has noted, these values—equality, individualism, achievement—can be traced to the fact that industrial capitalism emerged in the United States without having to confront the rigid status system of a feudal and aristocratic past.[35] Lipset's intent was to show how these values were responsible for some distinctive features of American unions, such as their bureaucratism and militance. But cultural norms are fluid, and can serve as ideological resources for a variety of purposes and groups. Although problematic in some respects—deference to superiors does not mesh well with it—America's dominant value system gave American employers a comparative ideological advantage in their fight with unions.

Take individualism, for example. Since the nineteenth century, American employers have argued that unions act to suppress individual rights, either by being undemocratic—members have to obey the orders of union bosses—or by being excessively democratic—dissenters must submit to the will of an occasionally reckless majority. Employers also attacked unions with arguments borrowed from classical (and today neoclassical) economics: unions were held to be harmful monopolies whose actions, such as trying to push wages up faster than productivity warranted, violated the market's natural laws. Because it was based on invidualism, classical economics appealed to Americans more than alternative philosophies that legitimated capitalism, such as European corporatism's emphasis on the economic and social functions of various estates, a theory congenial to unionism.[36]

Related to individualism is the American ethos of achievement—the "bitch goddess of success"—or as Lipset defined it, "the belief that everyone should try to be a 'success' regardless of background."[37] The stress on achievement explains why American culture has proven to be such a fertile spawning ground for gospels of self-improvement, for consumerism and conspicuous consumption, and for tales about striving entrepreneurs and rags-to-riches tycoons. The popularity of these tales suggests that even if they do not personally identify with the successful businessman, a sizable portion of the population continues to dream that they will someday have their own businesses or at least that their children will.[38] These visions breed public sympathy for managers who argue that no one should be allowed to interfere with their right to control, especially if managers base that right on hard work and "sweat equity" (as opposed to authority naturally flowing from property rights). It is important to remember, however, that the achievement ethos is fluid, and can be supportive of unionism as well as other forms of collective advancement (such as the cooperative visions of the Knights of Labor). Thus, employers can not take public support for granted but instead must constantly prove that they can do a better job of making people's dreams come true than can unions or government.

For this reason, the issue of relative living standards has always been of more than academic interest. Surprisingly, despite its importance, only recently have careful studies been developed that compare relative living standards and mobility rates in prewar America to those of other nations. The studies are somewhat ambiguous, showing, for example, that unskilled workers in the United States in the 1910s were no better off, and possibly worse off, than unskilled workers in England; that skilled workers in the United States were definitely better off; and that social mobility rates were roughly the same as those found in Europe.[39] Thus it is a measure of the persuasive power of what Lipset and Bendix term "ideological equalitarianism" that, despite the fact that hard data were unobtainable for many years and even now are inconclusive, public and academic opinion was nevertheless convinced that America was the land of high wages and upward social mobility. (Sombart referred to "reefs of roastbeef" that supposedly had beached American socialism.) Given this conviction, it was possible for employers to construct a growth coalition around the idea that business was a goose whose golden eggs would be laid only if the goose was left to labor undisturbed. So long as the country was prosperous and an achievement-oriented public was convinced that America was *the* land of opportunity, employers could find support for the argument that unionism or government intervention would kill the goose. Hence, when the Great Depression hit, the results were all the more devastating for American business. In this light, it is understandable that American unions and their supporters were attracted during the 1930s to an underconsumptionist explanation for the depression (the goose had been too stingy, and hereafter egg-laying could not be trusted to Mother Nature). The remedy, as the preamble to the Wagner Act spelled out, was to encourage unionism in order to boost purchasing power and prevent future catastrophes from occurring.[40]

PROOF IN THE ENGLISH PUDDING

The argument thus far has been that the weakness of unionism in the United States can be traced to employer, rather than labor, exceptionalism: American employers were more hostile to unions than other employers primarily because they had greater incentives and resources to be hostile, not merely because they faced less radical workers and unions. A final proof comes from a comparison of American and British experience: despite the similarity of British and American unions—both were politically moderate and emphasized job control—British employers, by and large, accepted collective bargaining. They were "passive in their relations with the unions, less aggressive individually than American employers [and] less willing to combine for defence and attack than employers in both continents."[41] Surely, then, one has to seek other explanations for British passivity and American hostility—polar opposites—than the common absence of radical unionism.

Like American unions, British unions were craft-oriented and sought to preserve the status of their highly skilled members through restrictive methods of job and labor market control, and through bargaining with employers. The New Unionism of the 1890s forced them to become less exclusive and admit relatively unskilled members. But this did not greatly radicalize British unions or change their basic approach (much like the American experience of the 1930s). The emphasis on the point of production and the absence of a strong political orientation in both labor movements is evident from comparative strike statistics. Britain and the United States have similar strike patterns that changed little over the course of the twentieth century—moderate frequency, size, and duration (although U.S. strikes are longer)—in contrast to continental Europe, where strikes are frequent, large, and brief, especially after the 1930s.[42]

Although British unions were more explicitly socialist than their American counterparts, theirs was a more moderate, less revolutionary brand of socialism than was found in the rest of Europe. With its roots in dissenting Methodism and similar traditions, British socialism was prone to alliances with sympathetic middle-class supporters like the Fabians, and to reformism. As one observer noted in 1871, "Average English workmen are not so political as continental workmen are. They have not the type of mind for which theoretical or philosophical politics have fascination" and seek to improve their position "by strikes and the strengthening of trade unions—and not by the establishment of entirely new social systems."[43] Though British labor *did* manage to establish its own political party, in stark contrast to the Americans, Labour can hardly be said to have constituted a serious threat to British capital.

Thus, given the great similarity between the American and British labor movements, one might have expected British employers to be quite hostile to unions. There was no need, as on the continent, to buy British workers out of their revolutionary militancy by proffering bargaining because British workers had little to sell. And, indeed, British employers did sometimes attack unions with American-style methods such as strikebreakers (blacklegs), lockouts, and the like, particularly between the 1890s and World War I when British industry began to encounter intensified competition in world markets.[44] Yet the employers who engaged in these activities were "few and unrepresentative" and less willing to use "American-style . . . unrestrained brutality and lawlessness."[45] As compared to the Americans, most British employers were considerably friendlier to organized labor and to collective bargaining. Arthur Shadwell, who in 1906 conducted a comparative social analysis of Britain, the United States, and Germany, said, "Nothing has struck me more in the course of this investigation than the remarkable difference of attitude displayed, in private, by employers in this country [Britain] and in the others." Not a word in favor of unions had been expressed by any American employer, whereas in Britain, he found employers who gave "fair and even friendly expressions of opinion."[46]

How are we to account for this? One could argue that, although British unions were not especially radical, they were far better organized, had wider support, and were more militant than those found in the United States. Hence, British employers may have been reluctant to adopt American-style tactics because they thought that the cost of dislodging the unions far exceeded any benefits to be gained from doing so. That is, British employers were hampered by Britain's early industrial and trade union development. By the time British employers realized the true costs of unionism, it was too late to develop alternatives; the unions had become too entrenched to dislodge. In the United States, however, employers could see the handwriting on the wall, and so took offensive action before matters went as far as they had in Britain.[47] Though plausible, this "late development" thesis has two problems. First, it is incorrect to suggest that British employers awoke to the dangers of unionism only at the end of the nineteenth century. Repression of trade unions took place after the passage of the Combination Acts of 1799–1800, and this was followed by sporadic employer attacks throughout the century, as in the lockouts of the 1850s. Moreover, in the wake of the Taff-Vale decision, when labor was vulnerable and employers had a chance to inflict major damage, most of them chose not to, but there were some who tried. Thus, British employers had numerous opportunities to repress unionism when it was vincible, but rarely did they seize the antiunion initiative in any concerted or sustained fashion. Second, there is the case of the steel industry. In the 1890s, both the American and the British steel industries were moderately well organized. But by 1914, the American industry had gone open shop, while in Britain the trend was in precisely the opposite direction. Attempts to explain this divergence in terms of American labor's relative immaturity or weakness fail to stand scrutiny: the Amalgamated Association of Iron, Steel, and Tin Workers in the 1890s was in some respects stronger than its British counterparts, and unions in both nations had to deal with divisive jurisdictional and ethnic disputes. The key difference was that "British employers were more willing to tolerate the existence of unions in their mills than their American counterparts."[48] And, I would argue, this tolerance was the mirror image of American hostility, being the result of British managers' having different values and relatively scarce economic and political resources with which to fight unions.

Values

A long-standing debate in the economic history literature concerns the relative efficiency of British managers, in particular, their responsibility for slow British growth at the end of the nineteenth century and again in recent years.[49] Two reasons are usually offered to support the claim of poor British managerial performance. First, as compared with the United States, entrepreneurship in Britain was not considered to be a prestigious career for an educated young person (and still is not), so that those attracted to business were neither the brightest nor the best.[50] Second, although the landed gentry disdained rank commercialism, they were willing to admit successful entrepreneurs into the upper classes if they had the proper attitudes. And rather than rejecting the offer, British businessmen seemed eager to prove that they were not mere moneygrubbers and to be accepted into high society. With the alacrity of *nouveaux* they took on such gentry values as the pursuit of leisure and a paternalistic noblesse oblige toward their employees, including tolerance toward unions and avoidance of conflict. Thus, "Under American egalitarianism the hard bargaining came about naturally between the parties negotiating a contract," whereas in Britain "there was dissonance between haggling and what were felt to be the proper relations of mutual support and respect between ranks."[51]

Economics

In several key respects, British employers lacked economic incentives and resources that drove their American counterparts to fight, and fight effectively, against unions. First, the district structure of British trade unionism led, in the earliest days of collective bargaining, to multiemployer agreements that standardized wage rates in what were then predominantly local labor and product markets. As national unions and national markets emerged, bargaining continued on a multiemployer basis and, when combined with relatively high union densities, this produced a uniformity of labor costs that removed the incentive for any single firm to go it alone and resist unionization. Reinforcing the tendency toward multiemployer bargaining in Britain were legislative developments such as the formation of joint industrial councils during World War I, and, more important, the structure of British manufacturing industries. British industry was characterized by relatively small firms that specialized in a single aspect of the production process; as a result, there were lower concentration ratios and less mass production than in the United States. Thus in Britain, with its "small-scale, competitive industries," company-level bargaining was less feasible than in the United States because "tolerance of cost differentials for even limited periods of time is very narrow [and] multi-employer bargaining is required."[52] Not only did Britain's smaller, often family-owned, firms have fewer financial resources to resist unionism, but they had fewer managerial resources to develop sophisticated programs for employee welfare and personnel management, which were of considerable importance in giving American companies a carrot to extend to their unorganized employees that augmented the stick of antiunionism[53] Family ownership too contributed to the lack of innovation in the personnel sphere, leaving managers "content to follow the settled ways of management handed down to them, and these left undisturbed the no less traditional practices of the trade unions."[54]

Politics

Although Britain resembled the United States in having a government that was reluctant to become involved in substantive direction of the economy and a judiciary that was exceedingly hostile to unionism, British employers received far less government support whenever they sought to use the state's repressive apparatus in disputes with organized labor. The government's reluctance to become involved in these disputes can be traced to the prior existence of feudalism in Britain, which created a more complex political structure than existed in the United States and made it harder for employers to achieve political hegemony. For much of the nineteenth century, Britain was ruled by its gentry, who, though not fond of unionism, were also disinclined to sanction state coercion simply for the purpose of furthering the employers' private gain. These landowners often had "little sympathy with the labour problems of manufacturers—and often a certain waspish impatience with examples of their shortsighed greed or stupidity when these threatened public peace and the social order."[55] As a result, at a relatively early date the British state began to apply pressure on its employers to eschew violence and to recognize unions and bargain with them, long before the emergence of Labour. No explicit laws defined how this was to take place, but the reports of the various royal commissions and the government's own arbitration activities sent a message to employers that tolerance and stability were preferable to hostility and open conflict.[56] As compared to American management in its reaction to the Wagner Act, British employers were more receptive to their government's message because of the respect accorded to a monarchical state and because, from the very beginning, necessity had forced them to get along with other powerful groups—including the gentry and the crown—whose interests were different from their own.

LABOR AND EMPLOYER EXCEPTIONALISM

An exceptionally high degree of employer hostility has had several important consequences for unionism in the United States. First, it was (and still is) a key factor behind the nation's low union density rates and the slow, erratic growth of its unions. Given that union recognition occurred through contests of strength with individual employers, unions often lost these contests except during unusual periods—wars and the New Deal era—when a normally reluctant federal government stepped in to lend its support by endorsing collective bargaining and by restraining repressive tactics.[57]

A second consequence of employer antiunionism was the absence in the United States of a sizable radical labor movement. Although labor exceptionalists attribute this to various unique characteristics of the American working class, not nearly enough weight has been given to the effects of repression, either carried out by employers acting on their own or, more commonly, by employers in concert with government forces. Each time that a radical labor organization emerged and began to gather strength—the American Railway Union, the Wobblies, the Western Federation of Miners—it was cut short by a potent combination of private and governmental repression. One student of the subject concludes that political repression "proved a major hindrance to the labor movement as a whole, but it was especially concentrated and consistent, and had especially pernicious effects, with regard to the most radical elements of the labor movement."[58] Of course, repression of radical labor was hardly unique to America. In other nations too, employers and governments worked together to undermine the most radical elements in their labor movements, and sometimes did so with explicit statutory authority, as under Bismarck's anti-socialist laws. But for reasons already noted—including an independent and antiunion judiciary, the dispersion of police forces, and the government's willingness to put those forces at the employer's service—repression was particularly effective in the United States. Some labor exceptionalists recognize the importance of repression but argue that it was more effective in the United States than in Europe because workers lacked strong class loyalties and so were easily scared away from radical labor movements by a minimal amount of coercion.[59] But that explanation seems implausible on several grounds: first, recent research shows that even today, social class remains an important source of emotional and cognitive identification in the United States, although the expression of class has not carried over to politics as much as it has in Europe; and second, that argument fails to consider that labor may have eschewed radicalism not as a result of weak class loyalties but instead because of a strategic calculation of how best to overcome the formidable obstacles that it faced.[60]

During the 1880s and 1890s when the AFL was forming, the leaders of the organization witnessed the disastrous consequences of radical unionism and mass strikes. The strikes of the 1870s and 1880s were followed by severe repression, as occurred at Haymarket in 1886 and subsequently at Coeur d'Alene and Pullman. About the latter, Perlman and Taft said, "the labor movement saw how the courts, the Federal executive, and the ruling forces in the country could be counted on to act as one in crushing any real or fancied industrial rebellion."[61]

There is little doubt that this repression played an important role in the evolution of the AFL's political and organizing strategies. During the 1870s and 1880s, Samuel Gompers had followed Marxist thinking on many issues, although he differed from most socialists in eschewing political action and instead emphasizing the organization of trade unions as the first step on the road to social transformation. But by the 1890s, Gompers had become wary of ultimate ends and increasingly saw trade unionism as an end in itself. Recalling how the police brutally broke up the Tompkins Square labor demonstrations, Gompers wrote in his autobiography that this taught him how "radicalism and sensationalism" inevitably led to repression that "nullified in advance normal, necessary activity" by the labor movement.[62] To achieve even the limited goals of trade unionism, Gompers thought that labor would have to make itself respectable—garnering the support of a middle class anxious for order and not giving employers or government a justification for repressing labor's activities. Out of this came the hyper-patriotism of the AFL, its distrust of government, its emphasis on pragmatism, and its attempt to find support from groups like the National Civic Federation in the 1910s and the American Legion in the 1920s. From the repression of radical labor and from their own repeated encounters with aggressively hostile employers,

> the leaders of the AFL concluded that under no circumstances could labor afford to arouse the fears of the public for the safety of private property as a basic institution. Labor needed the support of public opinion, meaning the middle classes both rural and urban, in order to make headway with its program of curtailing the abuses which attend the employer's unrestricted exercise of his property rights.[63]

The AFL made a strategic choice to adopt not only a philosophy but also an organizational form that would give it the greatest chance of making headway in an unfriendly environment. Job-control unionism combined an acceptable, achievement-oriented economism with a disciplined fighting organization capable of winning strikes. Recognizing that even respectability and conservatism would not win over hostile employers, the AFL unions attached great importance to the collection of dues, the administration of strike funds, and a quasimilitary, hierarchical structure that put control in the hands of a seasoned group of professional union officers. Because the government could not be relied upon to aid labor, the AFL made a virtue out of necessity and called it voluntarism. In later years organized labor was more willing to rely on government assistance, possibly unaware of the full costs of doing so, but nevertheless cognizant of the benefits of having at least a passive, and often an active, ally.[64]

But there is an ironic paradox here: although employer hostility led American labor leaders to choose a conservative form of unionism (or at least reassured them that they had made the right choice), that choice had the effect of sustaining and reinforcing employer opposition. First, as we have discussed, because job-control unionism involved an emphasis on issues that management considered sacrosanct, it raised the incentive for American employers to resist unions whenever they came knocking. Second—and here we come back to Ulman's argument—labor's choice closed off the European option of getting employers to accept collective bargaining as an alternative to more radical outcomes, although the AFL did regularly try to sell itself to employers by invidious comparisons with groups like the IWW and, later, the CIO. (Undoubtedly some employers recognized the AFL during World War I and in the 1930s because they believed that this would close any openings for the left.) Thus, a sort of feedback loop was created—the adversarial American system—in which employer hostility and conservative job-control unionism sustained one another.

Compare this to the British system, where the courts were essentially neutralized by 1906, the state was far friendlier to unionism, and employers were less aggressively hostile than in the United States. In light of these conditions, one could say that British labor had the *luxury* of combining job-control unionism with the pursuit of social democratic political objectives, notably the formation of the Labour party, a luxury that was unavailable to American labor at least until the New Deal. The British comparison is instructive in another regard, for it suggests that even if similar conditions had obtained in the United States before the 1930s, it is unlikely that the outcome would have been a radical labor movement such as emerged in, say, France. That is, although an important factor permitting the emergence of a radical, politically oriented union movement in France but not in the United States was the existence of a relatively pro-labor French state,[65] this did not mean that, if the American government had been friendlier to labor, the result would have been a flourishing of radical unionism in America. American labor's political reformism and job-control unionism were due not only to hostility from the state and from employers but also to a common Anglo-American tradition of strong craft unionism that existed well before the emergence of syndicalism and Marxian socialism in the 1870s. Craft unionism— with its sectional approach to labor market control and its sober, almost middle-class strain toward respectability—weakened work- ing-class unity and drained some of the appeal from a mass revolu- tionary politics. In other words, had the political and social environ- ment been less hostile to organized labor in the United States, the result would very likely have been something along British, rather than French, lines. In fact, that is what emerged, more or less, during the New Deal, when American labor hitched itself to the Democratic wagon in pursuit of ends similar to those achieved by the Labour party. But the resemblance to Britain went no further; because Amer- ican employers persisted in their antiunionism, American labor never attained the density levels found in Britain.

SINCE THE WAGNER ACT

One might ask, if American employers were so hostile to unions, how was organized labor able to achieve enormous membership increases during the 1930s and World War II? One way to approach this prob- lem is to compare France and the United States during this period. Before the 1930s, the labor movements in both countries faced ex- tremely hostile employers; and then, at about the same time, both countries experienced a wave of spontaneous strikes (including mas- sive sitdowns in France in 1936) followed by the enactment of legisla- tion favorable to union organization and collective bargaining. In the United States, the key legislation was the 1935 Wagner Act; in France, corresponding laws were passed in 1936, shortly after the Popular Front government was formed under Leon Blum. These laws, which were known as the "French New Deal," codified the Matignon Agree- ment that had been reached between the employers' federation and the Confederation generale du travail (CGT). They required compul- sory mediation and the negotiation of collective agreements between employers and the "most representative union" in a given bargaining area (note the influence of the Wagner Act). Each agreement was to contain guarantees of the freedom to organize without discrimination and of the right of workers to elect shop stewards. Prodded by the Ministry of Labor, French employers' associations (and some individ- ual employers) reluctantly negotiated over 8,000 collective agree- ments between 1936 and 1939, and the CGT's membership increased during this period from about one million to perhaps as many five million workers (as compared to a threefold increase in American union membership between 1933 and 1940). Yet collective bargaining was unable to establish itself in France at this time—employers often refused to abide by the terms of the new agreements and publicly repudiated the Matignon Agreement. However, in the United States, despite continuing employer hostility to unions and to the Wagner Act, collective bargaining took root, if not by 1940 then certainly by the end of the war.[66]

A number of factors contributed to the failure of the Blum experiments. First, as compared to the United States, in France the depression came on only gradually—reaching its trough in 1935—and so French employers had more time to prepare themselves for the developments that took American employers by surprise. Second, given the French government's long history of active involvement in industrial relations, French employers were better organized to negotiate and deal with the government and with other peak associations than were American employers, who did not form effective lobbying organizations until World War II.[67] Third, the Wagner Act was much more compatible with American unionism's bargaining traditions than were the Matignon reforms with French labor. The unions in France were as oriented to politics as French employers, a fact that helped them to win the reforms. But they were far less experienced than American unions in collective bargaining and in using workplace action to enforce their bargains when the government would not. Thus, a fourth and critical difference between France and the United States was the weakness and short life of the Popular Front. Although the Blum government was more pro-labor than the Roosevelt administration, it collapsed in 1938, leaving the unions to fend for themselves. In contrast, the Roosevelt administration was credited with saving the country from depression. Hence it grew more popular and powerful over time and was able to have the Wagner Act ratified by the Supreme Court in 1937. Finally, of course, France was occupied in 1940, before it had much of a chance to mobilize against the Germans. In the United States employer resistance to unionization continued right up until 1941 at major firms such as Ford, Westinghouse, and those of Little Steel, but war and the formation of the War Labor Board eradicated most pockets of employer belligerence. In short, the success of unionism in America depended on a variety of fortuitous circumstances: the timing and severity of the depression; the solidity of the Roosevelt administration; the passage of a bargaining law consistent with native traditions; and the advent of war without any threat to the country's territorial integrity. Their combined effect was to shrink (albeit temporarily) the ideological and political resources traditionally available to employers and to raise those available to unions. Had none of these events happened or had the timing been different, union density in the United States would have been much lower, perhaps as low in 1945 as it was in 1929.[68]

Finally, why was it that, despite the gains made between 1933 and 1945, American unions were unable to maintain the membership trajectory established during those years? Union density in the American private sector never reached European levels and moved steadily downward after the mid-1950s. Here again, I would stress the importance of employer hostility to unionism, a factor that industrial relations scholars underemphasized until quite recently. Most believed that the American industrial relations system was, or was becoming, pluralistic, with employers accepting unions as a legitimate pressure group engaged in joint rule making on behalf of employees, and government stepping in to rectify any imbalances.[69] Yet pluralism can hardly be said to have had wide acceptance in managerial circles. Instead, as observers began to warn in the late 1950s, most managers, including those within the heavily unionized core manufacturing industries, had an overwhelmingly conservative opinion of unions and adopted a seemingly flexible stance merely as a strategy. Were a more nuanced and extensive appraisal to be made, it would find pluralism a prescriptive norm urged upon managers by government officials and academics (as in the case studies published by the National Planning Association in the late 1940s and early 1950s)—not a widely accepted tenet of managerial belief.[70]

The onset of unionization in the 1930s came as a surprise to managers who thought that they had resolved the problem of unions in the 1920s. Managers of newly unionized companies suffered "an unparalleled loss of self-esteem and community standing," while other employers struggled to stave off unionization and to find an effective formula for maintaining their nonunion status.[71] A bellicose minority of the newly unionized firms intensified their application of the earlier nonunion model, hoping that it would shake loose what they mistakenly believed to be the tenuous hold that unionism had taken on their employees. They launched new company unions or breathed life into those that had become dormant; strengthened their personnel departments; devoted more resources to welfare programs; and tried to coerce their employees to stay out of unions through a range of what the Wagner Act held to be unlawful practices. Other firms—in fact, the vast majority—did many of these same things, although they eventually gave up on coercion in favor of building a modus vivendi with their new bargaining partners. Among these were companies such as General Motors, General Electric, and U.S. Steel, whose managers saw unions as an unpleasant new fact of life and strove to turn the situation as much to their benefit as possible. It was these companies that received the most attention from academic observers, few of whom, however, realized the weakness of the companies' commitment to collective bargaining. By the late 1940s, managements in these companies had regained some of their self-confidence and begun to take more aggressive steps to contain union inroads. The successful effort to pass the Taft-Hartley bill was one manifestation of this turnabout; others included the gradual relocation of plants to southern states (which major companies like General Electric and DuPont started to do immediately after the war) and the introduction of a new set of personnel policies intended to weaken the popularity of unions.

These polices were buttressed with two major props. First, there was the wider scope for employer antiunionism permitted under the Taft-Hartley Act, such as aggressive campaign tactics that fell under the act's "free speech provision" and the new decertification mechanism. Although the government's support for collective bargaining during the 1930s and World War II put a great deal of pressure on recalcitrant employers—one should not underestimate the importance of the Wagner Act, the National Labor Relations Board and the War Labor Board in opening a window of opportunity for unionism—nevertheless, as compared to policies of other countries, this support had critical limits and turned out to be short lived. The Wagner Act did not provide for mandatory recognition of unions, instead leaving this issue to be decided by "campaigns" for worker votes between individual companies and unions. Toward the end of the war, the government's previously pro-labor orientation began to shift in favor of business, as evidenced by the recomposition of the NLRB and a tilt in the board's decisions on critical issues such as free speech and company unions.[72]

Second, there was the gradual dissemination throughout industry of antiunion strategies that had been developed by companies which successfully avoided unionization after 1933, including sophisticated communications and survey techniques based on behavioral science; programs for employee participation in management; and campaign tactics based on clever transgressions of the law.[73] As well, there was a parallel development of tactics used by unionized companies to contain, weaken, and ultimately shed their unions, such as General Electric's practice of Boulwarism.[74] More was involved in this process than the diffusion of personnel "innovations." Because of the American emphasis on an achievement-oriented unionism, which promised to deliver the goods to members through job-control bargaining at the firm level, American unions had always been more innovative and insisted on a much wider range of issues subject to joint determination than was the case in Europe. But this strength on the union side was matched by active, sophisticated personnel management on the other: by the 1930s, most large American firms had sizable personnel departments. As these departments recovered from the shock of the New Deal, they proved a source of difficulty for unions in the competition for the hearts, minds, and loyalty of American workers.[75] Non-union firms increasingly were able to incorporate union gains—both financial and nonfinancial—into their personnel policies (called "threat effects" or "union substitution" by economists), while at the same time developing innovations of their own that allowed them to move ahead of the unions. In unionized firms, managers gradually turned their attention from the tasks of contract negotiation and administration to the incorporation of nonunion innovations into their own personnel programs. Only now are American unions beginning to appreciate how far behind they have fallen, although it is probably fair to say that both unions and personnel managers in the United States, at least until recently, were of necessity more technically sophisticated about plant-level personnel policies than their European counterparts, whereas the reverse was true in the arena of national social welfare and labor market policies.

CONCLUSIONS

Distinctive features of American unionism—its conservatism, job orientation, and low density—cannot be understood without taking into account national differences in management characteristics and policies. It is likely that American employers had values that predisposed them to be more hostile to collective bargaining than were European employers. But putting these contentious cultural issues to one side, it is still the case that American employers faced a different set of incentives and had more substantial resources to resist unionization than was true of employers elsewhere. These included economic and political factors not usually considered in either mainstream or Marxist analyses, such as the size and structure of firms and the state's role in the industrial relations system, which was more variable and complex than instrumental theories would have it. Through a comparative and historical analysis of American management, we can begin to piece together a more realistic picture of the features of American unions and of the unionization process itself.

This essay has been deliberately critical of the literature on labor exceptionalism. But this is not to deny that American working-class life had exceptional features—and still does—that colored organized labor in distinctive tones. The stress on management is not intended to substitute one set of causal factors for another but instead to broaden the range of relationships usually considered in this area. Too, because the essay was sketched with a broad brush, it did not discuss variations in employer antiunionism across industries or at particular firms. Of course, one can find cases of American managers welcoming unions for economic reasons—either as a stabilizing force in highly competitive industries such as apparel and coal, or as a prop to oligopolistic pricing practices in industries such as steel—and for normative reasons too (although pro-union managers such as Joe Wilson of Xerox or Cyrus Ching of U.S. Rubber were rare birds indeed).

Finally, a body of empirical scholarship is developing that measures the importance of employer resistance to unionism as a factor in the recent acceleration of labor's decline in the United States. Studies have shown that the union success rate in NLRB elections is significantly reduced by legal and illegal employer tactics such as communication programs, dilatory legal maneuvering, firings, threats, and the use of professional consultants.[76] Rather than being a new development, these tactics are consistent with what has been the historic tendency in the United States—for employers to resist and avoid unions whenever possible. The government opened up a window for unionism in the 1930s and 1940s, making it more difficult for employers to actualize their hostility, but the perceived legitimacy of the Wagner Act has gradually been fading and with that has come an increase in illegal employer resistance. At the same time, managements have become more skilled in providing workers with a positive, legal alternative to unionism. The outlook for organized labor in the United States is not bright. But American unions have always been creatively responsive to management actions, and they still may come up with a successful formula for arresting their decline.

Notes

■

MASTERS TO MANAGERS: AN INTRODUCTION

1. Comparative studies of the employer's role in contemporary industrial relations include H. A. Clegg, *Trade Unionism Under Collective Bargaining: A Theory Based on Comparisons of Six Countries* (Oxford, 1976); John P. Windmuller and Alan Gladstone, *Employers Associations and Industrial Relations: A Comparative Study* (Oxford, 1984); and Keith Sisson, *The Management of Collective Bargaining: An International Comparison* (Oxford, 1987). Various collections are available, including Richard Hyman and Wolfgang Streeck, eds., *New Technology and Industrial Relations* (Oxford, 1988); and Keith Thurley and Stephen Wood, eds., *Industrial Relations and Management Strategy* (Cambridge, Eng., 1983). For historical studies of European and Japanese employers, see Howard F. Gospel and Craig R. Littler, eds., *Managerial Strategies and Industrial Relations* (London, 1983); and Alastair Reid, Steven Tolliday, and Jonathan Zeitlin, eds., *Employment Strategies, Enterprise Management, and Industrial Relations: Britain in Comparative Perspective* (forthcoming).

2. Eric H. Monkonnen, "The Dangers of Synthesis," *American Historical Review* (December 1986), 91:1146–57.

3. In labor history, "old" refers to the approach developed early in this century at Johns Hopkins and at Wisconsin by Jacob Hollander, John Commons, and their students. As in the new business history pioneered in the 1960s by Alfred D. Chandler, the focus is on institutions—either unions or large corporations—and there is considerable concern with building or making use of social scientific concepts and theory. The new labor history, also a product of the 1960s, is "history from the bottom up," with a focus on the daily lives and concerns of working people and a tendency to eschew theoretically driven analysis in favor of "rich" description. A similar tendency existed in the old business history. The pioneering works of Richard Ehrenberg, Edwin F. Gay, and Arthur H. Cole rejected theory and aggregation in favor of micro-level case studies of firms and their managers. See David Brody, "The Old Labor History and the New: In Search of the American Working Class," *Labor History* (Winter 1979), 20:111–26; Sanford M. Jacoby, "Intellectual Foundations of Industrial Relations" (UCLA Institute of Industrial Relations working paper, November 1988).

201

4. Examples of the Harvard case studies include N. S. B. Gras, *The Massachusetts First National Bank of Boston, 1784–1934* (Cambridge, Mass., 1937); Ralph M. Howard, *History of Macy's of New York, 1858–1919* (Cambridge, Mass., 1943); and Evelyn H. Knowlton, *Pepperell's Progress: History of a Cotton Textile Company, 1844–1945* (Cambridge, Mass., 1948). Also see Alfred D. Chandler, Jr., *The Visible Hand: The Managerial Revolution in American Business* (Cambridge, Mass., 1977); Henry Eilbirt, "The Development of Personnel Management in the United States," *Business History Review* (1959), 33:345–64; Homer J. Hagedorn, "A Note on the Motivation of Personnel Management: Industrial Welfare, 1885–1910," *Explorations in Entrepreneurial History* (1957), 10:134–39; Norman J. Wood, "Industrial Relations Policies of American Management, 1900–1933," *Business History Review* (1960), 34:403–20; Leonard R. Sayles and George Strauss, *Managing Human Resources*, 2d ed. (Englewood Cliffs, N.J., 1981). Also see Charles Milton, *Ethics and Expediency: A Critical History of Personnel Philosophy* (Columbia, S.C. 1970).

5. Robert H. Wiebe, *Businessmen and Reform* (Cambridge, Mass., 1962); Gabriel Kolko, *The Triumph of Conservatism: A Reinterpretation of American History, 1900–1916* (Chicago, 1963); James Weinstein, *The Corporate Ideal in the Liberal State, 1900–1918* (Boston, 1968); Bruno Ramirez, *When Workers Fight: The Politics of Industrial Relations in the Progressive Era, 1898–1916* (Westport, Conn., 1978); Louis Galambos, *Competition and Cooperation: The Emergence of a National Trade Association* (Baltimore, 1966); Ellis W. Hawley, *The New Deal and the Problem of Monopoly* (Princeton, 1966); Richard H. Abrams, ed., *The Issue of Federal Regulation in the Progressive Era* (Chicago, 1963); Kim McQuaid, *Big Business and Presidential Power* (New York, 1982). For more cultural treatments, see Edward Kirkland, *Dream and Thought in the Business Community, 1860–1900* (Ithaca, N.Y., 1956); Samuel Haber, *Efficiency and Uplift: Scientific Management in the Progressive Era, 1890–1920* (Chicago, 1964); Reinhard Bendix, *Work and Authority in Industry* (New York, 1956); Thomas Cochran, *Business in American Life: A History* (New York, 1972); and Robert H. Wiebe, *The Search for Order: 1877–1920* (New York, 1967).

6. For examples of the "old" labor history see John R. Commons et al., *History of Labor in the United States*, 4 vols. (New York, 1918–1935); Philip Taft, *The AFL in the Time of Gompers* (New York, 1957); Milton Derber, *The American Idea of Industrial Democracy* (Urbana, Ill., 1970). Early bridges between old and new included David Brody, *Steelworkers in America: The Nonunion Era* (Cambridge, Mass. 1960) and Irving Bernstein, *The Lean Years: A History of the American Worker, 1920–1933* (Boston, 1960).

7. Brian Palmer, "Class Conception and Conflict: The Thrust for Efficiency, Managerial Views of Labor, and the Working Class Rebellion, 1903–1922," *Review of Radical Political Economics* (1975), 7:31–49; David Montgomery, *Workers' Control in America* (Cambridge, Mass., 1979); David Noble, *America by Design: Science, Technology, and the Rise of Corporate Capitalism* (New York, 1977). See also David Montgomery, "To Study the People: The American Working Class," *Labor History* (Fall 1980), 21:485–512.

8. David Kreps and Michael Spence, "Modelling the Role of History in Industrial Organization and Competition," in George Feiwel, *Issues in Contemporary Microeconomics and Welfare* (London, 1985), pp. 340–78.

The aggregate approach taken by economic historians is exemplified in such works as Stanley Lebergott, *Manpower in Economic Growth* (New York, 1964); H. J. Habakkuk, *American and British Technology in the Nineteenth Century* (Cambridge, Mass., 1962); Peter Temin, *Iron and Steel in Nineteenth-Century America* (Cambridge, Mass., 1964).

9. Daniel Nelson, *Managers and Workers: Origins of the New Factory System in*

the United States, 1880–1920 (Madison, Wis., 1975); Stuart Brandes, *American Welfare Capitalism, 1880–1940* (Chicago, 1976); Howell John Harris, *The Right to Manage: Industrial Relations Policies of American Business in the 1940s* (Madison, Wis., 1982); Walter Licht, *Working for the Railroad; The Organization of Work in the Nineteenth Century* (Princeton, 1983): Ronald W. Schatz, *The Electrical Workers: A History of Labor at General Electric and Westinghouse, 1923–1960* (Urbana, Ill., 1983); Susan Benson, *Counter Cultures: Saleswomen, Managers, and Customers in American Department Stores, 1890–1940* (Urbana, Ill., 1986); Nelson Lichtenstein, *Labor's War at Home: The CIO in World War II* (Cambridge, Eng., 1982); Stephen A. Marglin, "What Do Bosses Do? The Origins and Functions of Hierarchy in Capitalist Production," *Review of Radical Political Economics* (Summer 1974), 6:60–112; Katharine Stone, "The Origins of Job Structures in the Steel Industry," in Richard Edwards, Michael Reich, and David Gordon, eds., *Labor Market Segmentation* (Lexington, Mass., 1975), pp. 24–84; Harry Braverman, *Labor and Monopoly Capital: The Degradation of Work in the Twentieth Century* (New York, 1974); Richard C. Edwards, *Contested Terrain: The Transformation of the Workplace in the Twentieth Century* (New York, 1979); David Gordon, Richard Edwards, and Michael Reich, *Segmented Work, Divided Workers* (Cambridge, Mass., 1982); Kenneth L. Sokoloff, "Was the Transition from the Artisanal Shop to the Nonmechanized Factory Associated with Gains in Efficiency? Evidence from the U.S. Manufacturing Censuses of 1820 and 1850," *Explorations in Economic History* (1984), 21:351–72; David Landes, "What Do Bosses Really Do?" *Journal of Economic History* (September 1986), 46:585–683.

Also see Stephen Meyer, *The Five Dollar Day: Labor Management and Social Control in the Ford Motor Company* (Albany, N.Y., 1981); Robert M. Jackson, *The Formation of Craft Labor Markets* (New York, 1984); Sanford M. Jacoby, *Employing Bureaucracy: Managers, Unions, and the Transformation of Work in American Industry* (New York, 1985); Ruth Milkman, *Gender at Work: The Dynamics of Job Segregation by Sex During World War II* (Urbana, Ill., 1987); and Gerald Zahavi, *Workers, Managers, and Welfare Capitalism: The Shoeworkers and Tanners of Endicott Johnson, 1890–1950* (Urbana, Ill., 1988).

Precursors of the new employer history include Loren Baritz, *Servants of Power* (Middlebury, Vt. 1960); Sidney Pollard, *The Genesis of Modern Management* (Cambridge, Mass., 1965); and Stanley Buder, *Pullman: An Experiment in Industrial Order and Community Planning* (New York, 1967).

10. Data on unionization are in Richard Freeman, "Contraction and Expansion: Divergence of Private and Public Sector Unionism in the United States," *Journal of Economic Perspectives* (Spring 1988), vol. 2.

11. In an article published in 1967, Irwin Unger excoriated New Left historians for, among other things, having research interests that were governed "not by the natural dialogue of the discipline but by the concerns of the outside cultural and political world." Unger, "The New Left and American History," *American Historical Review* (1967), vol. 72, quoted in Peter Novick, *That Noble Dream: The "Objectivity Question" and the American Historical Profession* (Cambridge, Mass. 1988), p. 424.

12. Studies of contemporary industrial relations that rely on historical analysis include Thomas A. Kochan, Harry Katz, and Robert McKersie, *The Transformation of American Industrial Relations* (New York, 1986) and Michael Piore and Charles Sabel, *The Second Industrial Divide* (New York, 1984).

13. On the new institutionalism, see the following collections: Frank H. Stephen, ed., *Firms, Organization, and Labour: Approaches to the Economics of Work Organization* (New York, 1984); Louis Putterman, ed., *The Economic Nature of the Firm: A Reader* (Cambridge, Eng., 1986); William G. Ouchi and Jay Barney, *Orga-*

nizational Economics (San Francisco, 1986). See also Oliver E. Williamson, *Economic Institutions of Capitalism* (New York, 1985); Richard R. Nelson and Sidney G. Winter, *An Evolutionary Theory of Economic Change* (Cambridge, Mass., 1982); and Sanford Jacoby, "Learning from the Past: The New Institutional Labor Economics and the Old," *Industrial Relations*, forthcoming.

14. Joan Woodward, *Industrial Organization: Behavior and Control* (Oxford, 1970); Charles Perrow, *Complex Organizations: A Critical Essay*, 3d ed. (Glenview, Ill., 1986); Bill McKelvey, *Organizational Systematics* (Berkeley, 1982); Michael T. Hannan and John Freeman, *Organizational Ecology* (Cambridge, Mass., 1989); A. L. Stinchcombe, "Social Structure and Organizations," in James G. March, ed., *Handbooks of Organizations* (Chicago, 1965), pp. 142–94; Mayer Zald, "History, Sociology, and Theories of Organization" (working paper, University of Michigan Sociology Department, Ann Arbor, 1987); Theda Skocpol, ed., *Vision and Method in Historical Sociology* (Cambridge, Mass., 1984). For a critical appraisal of the shift from social to economic modes of analysis in industrial sociology, see Ida Harper Simpson, "The Sociology of Work: Where Have the Workers Gone?" *Social Forces* (March 1989), 67:563–81.

15. On deskilling, see Braverman, *Labor and Monopoly Capital;* Phil Kraft, *Programmers and Managers: The Rationalization of Computer Programming in the United States* (New York, 1977); Paul Adler, "Rethinking the Skill Requirements of New Technologies" (Harvard Business School working paper, Boston, 1984); Paul A. Attewell, "Work and Deskilling," *Work and Occupations* (August 1987), 14:323–46; Wassily Leontieff and Faye Duchin, *The Future Impact of Automation on Workers* (New York, 1986); Daniel Nelson, *Frederick W. Taylor and the Rise of Scientific Management* (Madison, Wis., 1980). On segmentation, see Gordon, Edwards, and Reich, eds., *Labor Market Segmentation*, or their *Segmented Work, Divided Workers;* Ivar Berg, ed., *Sociological Perspectives on Labor Markets* (New York, 1981); Paul A. Attewell, *Radical Political Economy Since the Sixties* (New Brunswick, N.J., 1984).

16. See Ronald Schatz, "Labor Historians, Labor Economics, and the Question of Synthesis," *Journal of American History* (June 1984), 71:93–100; Walter Licht, "Labor Economics and the Labor Historian," *International Labor and Working Class History* (Spring 1982), 21:52–62; Gavin Wright, "Labor History and Labor Economics," in Alexander J. Field, ed., *The Future of Economic History* (Boston, 1987), pp. 313–48; and David Landes and Charles Tilly, eds., *History as Social Science* (Englewood Cliffs, N.J. 1971).

17. Alfred D. Chandler, Jr., *Strategy and Structure: Chapters in the History of the American Industrial Enterprise.* (Cambridge, Mass., 1962) and Chandler, *The Visible Hand*. For a critical appraisal of this approach, see Richard P. Rumelt, "Evaluation of Strategy: Theory and Models" in D. E. Schendel and C. W. Hofer, eds., *Strategic Management: A New View of Business Policy and Planning* (Boston, 1979). For labor versions of Chandlerism, see Oliver Williamson, "The Organization of Work: A Comparative Institutional Assessment," *Journal of Economic Behavior and Organization* (March 1980), 1:5–38; William Lazonick, "Technological Change and the Control of Work: The Development of Capital-Labor Relations in the U.S. Manufacturing Industry," in Gospel and Littler, eds., *Managerial Strategies*, pp. 111–36; W. R. Garside and H. F. Gospel, "Employers and Managers: Their Organizational Structure and Changing Industrial Strategies," in Chris Wrigley, ed., *A History of British Industrial Relations, 1875–1914* (Brighton, 1982); and Howard F. Gospel, "The Management of Labor: Great Britain, the U.S., and Japan," *Business History* (January 1988), 30:104–15.

18. Braverman, *Labor and Monopoly Capital*. See also Dan Clawson, *Bureaucracy and the Labor Process* (New York, 1980).

19. The argument here follows G. K. Dow, "The Function of Authority in Trans-

action Cost Economics," *Journal of Economic Behavior and Organization* (March 1987), 8:13–38. The quotation is from Michael Burawoy, "Contemporary Currents in Marxist Theory," *American Sociologist* (February 1978), 13:54.

20. Paul David, "Clio and the Economics of QWERTY," *American Economic Review* (May 1985), 75:332–37.

21. Bennett Harrison and Barry Bluestone, *The Great U-Turn* (New York, 1988).

22. Ronald Dore, *Taking Japan Seriously: A Confucian Perspective on Leading Economic Issues* (Stanford, 1987); Chalmers A. Johnson, *The MITI and the Japanese Miracle: The Growth of Industrial Policy, 1925–1975* (Stanford, 1982). For a neoclassical economic analysis of these phenomena, see Benjamin Klein, Robert Crawford, and Armen Alchian, "Vertical Integration, Appropriable Rents, and the Competitive Contracting Process," *Journal of Law and Economics* (October 1978), 21:297–326.

23. Martin J. Sklar, *The Corporate Reconstruction of American Capitalism* (Cambridge, Eng., 1988), pp. 23–24.

24. See Mark Granovetter, "Economic Action and Social Structure: The Problem of Embeddedness," *American Journal of Sociology* (November 1985), 91:481–510.

25. P. K. Edwards, "Fiddles and Informality: How the Labor Contract Really Works" (working papers, Industrial Relations Research Unit, University of Warwick, Coventry, 1988); Richard Hyman, "Strategy or Structure? Capital, Labour, and Control," *Work, Employment, and Society* (March 1987), 1:25–55; David Lewin, "Industrial Relations as a Strategic Variable," in Morris Kleiner et al., eds., *Human Resources and the Performance of the Firm* (Madison, Wis., 1987), pp. 1–42; John Purcell, "The Structure and Function of Personnel Management," and Paul Marginson and Keith Sisson, "The Management of Employees," in Paul Marginson et al., *Beyond the Workplace: Managing Industrial Relations in the Multiestablishment Enterprise* (Oxford, 1988).

26. Jonathan Zeitlin, "From Labour History to the History of Industrial Relations," *Economic History Review* (May 1987), 40:159–84.

27. Frederick Rose, "In the Wake of Cost Cuts, Many Firms Sweep History Out the Door," *Wall Street Journal*, December 21, 1987.

1. THE TRANSITION FROM OUTWORK TO FACTORY PRODUCTION IN THE BOOT AND SHOE INDUSTRY, 1830–1880

Jens Christiansen and Peter Philips

1. Stephen A. Marglin, "What Do Bosses Do? The Origins and Functions of Hierarchy in Capitalist Production," *Review of Radical Political Economics* (Summer 1974), 6:60–112.

2. Ibid., p. 62.

3. For the traditional neoclassical (or orthodox) position see, among many others: David Landes, "What Do Bosses Really Do?" *Journal of Economic History* (September 1986), vol. 46; S. R. H. Jones, "Technology, Transaction Costs, and the Transition to Factory Production in the British Silk Industry, 1700–1870," *Journal of Economic History* (March 1987), 47:71–96. For the modern neoclassical (or transaction cost) approach see, e.g., Oliver E. Williamson, "The Organization of Work: A Comparative Institutional Assessment," *Journal of Economic Behavior and Organization* (March 1980), 1:5–38; Other recent contributions to the debate include Kenneth L. Sokoloff, "Was the Transition from the Artisanal Shop to the Nonmechanized Factory Associated with Gains in Efficiency? Evidence from the

206 *1. Transition from Outwork*

U.S. Manufacturing Censuses o 1820 and 1850," *Explorations in Economic History,* (1984), 21:351–82; Gregory Clark, "Authority and Efficiency: the Labor Market and the Managerial Revolution of the Late Nineteenth Century," *Journal of Economic History* (December 1984), vol. 44; Frank H. Stephen, ed., *Firms, Organization, and Labour: Approaches to the Economics of Work Organization* (London, 1984); Bruce Laurie and M. Schmitz, "Manufacture and Productivity: The Making of an Industrial Base, Philadelphia 1850–1880," in T. Hershberg, ed., *Philadelphia: Work, Space, Family, and Group Experience in the Nineteenth Century* (New York, 1981); Alfred D. Chandler, *The Visible Hand: The Managerial Revolution in American Business* (Cambridge, Mass., 1977); Louis Putterman, *The Economic Nature of the Firm: A Reader* (Cambridge, Eng., 1986).

4. The story has been told many times and in many places; see, e.g., David N. Johnson, *Sketches of Lynn or the Changes of Fifty Years* (Lynn, Mass., 1880); William Stone, "Lynn and Its Old Time Shoemakers' Shops," *Register of the Lynn Historical Society* (1911), pp. 79–100; Blanche Hazard, *The Organization of the Boot and Shoe Industry Before 1875* (Cambridge, Mass., 1921).

5. The number of shoemakers in a ten-footer ranged from 4 to 8. Massachusetts, State Sanitary Commission, *Report of the General Plan for the Promotion of Public and Personal Health* (Boston, 1850), p. 509; Charles Buffum, "History of Shoemaking," *Lynn Item,* October 15, 1909, found in newspaper clippings of the Lynn Historical Society, pp. 389–92.

6. For the sake of brevity, we will sometimes use the term "shoes" in the generic sense for boots and shoes. When a distinction needs to be made, it will be obvious from the context.

7. *Lynn Record,* September 13, 1837.

8. Alan Dawley, *Class and Community: The Industrial Revolution in Lynn* (Cambridge, Mass., 1976), pp. 27–28.

9. Blewett dates the decline of the family system of distributing shoe uppers as starting in 1810. However, as table 1.1 indicates, the proportion of women working within the Lynn outwork system remained constant between 1830 and 1840. The purpose of breaking up the family system was to expand the number of women relative to men either to ensure that female work would keep up with the work in the ten-footers, as Blewett suggests, or to drive down the female piece rate through an expansion of the effective supply of women workers. In either case, the effects of such an innovation in the outwork system are apparent only in the decade between 1840 and 1850, when the proportion of women in the system rises relative to men. Thus, we believe Blewett is correct in dating the beginnings of the decline in the family labor system back to 1810, but we suspect that the transfer of control over the gender division of labor to the shoe boss did not show its full fruits until the 1840s. Mary H. Blewett, "Work, Gender, and the Artisan Tradition in New England Shoemaking, 1780–1860," *Journal of Social History* (Winter 1983–1984), p. 225. Blewett gives more details to her argument in chapter 2 of *Men, Women, and Work: A Case Study of Class, Gender and Protest in the Nineteenth Century New England Shoe Industry* (Urbana, Ill., 1988).

10. *Lynn Weekly Reporter,* November 21, 1863, p. 2, c. 1.

11. Dawley, *Class and Community,* p. 245.

12. Slack effort is problematic even with piece rates because if workers fail to complete their batches, employers are unable to fill orders on time. In a competitive market, this can be very costly.

13. In general terms, this is Marglin's argument; with respect to the Lynn boot and shoe industry, Hazard argues along similar lines.

14. Some employers "had the reputation of being very particular." One of them was Christopher Robinson who often told shoemakers that "he wouldn't have any

more of that kind made." This led to the "quite common practice for one man to borrow a shoe of another, with which to go 'bossing.' It was an unfair thing to do, but it was done, and very often the man who did it found, when he carried the first lot in, that no more of his work was wanted." Stone, "Old Time Shoemakers," p. 88.

15. Hazard reports that scrap leather merchants would make the rounds of the ten-footers buying leftover leather from the shoemakers. Such a market phenomenon revealed to the absent shoe manufacturer the general amount and value of the scraps and highlighted the question of whether wasted leather could be saved by better or more honest cutting. Hazard, *Organization*, p. 43.

16. The cutter came into the central shop by the 1830s. Other workers, both men and women, entered the central shop in the late 1840s and 1850s. However, it is significant that the cutter was paid time rates while the other central shop workers were paid piece rates. Piece rate was not an effective payment system where there was a significant trade-off between speed of production and material use in production. Time-rate workers had to be managed in a different manner whereby they identified their interests with those of the shoe employer. On wage payment systems in the central shop see Hazard, *Organization*, p. 87. On the attachment of the cutter to the employer see Massachusetts, Bureau of the Statistics of Labor, [First Annual] *Report, 1870* (Boston, 1870), p. 336.

17. On occasion, materials were given to one worker in an outlying area who then independently subcontracted work out to others.

18. Each textile factory employed only a small number of full-time workers, while outwork firms employed larger numbers of females, but they tended to work part time. See Thomas Dublin, *Women at Work* (New York, 1979), ch. 3: "The Lowell Work Force, 1836, and the Social Origins of Women Workers." Blewett reports that by the 1820s, textile work in Essex county had shifted decisively out of the home and into the factories. Homebound workers were limited in their alternatives to hat making, sewing coats and shirts, and increasingly, to binding shoes. Blewett, "Work, Gender, and the Artisan Tradition," p. 225; and Blewett, *Men, Women, and Work*, pp. 14–15.

19. William H. Mulligan, Jr., "The Transition of Skill in the Shoe Industry: Family to Factory Training in Lynn, Massachusetts," in Ian M. G. Quimby, ed., *The Craftsman in Early America* (New York, 1984), pp. 234–46.

20. However, one shoemaker suggests that at least at times during the 1830 to 1850 period, all the members of a ten-footer would act in concert with regard to the piece rates and standards of a particular shoe boss. "We worked for 'Cris' [Robinson] for six years, and settled up once a year. We struck then for more wages, which was denied, and then called on Nathan Kimball at the next door, and was paid five cents a pair more for the same work, so that Cris had to pony up on his price to five brother workmen to keep them in his employ." This narrative suggests how the outwork system promoted competition among employers and between employers and workers. It also suggests that the system promoted cooperation among workers within any one ten-footer. It takes little imagination to also see how the system promoted competition among ten-footer work groups. Anonymous, "Shoe Business," *Lynn Daily Bee*, December 12, 1889, p. 2.

21. Ibid.

22. See, e.g., Martin Brown and Peter Philips, "Craft Labor and Mechanization in Nineteenth-Century American Canning," *Journal of Economic History* (September 1986) 46:743–56.

23. *Lynn Weekly Reporter*, October 7, 1865, p. 2, c. 4.

24. Various shoe manufacturers owned the exclusive rights to the Singer, Howe, and Grover-Baker machines, the three competing brands of the 1850s. The earliest

newspaper advertisement offering the sewing machine for sale to "operatives" were directed at home workers. *Lynn News*, January 28, 1853, p. 3, c. 6. Even as late as 1855, newspaper ads aimed at the home worker. A Grover Baker ad claimed: "After a trial of more than three years . . . no other can compare. . . . Easiest for New Beginner . . . we refer to the Manufacturers of Lynn who give the work done by these machines the preference." *Lynn Reporter*, September 22, 1855, p. 3. After 1855, the ads were aimed at both the home and the factory market. For instance, see *Lynn Reporter*, November 15, 1856, p. 3; *Lynn Weekly Reporter*, December 5, 1863, p. 4; ibid., January 28, 1865, p. 4.

Sewing machines were also rented by the manufacturers to the workers (see Blewett, *Men, Women, and Work*, p. 104). However, this practice stopped after a few years and is not mentioned further in contemporary reports. We assume that repair problems and questions of whether workers could be held responsible were too difficult to settle and thus made the practice unprofitable.

25. *Lynn News*, July 20, 1855, p. 2, c. 3.

26. Fifteen to forty women worked in the first stitching shops. *Lynn Reporter*, April 12, 1856, p. 3.

27. The establishment of stitching shops sped the diffusion of the new technology beyond the limits imposed by the number of women who could afford to buy these machines themselves. In 1855, there were 1,500 to 1,800 sewing machines in use in the Lynn outwork system both in homes and in stitching shops (*Lynn News*, July 20, 1855, p. 2, c. 3). At that time there were 6,476 women shoe binders in Lynn (Francis DeWitt, *Statistical Information* [Mass. Census] [Boston, 1856]. Ten years later 6,000 to 7,000 sewing machines were said to be in use in Lynn, almost one machine for every female binder in Lynn (*Lynn Weekly Reporter*, November 7, 1865, p. 2, c. 4).

As the use of sewing machines spread, the very high incomes of the home machine operators fell. Average incomes of all women, on the other hand, rose both absolutely and relative to men.

28. By 1860, the relative number of male workers (as compared to 1850) had increased even in the outwork system because the expansion of the system had forced employers to draw on less experienced and less productive shoemakers in the hinterland.

29. This ratio corresponds fairly accurately to the notion found in many contemporary reports of a fourfold productivity increase in machine over hand work.

30. Hazard, *Organization*, pp. 109–10.

31. War demands and labor scarcity account for the first adoption of the McKay machine, and the experimentation with a factory-based, detailed division of labor in men's work. Blewett argues that the wartime period was a mixed blessing for Lynn manufacturers with the loss of southern markets and their established lines of credit. Blewett, *Men, Women, and Work*, p. 394, n. 2 and p. 396, n. 14. The *Lynn Weekly Reporter*, February 28, 1863, p. 2, c. 3, noted the introduction of new machinery of various kinds in several factories "the introduction of which has been rendered necessary by the pressure of business and the increased demand for goods."

32. Johnson, *Sketches*, pp. 342–43.

33. Once the upper shoe leather had been shaped into its final form, it could not be transported without losing its shape again, and thus had to be bottomed in close proximity.

34. John Wooldredge used a steam-powered machine in his central shop in 1857 to cut heels out of the leather. By 1863, an estimated 800 to 1,000 heelers were working in Lynn heeling shops—much like women working in stitching shops. This did not necessarily threaten the demise of the ten-footers any more

than did the movement of cutting into the central shop thirty years before. This kind of job could be kept physically separate and apart from the other male tasks. In contrast, lasted shoes had to be bottomed (either in the ten-footers or, with the adoption of the McKay stitcher, in the factory) before they were transported. *Lynn Reporter*, February 28, 1863, p. 2, cc. 1–2; Ross David Thompson, "The Origins of Modern Industry in the United States: The Mechanization of Shoe and Sewing Machine Production" (Ph.D. diss. Yale University, 1976), pp. 15–16.

35. Bancroft and Purington's factory is described in *Lynn Weekly Reporter*, November 21, 1865, p. 2, cc. 1–2. While some shoe manufacturers may have tried to retrofit the manufacturing of bottoming into their central shop buildings, it appears that the leading manufacturers of the late 1860s poured considerable investment into shoe bottoming manufacturing during the Civil War. Bancroft and Purington, e.g., saw their property taxes rise in each year of the war to $774 in 1865. John Wooldredge, who bought a McKay stitcher in 1862, paid around $900 in property taxes until 1864, when his taxes rose to $1,187; in 1865, they nearly doubled again. Samuel Bubier, who was the leading postwar shoe manufacturer, apparently expanded immediately after the introduction of the McKay. His taxes, which were $456 in 1857 and $514 in 1862, rose to $1,297 in 1863, $2,189 in 1864 and $3,437 in 1865. *Lynn Weekly Reporter*, August 18, 1857, p. 2, c. 3; August 10, 1861, p. 2, cc. 5–6; August 9, 1862, p. 2, cc. 4–6; August 15, 1863, p. 2, cc. 3–4; August 20, 1864, p. 2, cc 5–6; August 23, 1865, p. 2, cc. 1–4.

36. Even as late as 1883, 93 percent of 3,872 Massachusetts shoe workers were paid piece rates suggesting that direct observation of work was not an early shoe factory managerial strategy and that the post facto inspection of work which was central to outwork management was retained in the first shoe factories. In this post facto inspection system, the factory had the advantage of shorter periods between inspections but had the disadvantage of no longer being able to utilize homebound workers. Massachusetts, Bureau of the Statistics of Labor, *Report, 1884* (Boston, 1884), p. 156.

37. Table 1.1 indicates that labor productivity was stagnant between the 1830s and the introduction of the sewing machine in 1852, with increased output resulting from increased use of labor and materials. The mid-1850s show an upturn in labor productivity that is probably associated with the sewing machine. No increase in labor productivity can be seen from the introduction of the McKay stitcher and factory production in men's work until after the Civil War. By the end of 1862, nine McKay stitchers were in use in Lynn. In 1873, 227 McKay machines were in Lynn, 43 more than all the machines in both New York and Philadelphia. By 1870, half of Lynn's shoe factories had steam power. While the factory system was introduced into Lynn only during the Civil War, it came to dominate production between 1865 and 1870. Blewett, *Men, Women, and Work*, pp. 142–46.

38. These early minor inventions were often the creations of workers within the factory. While it may be true that the detailed division of labor ultimately numbs the mind of workers in these narrowed tasks, during the initial transition from outwork to factory production, new factory prospects in Lynn acted as a stimulus for workers as well as employers to think up deskilling and labor-enhancing devices. Indeed, during this fluid period, a successful invention could catapult the factory worker to the status of factory owner. Only later, as capital requirements increased, market shares were stabilized, and the heritage of craft work receded would the stultifying effects of the division of labor impress its full weight upon the work force. Johnson, *Sketches of Lynn*, p. 343.

39. See Blewett, *Men, Women, and Work*, p. 153.

40. *Shoe and Leather Reporter* (New York), June 17, 1869, p. 2.

41. See Blewett, *Men, Women, and Work*, p. 152.

42. We measure just-in-time production by the inverse of months in operation: the fewer months a firm was producing, the more it was pursuing a just-in-time production strategy. Capital is measured by the total amount invested and labor by the number of employees per company. [All three coefficients in our estimation of just-in-time production as a function of the capital-labor ratio, capital, and percentage of shoes are statistically significant at the .01 level for factories, but insignificant for outwork firms (see table 1.3)

43. Effective labor is measured as the number of workers per company times the inverse of months in operation. The shorter the production period is per year (the fewer months in operation), the greater is the effort and the longer are the daily hours the workers are required to put in.

44. Actual piece rates paid per worker are not available in the Census manuscripts or elsewhere, but we can derive the amount of wages paid for each pair of boots or shoes (shoe piece rates) by dividing total wages per firm by output.

45. Statistically significant only at the .10 level.

46. The coefficient is not statistically significant, however.

47. Massachusetts, Bureau of the Statistics of Labor, *Report, 1871* (Boston, 1871), p. 238.

48. Ibid., p. 244.

49. Blewett, *Men, Women, and Work*, p. 388.

50. Recall the drastic, 40 percent decline in employment between 1865 and 1870 (see table 1.1).

51. Jones, "Technology," p. 94.

2. STUDYING WORK: PERSONNEL POLICIES IN PHILADELPHIA FIRMS, 1850–1950

Walter Licht

1. For the latest study of the evolution of personnel practices in American industry that is based on survey data, see James Baron, Frank Dobbin, and P. Devereaux Jennings, "War and Peace: The Evolution of Modern Personnel Administration in U.S. Industry," *American Journal of Sociology* (September 1986), 92:350–83. Notes in this article make reference to previous analyses of a similar nature.

2. In this plea for case study methodology, the author is all too aware of the problems of the approach. One or a small number of cases raise the difficult issue of representativeness; many cases often present a wealth of particulars that make patterns and generalizations almost impossible to find and draw. Nor does the author discount the value of surveys and censuses. They provide necessary cross-sectional views—the percentage of workers in white collar employment in 1900, the percentage of firms with personnel offices in 1945. They also provide some clues as to change over time—if large-scale firms tend to have personnel offices, then a link between size and formalization of procedures can be inferred. Still, the actual circumstances under which innovation takes place are not revealed; here is the importance of the case study approach. Finally, the case study allows the researcher not just to test abstractions but to avoid reification. Studying behavior at the level of the firm renders appreciation of the varied problems, inhibitions, and responses of employers, who never simply act as Capital; the realities of the workaday world for employees—struggles won, lost, and not fought—are also highlighted. Most important, the firm case study reveals the actual outcomes of interactions between management and labor.

3. Vertical integration is simply taken here as growth in firm size due to the taking on of new activities. Typically, vertical integration is noted when firms begin directly to access raw materials or market goods. New departments are formed with new employees, and the company expands. Creation of a personnel office represents a new task. I see no reason not to deem this a form of vertical integration.

4. Transcripts of meetings of the Business Problems Group can be found in the Charles Huston Correspondence, Lukens Steel Company Papers, Hagley Library, Wilmington, Delaware.

5. Alfred Chandler, *The Visible Hand: The Managerial Revolution in American Business* (Cambridge, Mass., 1977).

6. Harry Braverman, *Labor and Monopoly Capital: The Degradation of Work in the Twentieth Century* (New York, 1974).

7. For this more dialectical viewpoint see Michael Burawoy, *Manufacturing Consent: Changes in the Labor Process under Monopoly Capitalism* (Chicago, 1980); Walter Licht, *Working for the Railroad: The Organization of Work in the Nineteenth Century* (Princeton, 1983); and Sanford Jacoby, *Employing Bureaucracy: Managers, Unions, and the Transformation of Work in American Industry, 1900–1945* (New York, 1985).

8. Richard Edwards, *Contested Terrain: The Transformation of the Workplace in the Twentieth Century* (New York, 1979); David Gordon, Richard Edwards, and Michael Reich, *Segmented Work, Divided Workers: The Historical Transformation of Labor in the United States* (New York, 1982).

9. Baron, Dobbin, and Jennings, "War and Peace," pp. 362–77; Jacoby, *Employing Bureaucracy*, chs. 5, 8.

10. The firms discussed in this article were chosen in the following way. First, I conducted a search in local archives for company records; quantity and quality of materials pertaining to personnel matters determined choices, and six case studies were located in this manner. Second, I sent letters to more than 300 firms that had been in business in the city of Philadelphia for at least 100 years; a listing provided by the Philadelphia Chamber of Commerce facilitated this mailing. Responses from 42 firms and subsequent visits to 26 established possibilities for research in 14 businesses. Surviving documents and opportunities to interview veteran and retired workers, supervisors, and owners determined this selection.

11. Readers may detect an empiricist or antitheoretical bias in this article. I value conceptualization; theory provides guidance for research. At a certain point, though, immersion in the details is necessary not just to check theory but to redefine and reformulate theory if the evidence warrants. This suspension of conceptualization and penchant to delve into the particulars is the historian's stock in trade. There is a historian's bias to this article.

Representativeness is really not an issue here. The twenty firms chosen for research can reveal the range of practices manifest in firms with regard to personnel. No attempt is made to argue that the particular breakdown of practices illustrated in this article holds for the population of firms in Philadelphia (or elsewhere). Rather, the various possibilities of personnel relations are highlighted. In fact, the firms in this study do constitute a good representation of companies operating in Philadelphia in the time period under study. For confirmation, see Gladys Palmer, *Philadelphia Workers in a Changing Economy* (Philadelphia, 1956), pp. 5–60.

12. A history of the Wetherill Paint Company can be found in Miriam Hussey *From Merchants to "Colour Men": Five Generations of Samuel Wetherill's White Lead Business* (Philadelphia, 1956).

13. Ibid., pp. 16, 97–102.

14. Medical Records, M-52-ABC, Wetherill Paint Company Papers, Lippincott Library, University of Pennsylvania; Safety Committee Records, ibid.

15. Journal of Daily Occurences, John Gay & Sons Carpet Mill, 1876–1916, Historical Society of Pennsylvania, December 1, 1882; January 17, 1883; February 21, 1884.

16. Ibid., June 12, 1892, March 10, 1896; Lorin Blodget, *The Textile Industries of Philadelphia* (Philadelphia, 1880), pp. 45–50.

17. Journal of Daily Occurences, John Gay & Sons Carpet Mill, November 5, 1878; August 19, 1881; March 3, 1884; March 29, 1889; June 12, 1892; March 10, 1896; May 14, 1906; September 3, 1908; November 9, 1909; March 29, 1915.

18. Ibid., December 3, 1878; December 10, 1878; December 18, 1880; May 3, 1893; December 27, 1914.

19. Entries in the Journal of Occurences of the John Gay company reveal frequent job actions in the years listed.

20. Scrapbook, Newspaper Clippings, 1867–1888, William H. Horstmann Company Papers, Historical Society of Pennsylvania, article dated August 21, 1873; undated article from the *American Cabinet Maker;* article dated December 9, 1869, "The Silk Manufacturers of Patterson, N.J."; "American Silk Manufacturer," *Commercial Advisor*, May 17, 1875.

21. Scrapbook, Horstmann Company Papers: *Daily Register*, October 22, 1853; *American Gazette*, June 27, 1860; *Daily Chronicle*, May 20, 1870.

22. Computerized analysis of Horstmann Company Employee Register, 1850–1875, Horstmann Company Papers.

23. Scrapbook, Horstmann Company Papers, assorted invitations.

24. Ibid., article from *American and Gazette*, June 27, 1860. From numerous other clippings in the Horstmann Scrapbook, it is clear that William H. Horstmann played a leading role in the German-American community in Philadelphia.

25. This case study is based on interviews with George Kallish, manager of Swoboda & Sons for Trans-Continental Leather, Inc., and a small file of historical papers and items kept in the vault in Mr. Kallish's office (including a typewritten history of the firm prepared in the 1960s; no author listed).

26. This case study is based on extensive interviews with Edward K. Hueber, former owner and operating manager of Kelley & Hueber; Mr. Hueber referred to a few surviving papers and files of the firms.

27. This case study was compiled through interviews with Mrs. Lynn Walker, general manager of Herder Cutlery and descendant of Leopold Herder, and with Otto Schwartz, a grinder who started working with the firm in 1924.

28. This case study is based on interviews with Christian Spahr, one of the four owners of Lea & Febriger and a descendant of Matthew Carey, the founder of the company. Assorted records and materials deposited in the vault of the firm were also consulted.

29. Roll of Employees, 1890–1910, Lea & Febriger vault records.

30. Ibid.

31. A basic history of the Philadelphia Contributionship can be found in Nicholas Wainwright, *The Philadelphia Contributionship for the Insurance of Houses from Loss by Fire* (Philadelphia, 1952).

32. Carol Wojtowicz, "Office of the Philadelphia Contributionship," *227th Annual Report of the Philadelphia Contributionship* (1979).

33. Interviews with Carol Wojtowicz, Curator and Archivist, Philadelphia Contributionship, and Walter Smith, Secretary Treasurer, Philadelphia Contributionship.

34. The basic business and production history of Richard Remmey and Company can be found in the following articles supplied to the author by John Remmey, former president of the firm: W. Oakley Raymond, "Remmey Family: Ameri-

can Potters," *Antiques* (June 1937), pp. 296–97. W. Oakley Raymond, "Remmey Family: American Potters, Part II," *Antiques* (September 1937), pp. 132–34; "Laboratory Control and Flexible Operation Allow Wide Variety of Refractions," *Brick and Clay Record* (August 1940), pp. 44–46; "Remmey Refactories," *Noreaster* (February 1948), pp. 7–8; "The Remmeys and the Refactory Industry," *Reading Railroad Magazine* (n.d.), pp. 10–11, 24.

35. Interview with John Remmey.

36. This case study is based on interviews with S. E. Firestone, president of McCloskey Varnish, and Alice Carducci, whose father began working for the firm in the 1920s and who began working there herself in the early 1950s and has held various production and clerical jobs.

37. This case study is based on interviews with A. K. Taylor, Chairman of the Board of Directors of Ellisco Incorporated, and Robert Taylor, his son, who serves as vice-president of the firm. Both informants studied their files after a long agenda of questions was submitted to them; the author was not allowed direct access to written material.

38. The Insurance Company of North America is now Connecticut Insurance Group of North America (CIGNA).

39. For an overview of INA's history see: Thomas Montgomery, *A History of the Insurance Company of North America* (Philadelphia, 1885); Marquis James, *Biography of a Business, 1792–1942* (New York, 1942); and William Carr, *Perils Named and Unnamed* (New York, 1967).

40. Directors' minutes, vol. 7, September 4, 1877, p. 9; February 5, 1878, p. 16; March 5, 1870, p. 18; April 5, 1881, p. 67; vol. 9, October 1, 1895, p. 24; January 13, 1897, pp. 68–69, Archives of the Insurance Company of North America, Philadelphia, Pennsylvania. Also, James, *Biography of a Business*, pp. 104–7, 160; Montgomery, *History*, p. 47; Carr, *Perils*, p. 7.

41. "New Building Instructions, October 29, 1925," Record Group 9/14; untitled memorandum from Home Office Service Committee, Record Group 9/12.4; "Employment Application," Record Group 9/14, Archives of the Insurance Company of North America.

42. Record Group 9/6, ibid.

43. "Philadelphia Salary Market Analysis," Record Group 9/13, ibid.; interviews with Claudette Johns, archivist of INA, and Lee Corak, Assistant Director of Training at INA; "Interview with Harris Ebenbach, Personnel Department, Insurance Company of North America, September 12, 1956," Gladys Palmer Papers, box 167, Sociology Department, University of Pennsylvania, Philadelphia, Pennsylvania.

44. For a recent study that emphasizes the role of culture in affecting industrial relations, see Charles Dellheim, "The Creation of a Company Culture: *Cadbury's*, 1861–1931," *American Historical Review* (February 1987, 1:13–44.

45. This case study is based on interviews with Percy Lanning, president of Perseverance Iron, and perusal of assorted papers in his possession as well as informal interviews with veteran workers.

46. This case study is based on interviews with Harvard Wood and Harvard C. Wood, Jr., president and vice-president of H. C. Wood Incorporated. Their responses were based on memory and their searches of surviving records.

47. This case study is based on extensive interviews with William Hipp, Vice-President of Production at Schmidt's Brewery. Mr. Hipp's grandfather and father worked as brewmasters at Schmidt's, a position he also occupied before promotion to general plant manager. Mr. Hipp permitted the author access to various company papers, including union contracts and several unpublished company histories.

48. Edward Pry, "Analysis of Employer-Employee Relations in the John B.

Stetson Company" (unpublished MA thesis, University of Pennsylvania, 1941), pp. 2–15.

49. Ibid., pp. 15–25; "Employee Relations of the John B. Stetson Company," *National Association of Corporation Schools Bulletin* (December 1917), 12:22–25.

50. Pry, "Analysis," pp. 27–44.

51. "Brown, Richard Percy," entry in *National Cyclopedia of American Biography*, vol. G (1943–1946), pp. 112–13; "Edward Brown: Pacesetter," *Delaware Valley Announcer* (November 1959), pp. 28–29 (articles found in a vault at Honeywell Incorporated, Fort Washington, Pennsylvania).

52. Interviews with Carl Wagenhals (former production manager at Brown), Jack Wiley (veteran product line manager), Charles Cusick, John Moore, and James Cameron (retired engineers), Frank Rae (former chief of production at Brown), and Stuart Smith (Director of Personnel at Honeywell).

53. "Brown Instrument Co. and United Electrical, Radio, and Machine Workers of America (CIO)," printed article without references located in vault of Honeywell Incorporated, Fort Washington, Pennsylvania; copy in the possession of the author.

54. Interviews with Stuart Smith and Carol Holcombe (veteran Secretary at Brown).

55. Basic histories of the Baldwin Locomotive Works can be found in *Memorial of Matthias Baldwin* (Philadelphia, 1867); William Brown, *The History of the First Locomotives* (New York, 1871); *History of the Baldwin Locomotive Works, 1831–1923* (Philadelphia, n.d., no author listed); and *The Baldwin Locomotive Works of Philadelphia: The Story of Eddystone* (Philadelphia, 1928).

56. *The Baldwin Locomotive Works*, pp. 63–73.

57. Samuel Vauclain, *Optimism* (Philadelphia, 1924), pp. 45–46. This printed address was located in the files of the Samuel Vauclain Papers, Historical Society of Pennsylvania.

58. On the subcontracting system at Baldwin see Journal notes of William Austin, 1910, William Liseter Austin Collection, box 5, Hagley Library, Wilmington, Delaware.

59. Apprentice Contracts, 1835–1870, Baldwin Locomotive Papers, Historical Society of Pennsylvania; N. W. Sample, "Apprenticeship System at the Baldwin Locomotive Works, Philadelphia," *Annals of the American Academy of Political and Social Science* (1909), 33:175–77; Raghvendra Tripathi, "A Study of Labor Skills Required for Specific Production Jobs at the Baldwin Locomotive Works" (unpublished MA thesis, University of Pennsylvania, 1949), pp. 101–23; Philip Scranton and Walter Licht, *Work Sights: Industrial Philadelphia, 1890–1950* (Philadelphia, 1986), pp. 191–96.

60. The following two extensive biographies provide a wealth of information on John Wanamaker and his store: Herbert Adams Gibbons, *John Wanamaker*, 2 vols. (New York, 1926); Joseph Appel, *The Business Biography of John Wanamaker* (New York, 1930).

61. Gibbons, *Wanamaker*, 2:261–64, 272–79, 284–85; Appel, *Business Biography*, pp. 428–30; John Wanamaker, "The John Wanamaker Commercial Institute —A Store School," *Annals of the American Academy of Political and Social Science* (1909), 33:151–54.

62. Appel, *Business Biography*, p. 434; Herman Stern, "The Present Union—Management Relationship in Philadelphia Central City Department Stores" (unpublished MBA thesis, University of Pennsylvania, 1943), pp. 33–35.

63. Walton Forstall, "One Hundred Years of Philadelphia Gas Supply" (unpublished manuscript in possession of the Public Relations Department of the Philadelphia Gas Works, 1935), pp. 2–10.

64. *Philadelphia Gas Work News* (July–August 1950), 22:4–41, 58.

65. Forstall, "One Hundred Years," pp. 153–59.

66. Ibid., pp. 162–72; *Philadelphia Gas Work News* (July–August 1950), 22:42–49, 54, 60; Circular Letters 3093–97 of Personnel Office, Archives of Philadelphia Gas Works, Philadelphia, Pennsylvania.

67. *Philadelphia Gas Works News*, p. 54; Forstall, "One Hundred Years," pp. 255–58.

68. Braverman, *Labor and Monopoly Capitalism*.

69. Jacoby, *Employing Bureaucracy*.

70. David Brody, "The Rise and Decline of Welfare Capitalism," in Brody, *Workers in Industrial America: Essays on the Twentieth-Century Struggle* (New York, 1980), pp. 48–81.

71. David Brody, "The Emergence of Mass-Production Unionism," in ibid., pp. 82–119.

72. Baron, Dobbin, and Jennings, "War and Peace"; Edwards, *Contested Terrain;* and Howell John Harris, *The Right to Manage: Industrial Relations Policies of American Business in the 1940s* (Madison, Wis., 1982).

73. Chandler, *Visible Hand*, pp. 105–9; Licht, *Working for the Railroad*, pp. 16–17, 83.

74. "Data on Hiring in System Departments in Philadelphia," box marked "Personnel Records: Employee Recruitment and Hiring," Pennsylvania Railroad Company Papers, Hagley Library, Wilmington, Delaware; "A Program of Employee Selection, 1956," ibid.; "A Report on the Personnel Program, the Pennsylvania Railroad," box marked "Personnel Records: Personnel Department," ibid.; "Hiring Manual," Vice-President for Operations Files, box 5, ibid.

75. For the most recent biography of Taylor, see Daniel Nelson, *Frederick W. Taylor and the Rise of Scientific Management* (Madison, Wis., 1980).

76. Daniel Nelson, *Managers and Workers: Origins of the New Factory System in the United States, 1880–1920* (Madison, Wis., 1975), pp. 55–58, 62–63, 71–73.

77. Ibid., pp. 68–78; Edwards, *Contested Terrain*, pp. 97–104.

78. Kathy Burgess, "Self-Help and Scientific Management at the Link-Belt Company, 1890–1915" (unpublished manuscript in the possession of the author).

79. Employers of clerical help faced little pressure, at least before 1950, to innovate in personnel relations. They relied on outside agencies, namely schools, for the training of clerks in typing, stenography, filing, etc.; since these skills were standardized, in-house training programs were unnecessary. Since there apparently was also a ready supply, particularly of young women with commercial course degrees, little concern existed to encourage long tenure. The situation for production workers and sales forces was different. Human capital theory is helpful in this instance in understanding various strategies toward labor. This conforms to findings in Jurgen Kocka, *White Collar Workers in America* (London, 1980).

80. A question can be raised whether the patterns in personnel practices delineated in this article are peculiar to Philadelphia. In some sense, this criticism misses the point of this essay; the discussion here has aimed at identifying various possibilities. In other locations, the proportions of firms with particular personnel histories might be different; qualifications to the article would be in order if patterns *not* noted here were discovered elsewhere. Is the typology rendered here inclusive, in other words?

The particular distribution of practices described in this section, admittedly, is very much a mirror of particular aspects of Philadelphia's economic and social history. The Quaker influence in the city is obvious; that ethical values played a role in firm personnel histories in many instances is not surprising. Custom goods production dominated in the city, and a high proportion of the work involved skilled labor; that skilled workers played an important role in fixing practices is not surprising. Family-owned and -operated firms also were common to the city; this too made for cases of nonprogrammatic paternalism. Philadelphia similarly was composed of distinct and stable manufacturing districts; family and ethnic ties affected personnel matters within companies. An appreciation of Philadelphia's particular industrial history can be found in Philip Scranton and Walter Licht, *Work Sights: Industrial Philadelphia, 1890–1950* (Philadelphia, 1986).

The ultimate point, however, is not whether the findings are representative. Do they comprise the full gamut of personnel histories manifest in American business enterprises? That remains for other researchers to confirm or refute.

3. SCIENTIFIC MANAGEMENT AND THE WORKPLACE, 1920–1935

Daniel Nelson

1. Milton J. Nadworny, *Scientific Management and the Unions, 1900–1932* Cambridge, Mass., 1955); Samuel Haber, *Efficiency and Uplift* (Chicago, 1964); Hugh G. J. Aitken, *Taylorism at Watertown Arsenal, 1908–1915: Scientific Management in Action* (Cambridge, Mass., 1960); Daniel Nelson, *Frederick W. Taylor and the Rise of Scientific Management* (Madison, Wis., 1980).

2. See Sanford M. Jacoby, "Union-Management Cooperation in the United States: Lessons from the 1920's," *Industrial and Labor Relations Review* (October 1983), 37:18–33, and George C. Humphreys, *Taylorism in France, 1904–1920: The Impact of Scientific Management on Factory Relations and Society* (New York, 1986).

3. Harry Braverman, *Labor and Monopoly Capital: The Degradation of Work in the Twentieth Century* (New York, 1974); Katherine Stone, "The Origins of Job Structures in the Steel Industry," *Review of Radical Political Economics* (Summer 1974), 6:113–73; Richard Edwards, *Contested Terrain: The Transformation of the Workplace in the Twentieth Century* (New York, 1979); Dan Clawson, *Bureaucracy and the Labor Process: The Transformation of U.S. Industry, 1860–1920* (New York, 1980); David Montgomery, *Worker's Control in America* (New York, 1979); David Montgomery, *The Fall of the House of Labor: The Workplace, the State, and American Labor Activism, 1865–1925* (New York, 1967). Needless to say, this critique is limited to the issue of scientific management. These works deal with a variety of issues and have sparked much comment and controversy beyond the purview of this article. For a general survey see Paul Thompson, *The Nature of Work: An Introduction to Debates on the Labour Process* (London, 1983).

4. In the words of Stephen A. Marglin, whose essay on the European origins of industrial capitalism is still the most elegant statement of the radical view, "the social function of hierarchical work organization is not technical efficiency, but accumulation." Marglin, "What Do Bosses Do? The Origins and Functions of Hierarchy in Capitalist Production," *Review of Radical Political Economics* (Summer 1974), 6:62.

5. Robert J. Hoxie, *Scientific Management and Labor* (New York, 1918).

6. Montgomery, *Fall of the House of Labor*, p. 252.

7. Braverman, *Labor and Monopoly Capital*, p. 87.

8. David Gartman attempts to supply an antidote with a detailed examination of the auto industry. David Gartman, *Auto Slavery: The Labor Process in the American Automobile Industry, 1897–1950* (New Brunswick, N. J., 1986).

9. See H. Thomas Johnson and Robert S. Kaplan, *Relevance Lost: The Rise and Fall of Management Accounting* (Boston, 1987), pp. 47–60; Morris S. Viteles, *Industrial Psychology* (New York, 1932), pp. 9–19.

10. Horace Bookwalter Drury, *Scientific Management, A History and Criticism,* 3d. ed. (New York, 1922), p. 187.

3. *Scientific Management* **217**

11. Conversely, it was also possible to have a complicated incentive wage plan without other features of scientific management. The most famous example was Frederick A. Halsey's "premium" plan, which appeared in the 1890s and which Taylor vehemently rejected. The premium was still used in the 1920s, though in most cases it was probably combined with time study.

12. See E. S. Cowdrick, "Methods of Wage Payment," Bethlehem Steel Company Papers, Accession 1699, Hagley Library, Wilmington, Delaware. See also Donald R. Stabile, "The DuPont Experiments in Scientific Management: Efficiency and Safety, 1911–1919," *Business History Review* (Autumn 1987), 61:365–86.

13. See Daniel Nelson, "Le Taylorisme dans l'industrie americaine, 1900–1930," in Maurice Montmollin and Oivier Pastre, *Le Taylorisme* (Paris, 1984), p. 56. For discussions of Taylorism in other sectors see Margery Davies, *Woman's Place is at the Typewriter: Office Work and Office Workers, 1870–1930* (Philadelphia, 1982), pp. 97–128, and Susan Porter Benson, *Counter Cultures, Saleswomen, Managers, and Customers in American Department Stores, 1890–1940* (Urbana, Ill., 1986), pp. 41–44.

14. International Bedaux Company, Representative List of Clients, December 31, 1934. Courtesy of Steven Kreis.

15. Three other studies in the late 1920s are comparable with the 1928 NICB data. Michael Jucius and Adolph Langsner surveyed large firms, mostly in the Chicago area. R. W. King surveyed large and small firms in Connecticut. Their results were:

	Jucius	*Langsner*	*King*
Time wage	29.4	37.7	48
Piece rate	38.4	25.0	37.5
Premium and bonus	32.2	37.3	14.5

Jucius, who compared the four studies, emphasized the importance of plant size in explaining the disparities. The average plant in the Jucius and Langsner studies had four times as many employees as the average plant in the NICB and King studies. Michael J. Jucius, "The Use of Wage Incentives in Industry with Particular Reference to the Chicago Area," *Journal of Business* (January 1932), 5:81–82. See also Adolph Langsner, "A Survey of Compensation Methods and Incentive Plans in a Variety of Industries," *Trends in Industry* (Society of Industrial Engineers Sixteenth National Convention, 1929), pp. 45–46; R. W. King, "A Study of Wage-Payment Plans in Connecticut," *Factory and Industrial Management* (March, 1931), 81:411–13.

16. See U.S. Department of Commerce, Bureau of the Census, *Historical Statistics of the United States: Colonial Times to 1970* (Washington, 1975), pt. 1, pp. 126, 137.

17. See E. S. Horning, *Wage Incentive Practices*, Studies in Personnel Policy, no. 68 (New York, 1945), p. 1.

18. Also see Jucius, "The Use of Wage Incentives," pp. 81–82.

19. Internal evidence suggests that that was the Chevrolet axle plant in Detroit, an oddity in the General Motors empire.

20. For an excellent example, see Ernest B. Fricke, "The New Deal and the Modernization of Small Business: The McCreary Tire & Rubber Company, 1930–1940," *Business History Review* (Winter, 1982), 55:559–76.

21. National Industrial Conference Board, *Systems of Wage Payment* (New York, 1930), pp. 34–35.

22. Ibid., p. 35.

23. Frank and Lillian Gilbreth explicitly addressed this point in a 1924 article. Their work, they wrote, "presupposes that an unskilled worker is taught and placed *upward* to the job of machine tender. Scientific management does not

advocate nor practice demoting a highly skilled machinist to such work as feeding a machine with material." Frank B. and Lillian Gilbreth, "The Efficiency Engineer and the Industrial Psychologist," *Journal of the National Institute of Industrial Psychology* (1924), 2:43.

24. Cowdrick, "Methods of Wage Payment," Bethlehem Steel Company Papers, Goodyear report, p. 8.

25. Ibid.

26. Ibid., International Harvester report, p. 1.

27. Ibid., Westinghouse report, p. 1.

28. Ibid., U.S. Rubber report, p. 1.

29. Ibid., AT&T report, p. 5.

30. See, for example, David F. Noble, *Forces of Production, A Social History of Industrial Automation* (New York, 1984), esp. pp. 265–323. It should be noted, nevertheless, that "the grade of skill in machinery factories," which most radical accounts emphasize," is somewhat higher than in the manufacturing industries as a whole. ..." Harry Jerome, *Mechanization in Industry* (New York, 1934), pp. 391–92.

31. In 1918 Bethlehem substituted piece rates, without time studies, for the task and bonus in machine shop no. 2, where Taylor did most of his work. Cowdrick, "Methods of Wage Payment," Bethlehem Steel Company Papers, Bethlehem Steel report, p. 10.

32. Ibid., AT&T report, p. 7; Goodyear report, p. 1.

33. Ibid., General Electric report, p. 1. Also see H. Dubreuil, *Robots or Men? A French Workman's Experience in American Industry* (New York, 1930), pp. 170–71.

34. Cowdrick, "Methods of Wage Payment," Bethlehem Steel Company Papers, AT&T report, p. 7.

35. Stanley B. Mathewson to William M. Leiserson, August 15, 1929, box 2b, William M. Leiserson Papers, State Historical Society of Wisconsin, Madison.

36. Cowdrick, "Methods of Wage Payment," Bethlehem Steel Company Papers, Westinghouse report, p. 5.

37. Ibid., p. 12.

38. Ibid., Standard Oil report, p. 15.

39. Ibid., U.S. Rubber report, pp. 3, 8.

40. Ibid., International Harvester report, p. 3.

41. Ibid., General Motors report, p. 2.

42. For the "liberal" personnel movement, see Sanford Jacoby, *Employing Bureaucracy: Managers, Unions, and the Transformation of Work in American Industry, 1900–1945* (New York, 1985), pp. 126–80. See also Walter Dill Scott, Robert C. Clothier, and Stanley B. Mathewson, *Personnel Management: Principles, Practices, and Point of View* (New York, 1931).

43. Also see Dubrueil, *Robots or Men*, a similar account by a French union leader who worked in some of the same plants. Dubrueil emphasized the benign character of American industrial management.

44. See William B. Leiserson to Morris L. Cooke, November 13, 1928, box 9, Leiserson Papers.

45. Leiserson to Henry S. Dennison, November 2, 1926, box 11, Leiserson Papers. The research survey was published as Social Science Research Council, *Survey of Research in the Field of Industrial Relations* (New York, 1928). For the origins of the SSRC see Barry D. Karl, *Charles E. Merriam and the Study of Politics* (Chicago, 1974), pp. 125–36.

46. Stanley B. Mathewson, *Restrictions of Output Among Unorganized Workers* (New York, 1931), pp. 7–8.

47. Ibid., p. 8.

48. Leiserson to Mathewson, April 18, 1928, box 26, Leiserson Papers.
49. Leiserson to Mathewson, June 20, 1928, box 26, Leiserson Papers.
50. Mathewson, *Restriction of Output*, pp. 134–35.
51. Ibid., p. 135.
52. Ibid., p. 136.
53. Ibid., p. 137.
54. Ibid., p. 148.
55. Ibid., p. 153.
56. Ibid., pp. 146, 153, 151.
57. Henry S. Dennison to Leiserson, November 19, 1928," box 11, Leiserson Papers.
58. Walter V. Bingham, "The Personal Research Federation in 1928," box 10, Walter V. Bingham Papers, Carnegie-Mellon University, Pittsburgh, Pennsylvania.
59. *American Economic Review* (June 1931), 21:338.
60. Ibid.

4. FORD WELFARE CAPITALISM IN ITS ECONOMIC CONTEXT
Daniel M. G. Raff

1. David Hounshell, *From the American System to Mass Production 1800–1932: The Development of Manufacturing Technology in the United States* (Baltimore, 1984).
2. See, e.g., O. J. Abell, "Making the Ford Motor Car," *Iron Age* (June 13, 1912), 89:1454–60.
3. Hounshell, *From the American System*, p. 220.
4. Stephen Meyer, *The Five Dollar Day: Labor Management and Social Control in the Ford Motor Company 1908–1921* (Albany, 1976), p. 127, cites costs of roughly $108,000 per year in 1915. Employment in the home plant that year was about 19,000.
5. They met in meeting rooms on site and were taught by volunteers. The main ongoing item of expense probably would have been the electricity.
6. For more details of the calculations, see Daniel Raff, "Wage Determination Theory and the Five-Dollar Day at Ford," *Journal of Economic History* (1988), 48:389–92.
7. See, e.g., the famous passage in Stanley Matthewson, *Restriction of Output Among Unorganized Workers* (New York, 1931), pp. 125–26.
8. Perhaps the division of labor was radical enough that all such exercises of discretion were obvious to the supervisor.
9. See Meyer, *Five Dollar Day*, p. 54. This is opposite to what one would expect from a model in which pay can be substituted for supervision at the margin.
10. See, e.g., Allan Nevins, *Ford: The Times, the Man, the Company* (New York, 1954), p. 522. I should note that reports in contemporary newspapers suggest the strike seemed more alarming than Nevins wishes to acknowledge.
11. This is what I do in my *Buying the Peace: Wage Determination Theory, Mass Production, and the Five-Dollar Day at Ford* (forthcoming).
12. The reason only local reporters had been invited to the announcement was that the company wanted to communicate only with people who read Detroit newspapers (if they read any at all). Ford expressed considerable surprise later in the week about the amount of out-of-town interest the announcement had inspired. See H. H. Nimmo, "Talking It Over with Henry Ford," *Detroit Saturday Night*, January 10, 1914, pp. 9–10. One's credence in the surprise grows with the discovery that the company was utterly unprepared for the hoards of job seekers who

subsequently turned up. There is no evidence they prepared for any unusual number of inquirers at all.

13. W. A. Cole, *The Immigrant in Detroit* (Detroit, 1915), p. 14.

14. Ibid., p. 6.

15. "Report for the National Conference on Community Centers and Related Problems (Immigration)," in the file labeled "Correspondence . . . undated . . ." in the papers of the Americanization Committee of Detroit, Michigan Historical Collections, Bentley Historical Library, University of Michigan, Ann Arbor, Michigan.

16. See Boris Emmet, *Profit-Sharing in the United States*, U.S. Bureau of Labor Statistics Bulletin no. 208 (Washington, D.C., 1916), pp. 117–22.

17. Company archives, for example, record the following (Human Interest Story Number Nine, in the S. S. Marquis Papers, Ford Archives, Greenfield Village, Dearborn, Michigan:

"Life has been an uphill struggle for Joe since landing in America. He was a willing worker and not particular about the kind of employment he secured. For a time he worked digging sewers, then moved his family to [the Michigan beet fields] where he could support them in a way. Last spring he was unable to obtain . . . work and moved . . . to Detroit. . . . He went to the [Ford] Employment Office . . . and was . . . hired. Two days later an investigation was made to determine the man's eligibility to share in the profits of the company.

"The investigator found him located . . . in an old, tumbled-down one and a half story frame house. Four families lived there, one a negro family. Joe's apartment was one-half of the attic, consisting of three rooms, which were so low that a person of medium height could not stand erect—a filthy, foul-smelling hole.

"The family consisted of a wife and six children [ranging in age from a fifteen-year-old to a nursing baby] . . . [The] home was furnished with two dirty beds (one of which was occupied by the five children who slept crossways in same), a ragged and filthy rug, a rickety old table, and two bottomless chairs (the five children standing up at the table to eat). The wife and children were half clad, thin, pale, and hungry looking. . . .

"Their rent was past due; credit with the grocer and the butcher was exhausted; and six cents represented their cash on hand.

"A basket of provisions was taken to their home that very night. . . . [T]he officials of the company armed the investigator with a $50.00 bill and instructed him to relieve [the] family's immediate wants, and to help them make a start toward right living.

"Back rent was paid; grocery and meat bills settled and a five-room cottage rented a few blocks away. Enough moderate-priced furniture for comfort was bought; the kitchen was stocked with pots, pans, and provisions; coal supplied, and a liberal amount of soap was bought with instructions to use it freely, and cheap dresses were purchased for the wife and children."

Here ceases mere enterprise and expeditiousness: the rest is simply spectacle:

"When this was accomplished, the investigator had their dirty, old junk furniture loaded on a dray and under cover of night moved them to their new home. [The] load of rubbish was heaped in a pile in the back yard, a torch was applied, and it went up in smoke.

"There, upon the ashes of what had been their earthly possessions, this Russian peasant and his wife, with tears streaming down their faces, expressed their thanks and gratitude to Henry Ford, the FORD MOTOR COMPANY, and all those who had been instrumental in bringing about this marvellous change in their lives."

Both the rhetoric of these texts and their preservation by the Sociological Department clearly need to be discounted heavily for the natural motives of the reporters and their superiors. But unless one believes that the basic elements of the reports were simply invented, there are some facts to be made sense of here. It seems clear the company wished the workers to understand they were not simply paid in cash. The company offered them opportunities and interventions which were utterly beyond the workers' private efforts and ordinary market transactions.

18. "Meeting of the Sociological Department," May 12, 1915 in an untitled bound dittoed manuscript published by the Ford Motor Company Sociological Department in 1915, located in Small Accessions File 1018, box 25, p. 6, Ford Archives.

19. Ibid., p. 8.

20. Thus W. M. Purves: "[t]he objective of the investigation is to help and not to cause trouble for an employee." See "The Investigator's Standing with Employees and Others," memo dated June 21, 1915 in Accession 940, box 17, Ford Archives.

21. Lawrence Cremin, *The Transformation of the School: Progressivism in American Education, 1876–1957* (New York, 1961), p. 73.

22. The phrase is that of the lessons' author in a later book about Americanization. See Peter Roberts, *The Problem of Americanization* (New York, 1920), p. 226.

23. Samuel Marquis, "The Ford Idea in Education," in National Education Association, *Addresses and Proceedings* (1916), 64:916.

24. Samuel Levin, "The Ford Profit-Sharing Plan, 1914–1920 I. The Growth of the Plan," *Personnel Journal* (1927), 6:80.

25. "The Making of New Americans," *Ford Times* (1916), 10:151.

26. Ibid.

27. Stuart Brandes, *American Welfare Capitalism, 1880–1940* (Chicago, 1976), pp. 5–6.

28. U.S. Bureau of Labor Statistics, *Welfare Work for Employees in Industrial Establishments in the United States*, Bulletin no. 250 (Washington, 1919), p. 8.

29. See, most famously, William Tolman, *Social Engineering: A Record of Things Done by American Industrialists Employing Upwards of One and a Half Million People* (New York, 1909); Elizabeth Otey, *Employers' Welfare Work*, U.S. Bureau of Labor Statistics Bulletin no. 123 (Washington, 1913); and the BLS survey cited in note 28 above.

30. David Brody, *Workers in Industrial America* (New York, 1980).

31. Brandes thinks this owed to workers' eventual realization that the programs served management's ends above their own. Brody argues that the programs were actually quite successful in establishing an atmosphere of goodwill and benevolence. Only the Great Depression cut this off, by force majeure; and it was that experience of vulnerability rather than the recognition of inner contradictions that led to the growth of union representation during the thirties.

32. Brody, *Workers in Industrial America*, e.g., p. 49.

33. Ibid., p. 51.

34. *Automobile*, May 7, 1914, p. 959.

35. See Daniel Raff, "Efficiency Wage Theory, the Intra- and Inter-Industry Structure of Earnings, and the Structure of the Production Process, or, Making Cars and Making Money in the 1920s," typescript (Boston, 1988).

36. Letter dated July 15, 1915 to Detroit Mayor Oscar Marx, "Correspondence . . . 1914–1915 . . . ," Americanization Committee Papers.

37. "Minutes of the Meeting of the [Board of Commerce] Committee on Education . . . August 24 [1915]," p. 2, ibid.

38. Memo entitled "Information for the Committee on Education" dated Janu-

ary 17, 1916, passim, "Correspondence 1916–1917," Americanization Committee Papers.

39. Memo entitled "Information for the Committee on Education" dated January 10, 1916, p. 1, ibid.

40. Memo dated January 17, 1916, p. 1, ibid.

41. Compare "Minutes of the meeting of the [Board of Commerce] Educational Committee ... August 31, 1915," p. 2, "Correspondence ... 1914–1915 ... ," Americanization Committee Papers, with Cole, *The Immigrant in Detroit*, pp. 9 and 14.

42. This can be calculated from "Ford Motor Company: Statistics: Wages and Hours" dated October 1, 1946, Accession AR-68-26, box 1, Ford Industrial Archive, Redmon, Michigan, and "Changes in Cost of Living in the U.S.," *Monthly Labor Review* (February, 1925), 20:69.

43. Edward Berkowitz and Kim McQuaid, "Businessman and Bureaucrat: The Evolution of the American Social Welfare System," *Journal of Economic History* (1978), 38:124.

44. See, for example, National Industrial Conference Board, *Industrial Relations Programs in Small Plants* (New York, 1929), pp. 16–20.

45. I have in mind in particular members of the Special Conference Committee.

46. Howard Gitelman, personal communication. The Griffin index derives from John I. Griffin, *Strikes: A Study in Quantitative Economics* (New York, 1939).

5. GETTING IT TOGETHER: THE METAL MANUFACTURERS ASSOCIATION OF PHILADELPHIA, C. 1900–1930

Howell John Harris

1. Mira Wilkins, "Business History as a Discipline," in William Hausman, ed., *Business and Economic History* (1988), 17:4.

2. David Brody, *Steelworkers in America: the Non-Union Era* (Cambridge, Mass., 1960); Robert Ozanne, *A Century of Labor-Management Relations at McCormick and International Harvester* (Madison, Wis., 1967); Daniel Nelson, *Managers and Workers: Origins of the New Factory System in the United States, 1880–1920* (Madison, Wis., 1975). See also discussion in Jonathan Zeitlin, "From Labour History to the History of Industrial Relations," *Economic History Review* (1987), 40:159–84.

3. Howell Harris, *The Right to Manage: Industrial Relations Policies of American Business in the 1940s* (Madison, Wis., 1982); Sanford Jacoby, *Employing Bureaucracy: Managers, Unions, and the Transformation of Work in American Industry, 1900–1945* (New York, 1985).

4. Michael Piore and Charles Sabel, *The Second Industrial Divide: Possibilities for Prosperity* (New York, 1984); Charles Sabel and Jonathan Zeitlin, "Historical Alternatives to Mass Production: Politics, Markets, and Technology in Nineteenth-Century Industrialization," *Past and Present* (1985), 108:133–76; critiqued in Karel Williams et al., "The End of Mass Production," *Economy and Society* (1987), 16:405–30.

5. This debate between historians parallels that between microeconomists and administrative scientists on the benefits of internalization. See Oliver E. Williamson, *Markets and Hierarchies* (New York, 1975); Charles Perrow, "Economic Theories of Organization," *Theory and Society* (1986), 15:11–45.

6. Scranton, *Proprietary Capitalism: The Textile Manufacture at Philadelphia* (New York, 1983) and *Figured Tapestry: Production, Markets, and Power in Philadelphia Textiles, 1885–1940* (New York, 1989).

7. Mark Granovetter, "Small Is Bountiful: Labor Markets and Establishment Size," *American Sociological Review* (1984), 49:323–34.

8. Jeffrey Haydu, *Between Craft and Class: Skilled Workers and Factory Politics in the United States and Britain, 1890–1922* (Berkeley, 1988).

9. Principal primary sources for the MMA are its surviving papers, hereafter referred to as MMAP, Accession 44, Urban Archives, Temple University, Philadelphia, Pennsylvania. These include executive committee minutes, presidents' and secretaries' reports, financial statements, and miscellaneous documents—copies of collective bargaining agreements, wage data surveys, etc.

10. Milton Derber, "Employers' Associations in the U.S.A.," in John P. Windmuller and Alan Gladstone, eds., *Employers Associations and Industrial Relations: A Comparative Study* (Oxford, 1984); Keith Sissons, *The Management of Collective Bargaining: An International Comparison* (Oxford, 1987).

11. Studies near contemporary with the antiunion movement include Clarence E. Bonnett, *Employers' Associations in the United States* (New York, 1922); F. W. Hilbert, "Employers' Associations in the United States," in Jacob H. Hollander and George E. Barnett, eds., *Studies in American Trade Unionism* (London, 1906), pp. 185–200; Margaret L. Stecker, "The National Founders' Association," *Quarterly Journal of Economics* (1916), 30:352–86; William F. Willoughby, "Employers' Associations for Dealing With Labor in the United States," *Quarterly Journal of Economics*, (1905), 20:110–50.

From the collective bargaining era, see Jesse T. Carpenter, *Employers' Associations and Collective Bargaining in New York City* (Ithaca, 1950); Kenneth M. McCaffree, "A Theory of the Origins and Development of Employer Associations," pp. 56–68, and Max S. Wortman, Jr., "Influences of Employer Bargaining Associations in Manufacturing Firms," pp. 69–82, both in Gerald G. Somers, ed., *Proceedings of the Fifteenth Annual Meeting of the Industrial Relations Research Association* (Madison, Wis., 1963); Gerald G. Somers, "Pressures on an Employers' Association in Collective Bargaining," *Industrial and Labor Relations Review* (1957), 6:556–69; Daniel M. Slate, "Trade Union Behavior and the Local Employers' Association," *Industrial and Labor Relations Review* (1957), 11:42–55.

12. See, in addition to sources cited above, Albion G. Taylor, *Labor Policies of the National Association of Manufacturers* (Urbana, Ill., 1928); Howard Gitelman, "Management's Crisis of Confidence and the Origins of the National Industrial Conference Board, 1914–1916," *Business History Review* (1984), 58:153–77; Thomas Klug, "Employers' Strategies in the Detroit Labor Market, 1900–1929," in Nelson Lichtenstein and Stephen Meyer, eds., *On the Line: Essays in the History of Auto Work* (Urbana, Ill., 1989), ch. 3, esp. pp. 44–54; *Employers' Association of Detroit: Its Organization and Activities* (Detroit, 1921); Alfred H. Kelly, *The Illinois Manufacturers' Association* (Chicago, 1940).

13. William H. Chartener, "The Molders' and Foundry Workers' Union: A Study of Union Development," (Ph.D. diss., Harvard University, 1952), pp. 338; Mark Perlman, *The Machinists: A New Study in American Trades Unionism* (Cambridge, Mass., 1961), p. 206; U.S. Department of Labor, Bureau of Apprenticeship, *The Skilled Labor Force: A Study of Census Data on the Craftsman Population of the United States, 1870–1950*, Technical Bulletin no. T-140 (Washington, D.C., 1954). Cf. Leo Wolman, "The Extent of Labor Organization in the United States in 1910," *Quarterly Journal of Economics* (1916), 30:486–518, 601–24.

14. U.S. Department of the Interior, Bureau of the Census, *Twelfth Census Reports* (Washington, D.C., 1902), 7:ccxxx, ccxxxviii–ix.

15. Quantitative information on the MMA is drawn from a database including membership data compiled from MMAP, and reports on individual firms' work force size and industrial classification from the Commonwealth of Pennsylvania's *Second* through *Seventh Industrial Director[ies]* (Harrisburg, Pa., 1916–1930).

16. *Twelfth Census Reports,* 8:786–89.

17. Rowland Berthoff, "The Freedom to Control in American Business History," in David H. Pinkney and Theodore Ropp, eds., *A Festschrift for Frederick B. Artz* (Durham, N.C., 1964), pp. 158–80.

18. Larry Griffin et al., "Capitalist Resistance to the Organization of Labor Before the New Deal: Why? How? Success?" *American Sociological Review* (1986), 51:146–67.

19. U.S. Commission on Industrial Relations, *Industrial Relations: Final Report and Testimony. . . .* 64th Congr., 1st. sess. (1916), 3:2817–2922: See also Ken Fones-Wolf, "Mass Strikes, Corporate Strategies: The Baldwin Locomotive Works and the Philadelphia General Strike of 1910," *Pennsylvania Magazine of History and Biography* (1986), 110:447–57; Gerald G. Eggert, *Steelmasters and Labor Reform, 1886–1923* (Pittsburgh, 1981), esp. chs. 5–6.

20. Interview schedules, Philadelphia Labor Market Studies, in box 1 Accession 585, Gladys L. Palmer Papers, Urban Archives, Temple University, Philadelphia—occupational histories and comments from a sample of some 700 millwrights and machinists in May 1936.

21. Donald Tulloch, *Worcester: City of Prosperity* (Worcester, Mass., 1914).

22. Dorothea De Schweinitz, *How Workers Find Jobs: A Study of Four Thousand Hosiery Workers in Philadelphia* (Philadelphia, 1932); Joseph H. Willits, *Philadelphia Unemployment: With Special Reference to the Textile Industries* (Philadelphia, 1915); Frances A. Kellor, *Out of Work: A Study of Unemployment* (New York, 1915); Don D. Lescohier, *The Labor Market* (New York, 1919).

23. Eugene P. Ericksen and William C. Yancey, "Work and Residence in Industrial Philadelphia," *Journal of Urban History* (1979), 5:147–78; Gladys L. Palmer, *Philadelphia Workers in a Changing Economy* (Philadephia, 1956); William M. Hench, *Trends in the Size of Industrial Companies in Philadelphia from 1915 through 1930* (Ph.D. diss., University of Pennsylvania, 1938).

24. H. Larue Frain, *An Examination of Earnings in Certain Standard Machine-Tool Occupations in Philadelphia* (Philadelphia, 1929); Irving L. Horowitz, *The Metal Machining Trades in Philadelphia: An Occupational Study* (Ph.D. diss., University of Pennsylvania, 1939).

25. Anne Bezanson and Robert Gray, *Trends in Foundry Production in the Philadelphia Area* (Philadelphia, 1929); Alfred H. Williams, *Study of the Adequacy of Existing Programs for the Training of Journeymen Molders in the Iron and Steel Foundries of Philadelphia* (Ph.D. diss., University of Pennsylvania, 1924); Mildred Fairchild, "Skill and Specialization: A Study in the Metal Trades," *Journal of Personnel Research* (1930), 9:28–71, 128–75.

26. Commission on Industrial Relations, *Final Report,* 3:2889–2914. This testimony is confirmed by MMAP internal evidence.

27. J. Roffe Wike, *The Pennsylvania Manufacturers' Association* (Philadelphia, 1960).

28. Steven A. Sass, *The Pragmatic Imagination: A History of the Wharton School, 1881–1981* (Philadelphia, 1982), chs. 6–7.

29. James H. Soltow, "Origins of Small Business: Metal Fabricators and Machinery Makers in New England, 1890–1957," *Transactions of the American Philosophical Society* (December 1965), vol. 55, pt. 10.

6. THE CLOSED SHOP, THE PROPRIETARY CAPITALIST, AND THE LAW, 1897–1915

Daniel R. Ernst

1. The labor economist Edwin E. Witte counted a total of 1,845 labor injunctions obtained by employers, nonunion workers, and unions in state and federal courts between 1880 and 1930. Twenty-eight (2 percent) of Witte's injunctions were granted in the 1880s, 122 (7 percent) in the 1890s, 328 (18 percent) between 1900 and 1909, 446 (24 percent) between 1910 and 1919, and 921 (50 percent) between January 1, 1920 and May 1, 1930. Edwin E. Witte, *The Government in Labor Disputes* (New York, 1932), p. 84. William E. Forbath has recently revised Witte's figures. He estimates that courts issued at least 4,330 antistrike or antiboycott injunctions between 1880 and 1930. Of these 105 (2 percent) were issued in the 1880s, 410 (9 percent) in the 1890s, 850 (20 percent) in the 1900s, 835 (19 percent) in the 1910s, and 2,130 (49 percent) in the 1920s. William E. Forbath, "The Shaping of the American Labor Movement," *Harvard Law Review* (April 1989), 102:1249.

2. Examples include Christopher L. Tomlins, *The State and the Unions: Labor Relations, Law, and the Organized Labor Movement in America, 1880–1960* (New York, 1985); Nelson Lichtenstein, *Labor's War at Home: The CIO in World War Two* (New York, 1982); Karl E. Klare, "Labor Law as Ideology: Toward a New Historiography of Collective Bargaining Law," *Industrial Relations Law Journal* (1981), 4:450–82; Katherine Van Wezel Stone, "The Post-War Paradigm in American Labor Law," *Yale Law Journal* (June 1981), 90:1509–80; James B. Atleson, *Values and Assumptions in American Labor Law* (Amherst, Mass., 1983).

3. Examples include Sylvester Petro, "Injunctions and Labor Disputes: 1880–1932," *Wake Forest Law Review* (1978), 14:341–576; Richard A. Epstein, "A Common Law of Labor Relations? A Critique of the New Deal," *Yale Law Journal* (July 1983), 92:1357–1408; Howard Dickman, *Industrial Democracy in America: Ideological Origins of National Labor Relations Policy* (La Salle, Ill., 1987).

4. Naomi R. Lamoreaux, *The Great Merger Movement in American Business, 1895–1904* (New York, 1985), p. 2.

5. Leo Wolman, *The Growth of American Trade Unions, 1880–1923* (New York, 1924), pp. 33, 110–19; Frank T. Stockton, *The Closed Shop in American Trade Unions* (Baltimore, 1911), p. 40; David Montgomery, *Workers' Control in America* (New York, 1979), pp. 97, 98.

6. Julian Vallette Wright, "Which, the Open or Closed Shop?" *Open Shop* (January 1905), 4:10.

7. Bruno Ramirez, *When Workers Fight: The Politics of Industrial Relations in the Progressive Era, 1898–1916* (Westport, Conn., 1978), pp. 17–84; Clarence E. Bonnett, *Employers' Associations in the United States: A Study of Typical Associations* (New York, 1922), pp. 22–23; Lloyd Ulman, *The Rise of the National Trade Union* (Cambridge, Mass., 1966), pp. 519–35.

8. Robert H. Wiebe, *Businessmen and Reform: A Study of the Progressive Movement* (Cambridge, Mass., 1962), p. 165. For a model study of the interplay of the interests and beliefs of proprietary capitalists, see Philip Scranton, *Proprietary Capitalism: The Textile Manufacture at Philadelphia, 1800–1885* (New York, 1983).

9. I am indebted to Thomas Klug for references to the Detroit lawyers. This essay is part of a larger study of the AABA and its successor, the League for Industrial Rights. The best of the published studies on the group is Bonnet, *Employers' Associations*, pp. 449–74.

10. "Interview with Dudley Taylor, Counsel of the Chicago Employers' Associ-

ation, at His Office, September 30, 1914," box 20A, United States Manuscripts, State Historical Society of Wisconsin, Madison, Wisconsin.

11. The official was John H. Brine of the Allen-A Hosiery Company of Kenosha, Wisconsin; he addressed the Open Shop Committee of the NAM in October 1928. The unpublished report of his speech appears in box 251, NAM Papers, Eleutherian Mills Historical Library, Wilmington, Delaware.

12. Witte, *Government*, p. 113; see also David Montgomery, *The Fall of the House of Labor: The Workplace, the State, and American Labor Activism, 1865–1925* (New York, 1987), pp. 271–72.

13. Edwin E. Witte, "Injunctions in Labor Disputes," appendix E (Report, U.S. Commission on Industrial Relations, 1915), pp. 53–56 (microfilm ed., State Historical Society of Wisconsin); "Interview with Dudley Taylor"; Parshelsky Brothers to Harry Gould, July 2, 1911, Paine Lumber Co. v. Neal, 244 U.S. 459 (1917), record at 1936–37, *United States Supreme Court Records and Briefs* (Information Handling Services).

14. This point emerged from the conflicting testimony of Daniel Davenport and Walter Drew before the U.S. Commission on Industrial Relations. *Industrial Relations: Final Report and Testimony Submitted to Congress by the Commission on Industrial Relations Created by the Act of August 23, 1912*, 64th Cong., 1st sess., Senate Doc. no. 415 (1916), 11:10753.

15. Of a total of 314 cases in which labor unions or their members were defendants, Witte counted only 66 in which damages were recovered, and these included suits by nonunionists and expelled union members as well as by employers. Witte, *Government*, pp. 138–39.

16. The NAACP's campaign against segregation illustrates this point; so does litigation conducted by the Singer Manufacturing Company in the late nineteenth century to overturn state-imposed restrictions on their salesmen. Mark V. Tushnet, *The NAACP's Legal Strategy Against Segregated Education, 1925–1950* (Chapel Hill, N.C., 1987); Charles W. McCurdy, "American Law and the Marketing Structure of the Large Corporation, 1875–1890," *Journal of Economic History* (September 1978), 38:631–49.

17. Commonwealth v. Carlisle, Brightly's Rep. 36 (Pa. 1821); see Witte, *Government*, pp. 46–48; Haggai Hurvitz, "American Labor Law and the Decline of Entrepreneurial Property Rights: Boycotts, Courts, and the Juridical Reorientation of 1886–1895," *Industrial Relations Law Journal* (1986), 8:307–61.

18. "The Open Shop," *Shoe Workers' Journal* (April 1904), 5:6.

19. Curran v. Galen, 152 N.Y. 33 (1897).

20. Charles Fisk Beach, *A Treatise on the Law of Monopolies and Industrial Trusts* (St. Louis, 1898), pp. 344–45; Arthur J. Eddy, *The Law of Combinations* (Chicago, 1901), 1:435.

21. Ernest F. Eidlitz to Otto M. Eidlitz, April 19, 1900, box 1, Marc Eidlitz & Son Papers, New York Public Library, New York City.

22. "Third Annual Convention of the Citizen's Industrial Association of America," *Square Deal* (December 1905), 1:23.

23. Christensen v. Kellogg Switchboard and Supply, Co., 110 Ill. App. 61, 66–67 (1903). My summary of the Kellogg strike relies heavily upon Howard Barton Myers, "The Policing of Labor Disputes in Chicago" (Ph.D. diss., University of Chicago, 1929), pp. 433–59.

24. On the Chicago teamsters, see Selig Perlman and Philip Taft, *History of Labor in the United States, 1896–1932* (New York, 1935), pp. 61–70; Isaac F. Marcosson, "Labor Met by Its Own Methods," *World's Work* (January 1904), 7:4309–14; Hayes Robbins, "The Employers' Fight Against Organized Labor," *World To-Day* (May 1904), 6:624–25; Isaac F. Marcosson, "The Fight for the 'Open Shop,'" *World's Week* (December 1905), 11:6955–65.

25. William Hard, "A History of the Kellogg Strike," *Bulletin of the National Metal Trades Association* (January 1904), 3:25 (hereafter cited as *Bull. NMTA*); *Chicago Daily Tribune*, July 21, 1903.

26. *Bull. NMTA* (September 1903), 2:731; *Chicago Tribune*, July 23–24, 1903; *Eighth Annual Report of the State Board of Arbitration of Illinois* (Springfield, 1904), p. 41; Myers, "Policing," pp. 441–42.

27. This was Allen's formulation of the theory. For Holdom's somewhat muddier version, see Jesse Holdom, *Legal and Historical Progress of Trade Unions* (n.p. [1905]), p. 9.

28. Christensen v. Kellogg Switchboard & Supply Co., 110 Ill. App. 61, 73 (1903); *Jacob Christensen, et al., vs. Kellogg Switchboard and Supply Co., Brief and Argument and Decision of Appellate Court of Illinois* (Reprinted from the corporation's Auxiliary Company Bulletin, vol. 2, no. 3, for the American Anti-Boycott Association) (Cleveland, 1903), pp. 180, 228, 202. Wilkerson would later become a federal district judge and in that capacity follow this reasoning in issuing a sweeping injunction during the railroad shop-crafts strike of 1922. See Irving Bernstein, *The Lean Years: A History of the American Worker, 1920–1933* (Boston, 1966), pp. 211–12.

29. *Christensen*, 110 Ill. App. at 71, 74, 72, 75.

30. "War on Boycotters," *Bull. NMTA* (September 1903), 2:738; Christensen v. People, 114 Ill. App. 40, 53–54, 55–57 (1904).

31. *Christensen*, 114 Ill. App. at 64–66.

32. *Christensen*, 114 Ill. App. at 70–71, *affirmed*, O'Brien v. People, 216 Ill. 354 (1905).

33. "The Closed Shop," *Open Shop* (July 1905), 4:334–35, 328, 329.

34. "Is the Closed Shop Illegal and Criminal?" *National Civic Federation Monthly Review* (July 1904), 1:2 (hereafter cited as "NCF Symposium").

35. "Judicial Jumble on the 'Open Shop,'" *American Federationist* (July 1904), 11:585.

36. "NCF Symposium," pp. 2–3.

37. "Third Annual Convention," p. 23.

38. *Milwaukee Sentinel*, July 14, 1904; Jacobs v. Cohen, 99 A.D. 481, 485, 90 NYS 854 (1904); Berry v. Donovan, 188 Mass. 353, 74 N.E. 603 (1905).

39. See, for example, *Square Deal* (November 1907), 3:32.

40. State v. Stockford, 77 Conn. 277, 58 A. 769, 772 (1904).

41. *Jacobs*, 183 N.Y. at 210–11, 212, 215. For the AABA's attempt to overturn the decision, see AABA, *Quarterly Bulletin: February 1906* (n.p., 1906).

42. Kemp v. Division no. 241, 255 Ill. 213, 233–34, 248 (1912); AABA, *The Morals and Law Involved in Labor Conflicts* (New York [1908]), p. 29; Lindley D. Clark, "The Present Legal Status of Organized Labor in the United States," *Journal of Political Economy* (March 1905), 13:185; W. A. Martin, *A Treatise on the Law of Labor Unions* (Washington, D.C., 1910), p. 211; George Gorham Groat, *Attitude of American Courts in Labor Cases* (1911; reprint, New York, 1969), p. 168; C. B. Labatt, *Commentaries on the Law of Master and Servant*, 2d ed. (Rochester, N.Y., 1913), 8:8543.

43. *Jacobs*, 183 N.Y. at 213; Martin, *Law of Labor Unions*, p. 217.

44. Walter Gordon Merritt, *History of the League for Industrial Rights* (New York, 1925), pp. 93–95; Anon. to Martin Lawlor, April 23, 1912, box HRD-20, United Hatters of North America Papers, Robert F. Wagner Labor Archives, Tamiment Institute Library, New York City.

45. Connors v. Connolly, 86 Conn. 641, 650–51 (1913).

46. AABA, *July Bulletin*, July 27, 1914. On developments in the law of antitrust in this period, see Martin J. Sklar, *The Corporate Reconstruction of American Capitalism, 1890–1916* (New York, 1988), pp. 86–175.

228 *6. The Closed Shop and the Law*

47. Frederick Hale Cooke, *The Law of Combinations, Monopolies, and Trade Unions*, 2d ed. (Chicago, 1909), pp. 98–99, 113–15. See generally Herbert Hovenkamp, "Labor Conspiracies in American Law, 1880–1930," *Texas Law Review* (1988), 66:925–32.
48. *Industrial Relations*, 11:10654–55.
49. For an introduction to the historical literature on the rise of a consumer culture in America, see Robert M. Collins, "David Potter's *People of Plenty* and the Recycling of Consensus History," *Reviews in American History* (1988), 16:329–33.
50. James Willard Hurst, *Law and Social Process in the United States* (Ann Arbor, 1960), p. 301.
51. For a thoughtful survey of recent developments in the law of labor relations, see Theodore J. St. Antoine, "Federal Regulation of the Workplace in the Next Half Century," *Chicago-Kent Law Review* (1985), 61:631–62.

7. THE DECLINE OF PATERNALISM AND THE MAKING OF THE EMPLOYER CLASS: FRANCE, 1870–1914

Gerald Friedman

1. The literature on the development of labor movements in different countries is vast. For a few representative works, see Edward P. Thompson, *The Making of the English Working Class* (New York, 1963); John R. Commons et al., *History of Labor in the United States*, 4 vols. (New York, 1966); David Montgomery, *The Fall of the House of Labor* (Cambridge, Eng., 1987); Ira Katznelson and Aristide R. Zolberg, *Working-Class Formation* (Princeton, 1986). For France, in particular, see Edward Shorter and Charles Tilly, *Strikes in France, 1830–1968* (Cambridge, Eng. 1974); Edouard Dolléans, *Histoire du mouvement ouvrier, 1871–1936* (Paris, 1939); Michelle Perrot, *Les ouvriers en grève* (Paris, 1974); Yves Lequin, *Les ouvriers de la région lyonnaise (1848–1914)* (Lyon, 1975).
2. Employers barely appear even in such major works of French labor history as Edward Shorter and Charles Tilly's *Strikes in France* or Michelle Perrot's *Les ouvriers en grève*. The index to the Shorter and Tilly volume includes one line with ten references to "unions, employers' " compared with a full column of references to unions of workers. "Syndicalisme, patronal" similarly rates only two lines in Perrot's index, with only 8 references in 734 pages.
3. Perhaps the bourgeoisie remains, as Roland Barthes said, a "class that does not want to be known as such." Selig Perlman, one of the leading figures in American labor history, signaled the importance of studying capitalists and capitalist class formation in his pioneering work, *A Theory of the Labor Movement* (New York, 1928). His counsel has not been heeded, however. Only a handful of works directly address the development of capitalist class action in France; see, for example, André François-Poncet, *La vie et l'oeuvre de Robert Pinot* (Paris, 1927); Etienne Villey, *L'organization professionnelle des employeurs dans l'Industrie française* (Paris, 1923); Roget Priouret, *Origines du patronat français* (Paris, 1963); Georges Lefranc, *Les organisations patronales en France* (Paris, 1976); Louis Bergeron, *Les capitalistes en France (1780–1914)* (Paris, 1978); Bernard Bizay, *Le patronat: histoire, structure, stratégie du CNPF* (Paris, 1975); J. Lefort, *L'assurance contre les grèves* (Paris, 1911). Employer organizations are discussed tangentially in Michelle Perrot's "Le regard de l'autre: les patrons français vus par les ouvriers (1880–1914)," in M. Lévy-Leboyer, *Le patronat de la seconde industrialisation* (Paris, 1979), pp. 293–306; and in Jacques Houssiaux, *Le pouvoir de monopole* (Paris, 1958).

4. See, for example, Sanford Elwitt's study, *The Making of the Third Republic: Class and Politics in France, 1868–1884* (Baton Rouge, 1975); Jean Lhomme's classic, *La grande bourgeoisie au pouvoir, 1830–1880* (Paris, 1960). A more subtle approach is followed in the classic study of French industrial relations by Pierre Laroque, *Les rapports entre patrons et ouvriers* (Paris, 1938). Also see Michael Smith, *Tariff Reform in France, 1860–1900* (Ithaca, N.Y., 1980); Herman Lebovics, "Protection Against Labor Troubles," *International Review of Social History* (Spring 1986), 31:147–65; Henry Peiter, "Institutions and Attitudes: The Consolidation of the Business Community in Bourgeois France," *Journal of Social History* (June 1976), 9:510–25; Peter Stearns, *Paths to Authority* (Urbana, Ill., 1978).

5. F. Engels, "Trade Unions," in K. Marx and Engels, *Werke* (Berlin, 1963), 19:256, quoted in Peter Schottler, *Naissance des bourses du travail* (Paris, 1985), p. 203 (the English here is my translation from Schottler's French). Engels's words recall those of Adam Smith, *The Wealth of Nations* (Chicago, 1976, reprint of 5th ed.), p. 75: "We rarely hear, it has been said, of the combinations of masters. . . . But whoever imagines upon this account that masters rarely combine, is as ignorant of the world as of the subject. Masters are always and everywhere in a sort of tacit, but constant and uniform combination, not to raise wages of labor."

6. The new literature on the state (often inspired by Shorter and Tilly's *Strikes in France*) introduces state officials as independent actors with their own interests. See Peter Evans, et al., eds., *Bringing the State Back In* (Cambridge, Eng., 1985); Gerald Friedman, "French Republicanism in Theory and Decline" (unpublished manuscript, University of Massachusetts, 1987); Gerald Friedman, "The State and the Making of the Working Class," *Theory and Society* (May 1988), 17:403–30; Carol Conell, "Bring in the State: Arbitration in Nineteenth Century Massachusetts" (unpublished manuscript, Stanford University). For a perceptive critique of this approach, see Fred Block, *Revising State Theory: Essays in Politics and Postindustrialism* (Philadelphia, 1987).

7. This, of course, was Werner Sombart's approach in *Why Is There No Socialism in America?* (White Plains, N.Y., 1976 [translation and reprint of 1902 ed.]). For more recent examples, see Duncan Gallie, *Social Inequality and Class Radicalism in France and Britain* (Cambridge, Eng., 1983); Mike Davis, *Prisoners of the American Dream* (London, 1986). For discerning criticisms of this view, see Reeve Vanneman and Lynn Weber Cannon, *The American Perception of Class* (Philadelphia, 1987); Stearns, *Paths.*

8. Even outside agriculture there were nearly as many employers as workers, with one employer for every two French nonagricultural workers and one for every one and one-half manufacturing workers.

French employers were relatively numerous compared with those in other developed, capitalist economies; see Gerald Friedman, *Politics and Unions* (Ph.D. diss., Harvard University, 1986), pp. 101–2.

9. Brizay, *Le patronat*, p. 11.

10. See the discussion in Lefranc, *Les organisations*, pp. 31–32; Peiter, "Institutions"; Stearns, *Paths*, pp. 13–34; Alfred Cobban, "The 'Middle Class' in France," *French Historical Studies* (Spring 1967), pp. 42–51; Judith Stone, *The Search for Social Peace Reform Legislation in France, 1890–1914* (Albany, 1985), pp. 170–73.

11. See Archives Nationales de France (AN), box F7 4667, for one case where the strikers were subsidized by a firm's competitors. Employers were also rumored to be subsidizing a Limoges pottery strike described in John Merriman, *The Red City* (Oxford, 1985), p. 114. See also Peter Stearns, "Against the Strike Threat: Employer Policy Toward Labor Agitation in France, 1900–1914," *Journal of Modern History* (1968), 40:474–500. Gérard Noiriel, *Les ouvriers dans la société française* (Paris, 1986), p. 114, notes that employers' resistance to militant labor in the early

230 *7. The Decline of Paternalism*

1890s often failed because of their "disarray" in confronting "powerful strike movements."

12. Stanley Hoffmann, "Paradoxes of the French Political Community," in Hoffmann ed., *In Search of France* (New York, 1963); M. Crozier, *La société bloquée* (Paris, 1980); Stone, *Search for Social Peace.*

13. Lorwin, *French Labor Movement,* p. 16.

14. David Landes, "French Entrepreneurship and Industrial Growth in the Nineteenth Century," *Journal of Economic History* (1949), 9:45–61; David Landes, *The Unbound Prometheus* (Cambridge, Mass., 1969); Thomas Kemp, *Industrialization in Nineteenth-Century Europe* (Oxford, 1982). This image is most appropriate for employers in some industries. Textile firms were often family firms even while metallurgical firms, mines, and chemical firms were large joint stock businesses dependent on bank credit. Enterprises were very small in most other industries, including printing, food processing, clothing, construction. On average, French industrial establishments had half as many employees as their American counterparts; see Friedman, *Politics,* pp. 164–102.

An alternative literature has developed emphasizing the successes of French industrialization. See, for example, R. Roehl, "French Industrialization: A Reconsideration," *Explorations in Economic History* (1976), 13:233–81; Patrick O'Brien and Caglar Keyder, *Economic Growth in Britain and France* (Oxford, 1976).

15. C. Robert in *La suppression des grèves par l'association aux bénéfices* (Paris, 1870), quoted in Alberto Melucci, "Action patronale, pouvoir, organisation: réglements d'usine et contrôle de la main-d'oeuvre au XIXᵉ siècle," *Le mouvement sociale* (1976), 97:143.

16. A. Gratiot, *Distribution des prix faite aux enfants* (Lille, 1848), quoted in Melucci, "Action patronale," p. 140.

17. Donald Reid, "Labor Management and Labor Conflict," *Social History* (January 1988), 13:39.

18. Henri Ameline, *Conférence des institutions ouvrières au dix-neuvième siècle* (Paris, 1866), pp. 25–26.

19. Melucci, "Action Patronale," p. 158.

Not all French employers were paternalists. While paternalism provided the model and the ideological justification for employers' domination of the labor process, it was concentrated in large establishments, especially in mining, metalworking, and textiles; Stearns, *Paths,* p. 89.

20. See Donald Reid, "Industrial Paternalism: Discourse and Practice in Nineteenth-Century French Mining and Metallurgy," *Comparative Studies in Society and History* (October 1985), 27:579–608; Michelle Perrot, "The Three Ages of Industrial Discipline in Nineteenth-Century France," in John Merriman, *Consciousness and Class Experience in Nineteenth-Century Europe* (New York, 1979).

In single-industry towns in isolated areas, employers also provided public goods. Because they know their own plans, employers could improve on the operation of product markets by providing housing and other services in areas where outside entrepreneurs might hesitate to invest for fear that their investment would be completely dependent on the behavior of a single company.

21. Reid, "Industrial Paternalism," p. 584. Also see Gérard Noiriel, "Du 'patronage' au 'paternalisme': la restructuration des formes de domination de la main-d'oeuvre ouvrière dans l'industrie métallurgique française," *Le mouvement social* (July–September 1988), 144:17–36.

For the ideological association between the church and paternalist employers, see Pierre Pierrard, *L'église et les ouvriers en France (1840–1940)* (Paris, 1984), pp. 116–20, 254–56, 397–405; and Alain Cottereau, "The Distinctiveness of Working-Class Cultures in France, 1848–1900," in Ira Katznelson and Aristide R. Zolberg,

Working-Class Formation (Princeton, 1986), pp. 147–48. Paternalist employers subsidized the church throughout France; see, for example, Reid, *Decazeville*, p. 20; Elinor Accampo, *Industrialization, Family Life, and Class Relations: Saint Chamond, 1815–1914* (Berkeley, 1989), pp. 152–54, 167; and Alberto Melucci, "Action patronale," p. 155. In response, by the late nineteenth century French working-class activists held anticlerical values; see Henry Steele, *The Working Classes in France: A Social Study* (London, 1904), pp. 52, 68; Noiriel, *Les ouvriers*, p. 101.

22. Paternalists implicitly admitted this when they complained of the impact on their workers of outside agitators—"traveling salesmen of social revolt"—and strikes; Serge Bonnet and Roger Humbert, *La ligne rouge des hauts fourneaux* (Paris, 1981), p. 87; Stearns, *Paths*, p. 86.

23. Reid, *Decazeville*, p. 39.

24. Priouret, *Origines*, pp. 59, 60, 63; Brizay, *Le patronat*, pp. 12, 15. While these organizations are the best known, among the earlier ones are the Parisian Réunion des fabricants de bronze, formed in 1818; see Lincoln, "Le syndicalisme patronal."

25. Legislation enacted in 1854 gave workers the right to hold their *livrets*. In practice, however, managers continued to hold them, preserving their right to prevent workers from leaving or to punish workers who quit. In 1868, l'Association des Filateurs de Lille declared that "following a time-honored usage, the *livret* stays in the factory office, that is to say in the hands of the *patron*. We feel that this is proper; the law [i.e. the 1854 amendment] is wrong and usage right." Quoted in Melucci, "Action patronale," p. 143.

Note, however, that legal restrictions on labor mobility were not always enforced, especially in tight labor markets; Stearns, *Paths*, pp. 81–82.

26. Monique Kieffer, "La législation prud'hommale de 1806 à 1907," *Le mouvement social* (October–December 1987), 141:9–24.

27. Except briefly under the Second Republic.

28. Perrot, "Three Ages," p. 160.

29. Henry Noëll, *Au temps de la République Bourgeoise* (Paris, 1957); Elwitt, *Making*; E. Beau de Lomenie, *Les responsabilités des dynasties bourgeoises*, 3 vols. (Paris, 1954); Lhomme, *La grande bourgeoisie*.

30. Perrot, *Les ouvriers*, pp. 182–183. See also Jean Bouvier, "Aux origines de la Troisième Républiques: les réflexes sociaux des milieux d'affaires," *Révue historique* (1953), pp. 271–301.

31. Lhomme, *La grande bourgeoisie*, pp. 278, 280.

32. Katherine Auspitz, *The Radical Bourgeoisie* (Cambridge, Eng., 1982); Daniel Halévy, *La fin des notables* (Paris, 1930). On the social origins of republican deputies, see Mattei Dogan, "Les filières de la cariere politique en France," *Revue française sociologique* (1967), pp. 468–92.

33. See Auspitz, *Radical Bourgeoisie*, pp. 131–34; Merriman, *Red City*, pp. 110–15. Many businessmen also opposed the Empire in its last years, partly because of opposition to "oppressive centralization," the legalization of strikes in 1864, and the Cobden-Chevalier free trade treaty of 1860; see Priouret, *Origines*, pp. 159–89.

34. See Auspitz, *The Radical Bourgeoisie*, passim; Halévy, *La fin des notables*. On working-class hopes for the new republic, see, for example, Yves Lequin, *Les ouvriers de la région lyonnaise (1848–1914)* (Lyon, 1977), 2:204–20. On business support for the antirepublican opposition, see Friedman, "French Republicanism," p. 26.

35. In addition to Auspitz, *Radical Bourgeoisie*, see Jean Touchard, *La gauche en France depuis 1900* (Paris, 1981), pp. 20–52.

36. See Auspitz, *Radical Bourgeoisie*; Léon Bourgeois, *Solidarité* (Paris, 1902); A. Charpentier, *Le Parti Radical et Radical Socialiste à travers ses congrès, 1901–1911* (Paris, 1913); Leo Loubère, "The French Left-Wing Radicals: Their Views on Trade

Unionism, 1870–1898," *International Review of Social History* (1962), 7(2):203–30; Albert Milhaud, *Histoire du Radicalisme* (Paris, 1951); David Watson, *Georges Clemenceau* (Plymouth, 1974).

37. Quoted in Reid, "Industrial Paternalism," p. 581.

38. Paul Brousse in France, *Annales de la Chambre des députés, 1884*, p. 659; Georges Clemenceau and then Alain Tolain in France, *Annales du Chambre des députés, 1885*, pp. 899–900.

39. Brousse, *Annals, 1884*, p. 659.

40. Francis Laur quoted in Donald Reid's superb study, *The Miners of Decazeville: A Genealogy of Deindustrialization* (Cambridge, Mass., 1985), p. 103.

41. Gerald Friedman, "Union Strikes and Striking Unions" (unpublished manuscript, University of Massachusetts, November, 1987).

42. Donald Reid, "Putting Social Reform into Practice: Labor Inspectors in France, 1892–1914," *Journal of Social History* (1986), 20(1):67–87; Perrot, *Les ouvriers*, pp. 715–16; Peter Schottler, *Naissance des bourses du travail;* Friedman, "French Republicanism."

43. See, for example, the activities of the Limoges *bourse* described in Merriman, *Red City*, pp. 210–21.

44. Donald Reid, "Labor Management and Labor Conflict in Rural France: The Aubin Miners' Strike of 1869," *Social History* (1988), 13(1): 25–44.

45. Friedman, "Strike Success"; Shorter and Tilly, *Strikes*, pp. 21–45.

46. Pierre Sorlin, *Waldeck-Rousseau* (Paris, 1966); Joseph A. Roy, *Histoire de la famille Schneider et du Creusot* (Paris, 1962), pp. 97–100; Léon de Seilhac, *Les grèves* (Paris, 1903).

47. Under Waldeck-Rousseau's arbitration award, LeCreusot had to establish a system of workers' delegates in its works. Shortly afterward, however, LeCreusot, one of France's largest firms, with extensive holdings and political influence throughout the world, was able to transform this system into a "yellow," or employer-dominated, union.

48. Membership grew even faster before 1900, increasing by nearly 14 percent a year. Note that the French labor force scarcely grew during this period. The number of wage earners grew by 0.3 percent a year in 1886–1911, only 2.0 percent a year outside agriculture. See Friedman, *Politics*, p. 418.

49. Gerald Friedman, "Union Strikes"; Shorter and Tilly, *Strikes*, pp. 104–18. The economic recovery after the mid-1890s may have contributed to rising unionization and strike activity; but for an alternative explanation of union growth see Gerald Friedman, "Why Economic Models Can't Explain Early Union Growth" (unpublished manuscript, University of Massachusetts at Amherst, October 1985).

50. This was not true for all paternalists. In the eastern textile mills, for example, there were few strikes, only weak unions, and little Socialist political activity. On collective action and the importance of networks of social institutions see Reid, *Decazeville*, p. 52; Charles Tilly, *From Mobilization to Revolution* (Reading, Mass., 1978); Clark Kerr and Abraham Siegel, "The Inter-industry Propensity to Strike," in Arthur Kornhauser, et al., *Industrial Conflict* (New York, 1954), pp. 189–212; John D. McCarthy and Mayer N. Zald, "Resource Mobilization and Social Movements," *American Journal of Sociology* (1977), 82:1212–46.

51. Peter Campbell, *French Electoral Systems* (Hamden, Conn., 1965). Socialist support was concentrated among workers and miners in areas of strong union membership; see table 7.5.

52. Union Industrielle de l'Industrie Française, *Programme 1900* (Paris, 1901), p. 1; Peiter, "Institutions and Attitudes," p. 513. These claims about France's competitors were somewhat self-serving; see Arno Mayer, *The Persistence of the Old Regime* (New York, 1977).

53. Leon Bourgeois as prefect in the Tarn in 1883, quoted in Perrot, *Les ouvriers,* p. 700. Gauthier in France, Chamber of Deputies, *Journal officiel* (hereafter cited as *JO*) (May 7, 1907), p. 913; also note in the same debate (over banning the CGT), Deschanel, *JO* (May 8, 1907), pp. 936–38 and Ribot, *JO* (May 14, 1907), pp. 991–92. Employers sought to have strikers persecuted under article 1780 of the criminal code for violating the contract of employment by leaving work without notice. See Isidore Finance, *Les syndicats professionnels devant les tribunaux et le parlement depuis 1884* (Paris, 1911); C. Perreau, "Si la grève suspend le contrat de travail," in C. Gide, *Le droit de grève* (Paris, 1909), pp. 101–26.

54. Quoted in Peiter, "Institutions," p. 513.

55. A delegate to the 1901 founding convention of *Parti commercial et industriel français,* quoted in Philip Nord, "Le mouvement des petits commerçants et la politique en France de 1888 à 1914," *Le mouvement social* (January–March 1981), 114:46.

56. These were all precursors of the *Confédération nationale du patronat français;* see Nord, "Les petits commerçants," pp. 44–52; Brizay, *Le patronat,* pp. 12–15; Lefranc, *Les organisations,* pp. 38–43.

57. François-Poncet, *Robert Pinot,* p. 186.

58. P. Saint-Girons, quoted in Villey, *L'organisation professionnelle,* pp. 236–37. This work utilizes three data sets either new or never before used to study employer associations. First, I located employer associations from the registration records for associations registering under the 1884 law legalizing professional associations in France; Direction du Travail, *Annuaire des syndicats professionnels, 1911* (Paris, 1911). I collected data on each of the over 4,600 registered employer associations in continental France in 1910, recording the occupation of the members, the number of members, the existence of formal benefit funds, and the year of first organization. Data on total membership in employer associations by industry and department were matched with the French census of 1906 on the number of employers and self-employed by industry and department, as well as other characteristics of the industry and department. (These data are similar to those used in Friedman, *Politics.*)

To measure the impact of employer aassociations on strikes, I utilized the data on individual French strikes collected by Shorter and Tilly, including whether the struck employers belonged to a formal employer association. These data, and some additions I made to what Shorter and Tilly collected, are described in Friedman, *Politics;* and Gerald Friedman, "Strike Success and Union Ideology," *Journal of Economic History* (March 1988), 48(1):1–26.

I also collected data to measure the impact of membership in employer associations on political activity. The share of employers belonging to associations in a department was matched with election data for voting in the first round of the 1910 elections to the French Chamber of Deputies. These election data are described in Friedman, "French Republicanism."

59. Employer associations were formed an average of two years after the organization of a labor union in the industry and department.

60. Employer associations were especially common in strikes. While only 4 percent of all employers belonged to employer associations in 1910, the share of strikes where there was an employer association increased from 27 percent in 1895–1899 to 48 percent in 1910–1914.

The increase in the share of strikes with an employer union in 1910–1914 compared with 1895–1899 reflects the growth of labor militancy. Employer unions are most common in strikes in strike-prone areas, in urban areas, and in socialist strongholds. They are also most common in labor union–led strikes. The presence of a union on the employee side is associated with an increase in the probability that the employers will have a union, of 76 percent in 1895–1899 and 109 percent in 1910–1914. When other strike characteristics are controlled, including the presence of a union on the employee side, the likelihood that a strike will have an employer association actually peaks in 1896; all the increase in the share of strikes with employer associations after that is because of rising strike rates, socialist voting, and unionization.

61. Union Fédérale . . . métallurgie, *L'organisation patronale* (Paris, 1909), pp. 1, 13; Perrot, "Le regard," pp. 302–4. On Merrheim, see Nicholas Papayanis, *Alphsonse Merrheim: The Emergence of Reformism in Revolution* (Boston, 1985).

62. Union Fédérale, *L'organisation*, pp. 14, 31–34; Papayanis, *Merrheim*, pp. 14, 33–34. Some employer association leaders also emphasized their ability to support their members during strikes; A.-E. Sayous, "Le patronat et la grève," in Charles Gide, *Le droit de grève* (Paris, 1909), pp. 134–35; Stearns, "Against the Strike Threat."

63. Georges Berry, monarchist *rallié*, deputy from the Seine, and Père Danset, both quoted in Lefranc, *Les organisations*, pp. 47, 46.

64. Laroque, *Rapports*, p. 133.

65. Note that these only include associations registered under the 1884 law legalizing professional associations. While registration was free, there was rarely any penalty for not registering and some associations may have chosen not to comply with the law; it is possible that these associations were better organized and had more resources.

Laroque (*Rapports*, p. 135) suggests that after 1906 more employer associations had strike funds and other financial supports for struck employers. I have no evidence, however, that associations formed after 1906 had more benefit funds or were more effective in aiding strikes; François-Poncet makes the same claim for associations after 1906 (*Robert Pinot*, pp. 143, 177), as does Villey (*L'organisation*, p. 236).

66. Note that the share of employer associations with benefit funds is even lower than the share of unions with benefit funds; see Friedman, *Politics*, p. 99.

67. "Labor union" strikes are those involving formal organization on the part of the striking employees; even after 1900, nearly a third of strikes were conducted without any formal worker organization.

The effect of employers associations is calculated at the mean of the independent variables.

68. This result is from strike duration regressions controlling for the strike's location, issues, and outcome. These regressions are available from the author upon request.

69. Lefranc, *L'organisation*, p. 52. A similar point is made by Melucci, "Action patronale," p. 151.

70. Laroque, *Rapports*, p. 134, 135. Note that Laroque had personal experience of employer association's political activity during the Popular Front governments of the late 1930s.

71. François-Poncet, *Robert Pinot*, 173–75.

72. Even when they could not prevent mediation, employer associations limited the impact of intervention, lowering the positive effect of state intervention on strike success by nearly 20 percent. (This result is from regression similar to those in table 7.3 but including additional variables, including the effect of government mediation. These regressions are available from the author upon request.)

73. François-Poncet, *Robert Pinot*, pp. 164–65, 169.

74. Nord, "Les petits commerçants," p. 44. On the French right generally, see the classic, René Rémond, *Les droites en France* (Paris, 1982).

75. Nord, "Les petits commerçants," p. 53.

76. The effect of employer association and union membership on voting is calculated controlling for the industry distribution of the labor force and the share of wage earners and employers. The estimate of the impact of associations and unions on voting is made at the mean value of the dependent variables.

77. See Stone, *The Search for Social Peace;* Jean Touchard, *La gauche en France,* pp. 89–178.

78. The following argument is developed more fully in Gerald Friedman, "Capitalism versus Democracy: The American Case, 1870–1914" (unpublished manuscript, University of Massachusetts, September, 1988).

79. George Storm in United States Senate, *Relations Between Labor and Capital* (Washington, 1885), p. 99.

80. John Swinton in *John Swinton's Paper* (February 13, 1887), p. 1.

81. See F. W. Hilbert, "Employers' Associations in the United States," in George Barnett and Jacob Hollander, *Studies in American Trade Unionism* (New York, 1907), pp. 183–219; Clarence Bonnett, *Employers' Associations in the United States* (New York, 1922). On government policy, see Robert J. Goldstein, *Political Repression in Modern America* (Cambridge, Mass., 1978); David Montgomery, "Liberty and Union: Workers and Government in America, 1900–1940," in Robert Weible, et al., eds., *Essays from the Lowell Conference on Industrial History, 1980 and 1981* (Lowell, Mass., 1981), pp. 145–57.

82. John R. Commons, "Is Class Conflict in America Growing and Is It Inevitable?" *American Journal of Sociology* (1908), 13:763.

83. Hilbert, "Employers," p. 210.

84. Samuel Gompers, *Seventy Years of Life and Labor* (New York, 1925), p. 127.

85. On occasion, however, even American employers mobilize, as happened in the 1970s in the face of labor militancy and the growth of movements of environmentalists, consumers, blacks, women, and others protesting corporate policy. See, Thomas Edsell, *The New Politics of Inequality* (New York, 1985).

86. Papayanis, *Merrheim,* pp. 59–70; Christian Gras, "La Fédération des Métaux en 1913–1914 et l'évolution du syndicalisme révolutionnaire français," *Le Mouvement social* (1971), pp. 86–111; Jacques Julliard, *Clemenceau: briseur de grève* (Paris, 1965).

8. AMERICAN EXCEPTIONALISM REVISITED: THE IMPORTANCE OF MANAGEMENT

Sanford M. Jacoby

1. Gerald C. Friedman, "Politics and Unions: Government, Ideology, and the Labor Movement in the United States and France, 1880–1914" (Ph.D. diss., Harvard University, 1985), pp. 30–31; Richard Freeman, "Contraction and Expansion: The Divergence of Public and Private Sector Unionism in the United States," *Journal of Economic Perspectives* (September 1988), vol. 2.

2. Selig Perlman, *A Theory of the Labor Movement* (New York, 1928); John R. Commons, "Labor Movements" in E. Seligman, ed., *Encyclopaedia of the Social Sciences* (New York, 1932), vol. 8; Louis Hartz, *The Liberal Tradition in America* (New York, 1955); John H. M. Laslett and Seymour M. Lipset, *Failure of a Dream? Essays in the History of American Socialism* (Garden City, N.Y., 1974); Mike Davis, *Prisoners of the American Dream: Politics and Economy in the History of the U.S. Working Class* (London, 1986).

3. Sean Wilentz, "Against Exceptionalism: Consciousness and the American Labor Movement, 1790–1920" *International Labor and Working Class History* (Fall

1984), 26:1–24. By "feudalism" I do not mean an ideal construct but the existence of estates or visible social classes in a society emphasizing aristocracy and monarchy.

4. Aristide Zolberg, "How Many Exceptionalisms?" in Ira Katznelson and Zolberg, eds., *Working-Class Formation: Nineteenth-Century Patterns in Western Europe and the United States* (Princeton, 1986).

5. P. K. Edwards, *Strikes in the United States, 1881–1974* (Oxford, 1981); Michael Wallerstein, "Union Growth from the Unions' Perspective: Why Smaller Nations Are More Highly Organized," UCLA Institute of Industrial Relations working paper, Los Angeles, August 1987.

6. Lloyd Ulman, "Who Wanted Collective Bargaining in the First Place?" In *Thirty-ninth Annual Proceedings of the Industrial Relations Research Association* (New York, 1986), p. 2.

7. Lloyd Ulman, "Some International Crosscurrents in Labor Relations" in Eric Flamholtz, ed., *The Future Direction of Employee Relations* (Los Angeles, 1985), p. 105.

8. David Granick, *Managerial Comparisons of Four Developed Countries: France, Britain, United States, and Russia* (Cambridge, Mass., 1972).

9. Geert Hofstede, *Culture's Consequences: International Differences in Work-Related Values* (Beverly Hills, 1984); Hofstede, "Nationality and Espoused Values of Managers", *Journal of Applied Psychology* (April 1976), 61:148–55; Hofstede, "Businessmen and Business School Faculty: A Comparison of Value Systems," *Journal of Management Studies* (February 1978), 15:77–89. See also George W. England, *The Manager and His Values: An International Perspective* (Cambridge, Mass., 1975).

10. Reinhard Bendix, *Work and Authority in Industry* (New York, 1956); Francis X. Sutton, Seymour Harris, Carl Kaysen, and James Tobin, *The American Business Creed* (Cambridge, Mass., 1956).

11. David Vogel, "Why Businessmen Distrust Their State: The Political Consciousness of American Corporate Executives," *British Journal of Political Science* (January 1978), 8:63. See also Thomas K. Mc Craw, "Business and Government: The Origins of the Adversary Relationship," *California Management Review* (Winter 1984), 26:33–52.

12. John G. Cawelti, *Apostles of the Self-Made Man* (Chicago, 1965).

13. Rowland Berthoff, "The 'Freedom to Control' in American Business History," in David Pinkney and Theodore Ropp, eds., *A Festschrift for Frederick B. Artz* (Durham, N.C., 1964).

14. Everett M. Kassalow, *Trade Unions and Industrial Relations: An International Comparison* (New York, 1969); L. Hamburger, "The Extension of Collective Agreements to Cover Entire Trades and Industries," *International Labour Review*, (August 1939), 40:153–94; Tadashi A. Hanami, "The Function of the Law in Japanese Industrial Relations," in Taishiro Shirai, *Contemporary Industrial Relations in Japan* (Madison, Wis., 1983); William B. Gould, *Japan's Reshaping of American Labor Law* (Cambridge, Mass. 1984).

Of course, partial unionism not only imposes costs on employers but also creates opportunities: American employers have the opportunity to move to the unorganized hinterlands in the south and overseas. Though this was less of an option before these regions were industrialized during and after World War II, today the threat of capital flight has sharply reduced the bargaining power of American unions except in those situations where employers are reluctant or unable to move.

15. On industrial size structure, see Mark Granovetter, "Small Is Bountiful: Labor Markets and Establishment Size," *American Sociological Review* (June 1984),

49:323–34; and data cited in David Marsden, *Beyond Economic Man* (Brighton, 1986), p. 183.

One could argue that export-dependent European employers had a reason to resist unionism that was every bit as effective as the presence of a low-wage, nonunion hinterland in the United States: the "hinterland" made up of international competitors. But the two hinterlands were not entirely analogous. Whereas nearly all unionized American firms faced unorganized domestic competitors, only a minority of European employers (though sometimes a large one) produced for export. Moreover, the corporatist politics produced by high European union densities gave European employers something to offer in return for wage restraint (e.g., political influence and social welfare programs); American employers could offer no such thing in return.

16. Geoffrey Ingham, *Strikes and Industrial Conflict* (London, 1974); Arthur M. Ross, "Prosperity and Labor Relations in Europe: The Case of West Germany," *Quarterly Journal of Economics* (August 1962), 76:331–59.

17. Walter Galenson, "Scandinavia," in Galenson, ed., *Comparative Labor Movements* (New York, 1968).

18. Berndt Schiller, "Years of Crisis, 1906–1914," in Steven Koblik, ed., *Sweden's Development from Poverty to Affluence, 1750–1970* (Minneapolis, 1975); T. L. Johnston, *Collective Bargaining in Sweden* (Cambridge, Mass. 1962).

19. Stephen Bornstein, "States and Unions: From Postwar Settlement to Contemporary Stalemate," in Stephen Bornstein, David Held, and Joel Krieger, eds., *The State in Capitalist Europe* (London, 1984); Jonathan Zeitlin, "Shop-floor Bargaining and the State: A Contradictory Relationship," in Steve Tolliday and Jonathan Zeitlin, eds., *Shop Floor Bargaining and the State* (Cambridge, Eng., 1985).

20. Friedman, "Politics and Unions," p. 70.

21. Val R. Lorwin, "Reflections on the History of the French and American Labor Movements," *Journal of Economic History* (March 1957), 17:37.

22. Gerald Feldman, *Army, Industry, and Labor in Germany, 1914–1918* (Princeton, 1966), p. 18. See also Nathan Reich, *Labour Relations in Republican Germany: An Experiment in Industrial Democracy, 1918–1933* (New York, 1938).

23. James J. Sheehan, *The Career of Lujo Brentano: A Study of Liberalism and Social Reform in Imperial Germany* (Chicago, 1966).

24. Feldman, *Army, Industry, and Labor*, p. 6. In Japan, a nation often compared to Germany, the government took a more repressive stance toward organized labor, acting under the authority of the Peace Police Law of 1900. Yet even in Japan, it is possible to observe parallels to the general European late development pattern. Thus, in the late Meiji era the government feared that "industrialists left to their own devices in the management of labor would undermine social and political order in factories and in society at large." Though it did not go so far as to encourage unionism, after World War I the government came to tolerate moderate union activity "in an application of the candy-and-whip (ame to muchi) theory of social control." Andrew Gordon, *The Evolution of Labor Relations in Japan: Heavy Industry, 1853–1955* (Cambridge, Mass., 1985), pp. 65, 208.

25. Elaine Glovka-Spencer, *Management and Labor in Imperial Germany: Ruhr Industrialists as Employers, 1896–1914* (New Brunswick, N.J. 1984), p. 143.

26. Philip Taft and Philip Ross, "American Labor Violence: Its Causes, Character, and Outcome," in Hugh D. Graham and Ted Robert Gurr, eds., *Violence in America: Historical and Comparative Perspectives* (Washington, D.C., 1969), p. 221.

27. Hugh Armstrong Clegg, *The System of Industrial Relations in Great Britain*, 3d ed. (Oxford, 1976); Stuart Jamieson, *Industrial Relations in Canada*, 2d ed. (New York, 1973); Robert J. Goldstein, *Political Repression in Nineteenth-Century Europe* (London, 1983).

A topic of considerable recent interest is the significant difference in unionization rates between the United States and Canada, a gap that has been attributed to Canada's more pro-union labor laws and to the greater propensity of Canadian workers to join unions. Without getting too tangled up in this debate, let me simply suggest that there are differences between Canadian and American employers that are consistent with the argument presented in this essay. At the level of values, comparative studies indicate that Canadian employers are much more likely to come from an upper class background than American employers (61 versus 36 percent), which has two significant consequences. First, like their British counterparts (see below), Canadian managers are less likely to be aggressive innovators and entrepreneurs; this lack of aggression presumably carries over to labor relations. Second, the Tory counterrevolutionary ethos imbued the Canadian elite with a long tradition of noblesse oblige, along with which goes tolerance of the welfare state, of government intervention, and of other forms of communal collectivism such as trade unions—very different from the antistatist individualism found in America.

As for incentives and constraints, the following are relevant. First, there are no right-to-work laws and no nonunion hinterland to which Canadian employers can retreat. Hence although union density rates in the provincial private sector vary, the coefficient of variation is smaller than in the United States (.32 versus .48; with Newfoundland excluded the Canadian figure drops to .25). Perhaps as a result, the union-nonunion pay gap is smaller in Canada than in the United States. Second, Canada's counterrevolutionary tradition has produced a stronger and more interventionist state, one that is far more willing to circumscribe employer actions.

See Seymour Martin Lipset, "North American Labor Movements: A Comparative Perspective" in Lipset, ed., *Unions in Transition* (San Francisco, 1986); Lipset, "Historical Traditions and National Characteristics: A Comparative Analysis of Canada and the United States," *Canadian Journal of Sociology* (Summer 1986), 11:113–55; Wallace Clement, *Continental Corporate Power* (Toronto, 1977); and Noah Meltz, "Interstate vs. Interprovincial Differences in Union Density" (unpublished manuscript, Centre for Industrial Relations, University of Toronto, December 1987).

28. Simha Landau, "Trends in Violence and Aggression: A Cross-Cultural Analysis," *International Journal of Comparative Sociology* (September 1984), 25:133–58; Howard M. Gitelman, "Perspectives on American Industrial Violence," *Business History Review* (Spring 1973), 47:1–23.

29. Gitelman, "Perspectives," p. 21.

30. Jerry M. Cooper, "The Army and Civil Disorder: Federal Military Intervention in American Labor Disputes, 1877–1900" (Ph.D. diss., University of Wisconsin, 1971); Robert Justin Goldstein, *Political Repression in Modern America* (Cambridge, Mass., 1978); David Brody, *Labor in Crisis: The Steel Strike of 1919* (Philadelphia, 1965); Jeremy Brecher, *Strike!* (Greenwich, Conn., 1972).

31. James Weinstein, *The Corporate Ideal in the Liberal State, 1900–1918* (Boston, 1968); Samuel P. Hays, "The Politics of Reform in Municipal Government in the Progressive Era," *Pacific Northwest Quarterly* (October 1964), 55:157–69.

32. John R. Commons, *Labor and Administration* (New York, 1913), p. 153.

33. Irving Bernstein, *The Lean Years* (Boston, 1960), p. 221; Sanford M. Jacoby, "The Duration of Indefinite Employment Contracts in England and the United States: An Historical Analysis," *Comparative Labor Law* (Winter 1982), 5:85–128; Howell John Harris, "The Snares of Liberalism? Politicians, Bureaucrats, and the Shaping of Federal Labour Relations Policy in the United States, ca. 1915–1947," in S. Tolliday and J. Zeitlin, eds., *Shop Floor Bargaining and the State* (Cambridge, Mass., 1985). Note that at least 5,600 injunctions were issued between 1880 and

1930. Although this number was only a small proportion of all strikes that occurred during those decades, it was a significant proportion. One-quarter to one-half of all sympathy strikes were enjoined in the 1910s and 1920s and injunctions figured in most railroad strikes and in "virtually every strike in which industrial unionism or 'amalgamation' or 'federation' was at issue." William Forbath, "The Shaping of the American Labor Movement," *Harvard Law Review* (April 1989), 102:1109–1256.

34. Vogel, "Businessmen Distrust," p. 64.

35. Seymour Martin Lipset, "Trade Unions and Social Structure: II," *Industrial Relations* (February 1962), 1:89–110.

36. Sutton et al., *Business Creed*. This accounts for the dominance of neoclassical economics in the United States as compared to continental Europe.

37. Seymour Martin Lipset, "Trade Unions and Social Structure: I," *Industrial Relations* (October 1961), 1:78.

38. Ely Chinoy, *Automobile Workers and the American Dream* (Garden City, N.Y., 1955); Richard Sennett and Jonathan Cobb, *The Hidden Injuries of Class* (New York, 1972).

39. Peter R. Shergold, *Working-Class Life: The "American Standard" in Comparative Perspective 1899–1913* (Pittsburgh, 1982); Reinhard Bendix and Seymour Martin Lipset, *Social Mobility and Industrial Society* (Berkeley, 1959).

40. Daniel J. B. Mitchell, "Inflation, Unemployment, and the Wagner Act: A Critical Reappraisal," *Stanford Law Review* (April 1986), 38:1065–95.

41. Henry Phelps Brown, *The Origins of Trade Union Power* (Oxford, 1986), p. 116.

42. Edward Shorter and Charles Tilly, *Strikes in France, 1830–1968* (London, 1974). Edwards attributes the persistent length of American strikes to the intensity of labor-management conflict in the United States, which, he argues, is largely due to the unwillingness of American employers to accept unions and collective bargaining. As a result, each strike becomes a contest of strength that could (dangerously or hopefully) undermine unionism. Edwards, *Strikes*, p. 238.

43. Quoted in Alan Fox, *History and Heritage: The Social Origins of the British Industrial Relations System* (London, 1985), p. 128.

44. Kenneth D. Brown, *Essays in Anti-Labour History: Responses to the Rise of Labour in Britain* (London, 1974); W. R. Garside and H. F. Gospel, "Employers and Managers," in Chris Wrigley, ed., *A History of British Industrial Relations, 1875–1914* (Brighton, 1982).

45. Fox, *History and Heritage*, p. 189.

46. Quoted in ibid., p. 217.

47. Ronald Dore, *British Factory–Japanese Factory: The Origins of Diversity in Industrial Relations* (Berkeley, 1973).

48. James Holt, "Trade Unionism in the British and U.S. Steel Industries, 1880–1914," *Labor History* (Winter 1977), 18:30.

49. Donald N. McCloskey, *Economic Maturity and Entrepreneurial Decline: British Iron and Steel, 1870–1913* (Cambridge, Mass. 1973).

50. Granick, *Managerial Comparisons*.

51. Phelps Brown, *Origins*, p. 211. See also Fox, *History and Heritage;* and Martin J. Wiener, *English Culture and the Decline of the Industrial Spirit, 1850–1980* (Cambridge, Eng. 1981).

52. Lloyd Ulman, "Connective Bargaining and Competitive Bargaining," *Scottish Journal of Political Economy* (June 1974), 21:103; Jonathan Zeitlin, "From Labor History to the History of Industrial Relations," *Economic History Review* (May 1987), 40:159–84.

53. Sanford M. Jacoby, *Employing Bureaucracy: Managers, Unions, and the Transformation of Work in American Industry, 1900–1945* (New York, 1985).

54. Phelps Brown, *Origins*, p. 117.

55. Fox, *History and Heritage*, p. 78.

56. Roger Davidson, "Government Administration," in Chris Wrigley, ed., *A History of British Industrial Relations* (Brighton, 1982).

57. Even after the Wagner Act, an organizing drive was expensive, and, although recognition strikes in theory were made unnecessary by the act, strikes during organizing drives or to win first contracts still occurred.

58. Goldstein, *Political Repression*, p. 550. Also see Daniel Fusfeld, "Government and the Suppression of Radical Labor," in Charles Bright and Susan Harding, eds., *Statemaking and Social Movements* (Ann Arbor, 1984).

59. Davis, *Prisoners*.

60. Mary Jackman and Robert Jackman, *Class Awareness in the United States* (Berkeley, 1973).

61. Selig Perlman and Philip Taft, *History of Labor in the United States, 1896–1932* (New York, 1935), p. 5.

62. Samuel Gompers, *Seventy Years of Life and Labor: An Autobiography* (New York, 1925), 1:97.

63. Perlman and Taft, *History of Labor*, p. 5. A similar analysis was made by Slichter, Healy, and Livernash, who noted that "The American environment has produced strongly individualistic and highly competitive employers who have been aggressively hostile to unions and who have been willing to go great extremes to destroy them." Along with labor exceptionalism, they argue, this produced "business unionism—that is, unionism which has little or no interest in social reforms but which is frankly out to advance the selfish aims of its members." Sumner Slichter, James J. Healy, and E. Robert Livernash, *The Impact of Collective Bargaining on Management* (Washington, D.C., 1960), p. 34.

64. Note that this is rather different from the analysis of Christopher Tomlins in *The State and the Unions: Labor Relations, Law, and Organized Labor in America, 1880–1960* (New York, 1985). Today, however, there is again distrust of government reemerging as a result of labor's experiences with Reagan-appointed circuit court judges and NLRB members.

65. This is the argument made by Friedman in "Politics and Unions."

66. Val R. Lorwin, *The French Labor Movement* (Cambridge, Mass., 1954); Henry W. Ehrmann, *French Labor from Popular Front to Liberation* (New York, 1947).

67. Howell John Harris, *The Right to Manage: Industrial Relations Policies of American Business in the 1940s* (Madison, Wis., 1982).

68. One might have expected French labor to rebound at the end of the war, since many workers perceived their employers as collaborators and the CGT was taken over by the Communists, who were associated with the Resistance. But this failed to happen, in part because the labor movement was sharply divided and in part because the economy was a wreck for a long time after the war. Duncan Gallie, *Social Inequality and Class Radicalism in France and Britain* (Cambridge, Eng. 1983). Note that, just as France had looked to the Wagner Act as an industrial relations model in the 1930s, it did the same thing in 1945. Making reference to the labor-management production committees that were created in the United States during the war, the preamble to a 1945 ordinance that legalized plant-level worker committees in France said, "No doubt—as the experiences of the last four years in . . . the United States and Canada have shown—the participation of the personnel in committees of this kind can have the happiest effect." Adolf Sturmthal, *Workers Councils: A Study of Workplace Organization on Both Sides of the Iron Curtain* (Cambridge, Mass., 1964).

69. Sylvia K. Selekman and Benjamin M. Selekman, *Power and Morality in a Business Society* (New York, 1956).

70. Douglass V. Brown and Charles A. Myers, "The Changing Industrial Relations Philosophy of American Management," Ninth Annual Proceedings of the Industrial Relations Research Association, Madison, Wisconsin, 1958; Clinton S. Golden and Virginia D. Parker, eds., *Causes of Industrial Peace Under Collective Bargaining* (New York, 1955).

71. Daniel Nelson, "History of the Rubber Workers" (unpublished manuscript, University of Akron, 1986).

72. James A. Gross, *The Reshaping of the National Labor Relations Board: National Policy in Transition, 1937–1947* (Albany, N.Y., 1981).

73. Sanford M. Jacoby, "Employee Attitude Testing at Sears Roebuck, 1938–1960" *Business History Review* (Winter 1986), 60:602–32; Jacoby, "Norms and Cycles: The Dynamics of Nonunion Industrial Relations in the United States, 1897–1985," in Katherine Abraham and Robert McKersie, eds., *New Developments in Human Resources and Labor Markets* (Cambridge, Mass., forthcoming).

74. Herbert Northrup, *Boulwarism* (Ann Arbor, 1964). Two other props (more accurately permissive factors) were the shift in public opinion after the war in favor of business and against unions, and the industrialization of the south that started during the war.

75. Jacoby, *Employing Bureaucracy.*

76. Henry Farber, "The Decline of Unionization in the United States: What Can Be Learned from Recent Experience," National Bureau of Economic Research, working paper no. 2267, May 1987; Richard Freeman and James Medoff, *What Do Unions Do?* (New York, 1984).

Index

■

AABA, *see* American Anti-Boycott Association
Accounting, management, 76
AFL, 171; contract regulation, 60-61; formation, 192-94; and judiciary, 133; and voluntarism, 194
Aitken, Hugh, 74, 82
Allen, Alexander C., 136, 140-42
American Anti-Boycott Association, 136, 140-42
American Federation of Labor, *see* AFL
Americanization, immigrants and, 96-100
American Legion, 193
Anti-trust legislation, 101, 147, 179
Apprenticeship, 24, 55, 57, 66, 126; and demand for labor, 26; family influence, 28; and female workers, 30; unions and, 61
Assembly line, 19, 92
Association, employer, 108-9, 115-27, 228*n*3, 233*nn*36, 59, 234*nn*65, 67, 72; in France, 150, 154-71, 195; international, 116; law and, 136-48; membership, 163, 164 tab.; open shop and, 135-36; political influence, 168-69, 233*n*58; as service, 117, 121-27, 136-38; and strikes, 165-67, 171, 233*n*58; and unions, 120-21, 163, 235*n*76
Auspitz, Katherine, 159

Automation, 58, 65, 68; *see also* Mechanization

Barth, Carl, 74
Bendix, Reinhard, 149
Benefits: evolution of, 57; paternalism and, 63; unions and, 61-62
Bismarck, Otto von, 192
Blacklisting, 120, 184
Blum, Leon, 195-96
Boulwarism, 198
Bourgeoisie, 153, 159, 228*n*3
Brandeis, Louis D., 143, 145
Brandes, Stuart, 4, 100-1
Braverman, Harry, 4, 6-7, 9, 47, 75
Brody, David, 101
Business: and government, 3, 180; history, 2-3, 131, 201*n*3; Third Republic and, 154, 159-62

Canada, unionization in, 237*n*2
Capital: access to, 24, 31, 41, 42; human, 67; mass production and, 104
Capitalism, 2; corporate, 3; Engels and, 153-54; industrial, 216*n*4; proprietary, 107-9, 134, 147, 149; and Taylorism, 75
Capital-labor ratio, 33, 36
Centralization, 231*n*33